AF606757

CURATING RESEARCH

Paul O'Neill & Mick Wilson (Eds.)

Open Editions

45 Handforth Road
London SW9 0LL
United Kingdom

+ 44 (0)20 7820 9779
info@openeditions.com
www.openeditions.com

de Appel Arts Centre

Prins Hendrikkade 142
1011 AT Amsterdam
Netherlands

+31 20 625 5651
www.deappel.nl

First published in London 2015

British Library Cataloguing in Publication Data:
A catalogue record for this book is available from the British Library

ISBN 978-0-949004-03-1

Printed and bound in Europe

CURATING RESEARCH

Occasional Table

Open Editions / de Appel

Hyunjoo Byeon
Carson Chan & Joanna Warsza
Chris Fite-Wassilak
Olga Fernández López
Kate Fowle
Maja & Reuben Fowkes
Liam Gillick
Georgina Jackson
Sidsel Nelund
Simon Sheikh
Henk Slager
tranzit.hu
Jelena Vesić
Marion von Osten
Vivian Ziherl

Paul O'Neill & Mick Wilson (Eds.)

Table of Contents

AN OPENING TO CURATORIAL ENQUIRY: INTRODUCTION TO CURATING AND RESEARCH

Paul O'Neill & Mick Wilson

The Contexts

The texts assembled in this volume are responses to the editors' invitation to consider the relationship between curating, the 'curatorial' and the practices of 'research'. This invitation has been formulated in response to what we perceive to be a key moment of consolidation in the discursive field around curating, whereby many protagonists are attempting to inscribe certain limitations upon, and definitions of, what curating should be, or seek to be, and to determine which bodies of knowledge shall have enduring consequence for its practice and associated discourses and histories. This tendency has been particularly apparent in recent attempts to construct concepts of the 'curatorial', conceived as forms of practice operating away from, alongside or supplementary to the main work of curating-as-exhibition-making. It is illustrative of the contested nature of the territory around concepts of the 'curatorial' that, for many authors, as will be outlined later, these concepts cannot be reduced to a set of positions that exist in opposition to notions of curating as exhibition-production. Rather, the 'curatorial' is most often expressed with reference to modes of becoming – research-based, dialogical practices in which the processual and serendipitous overlap with speculative actions and open-ended forms of production. Certainly, varied definitions of the curatorial can be read as resisting the narrative-orientated authorial model of curating, which might be defined as commissioning or working with extant artworks for a public manifestation within an exhibitionary frame or organising principle defined by a curator.

With this in mind, it appears that the 'curatorial' and certain understandings of 'research' have become aligned with each other, perhaps as a means of moving beyond an understanding of exhibitions as the main outcome of curating-as-production. In relation to the possible conjunctions and divergences between curating, the 'curatorial' and research, our original invitation identified possible topics to include: research within the exhibition-making process; the exhibition as a research action in itself; expanded notions of the curatorial and the role of research models and methodologies within these; the distinction between research finding its way into curatorial practice/exhibition models and the curatorial, in itself, as a mode of research practice. This book attempts to draw upon some of these distinctions as a way of clarifying certain differences in approach, whilst aspiring to demonstrate a multiplicity of authorial positions in relation to understandings of the intersection between curatorial practice and research paradigms.

As indicated above, we are engaging with the question of research at a time when there is an intensification of the contestation over curating and the curatorial as frameworks of critical practice within contemporary art. Indicative of the clash between different models of curating is the way in which contemporary art journalism is littered with expressions of dismissal and/or weariness in the face of claims surrounding the agency and critical import of curating and its rhetorical production. The following three examples may be taken as indicative:

For a long time being a curator was not a big deal. It was a craft based in understanding. But in the 1990s the role of the curator changed. Curators wanted to acquire the mystique of artists. Which I've always taken to be a sign of weakness actually [...] (1)

The last 25 years have seen not only the rise (and recent waning?) of the independent curator, but also curating's rapid institutionalization. Little more than a decade ago, for instance, there were only five curatorial studies programmes in the world, with barely half a dozen publications available on the subject. While the amount of publishing on curating is now difficult to keep track of [...] (2)

It seems that no one in the art world is just one thing anymore. We are all some hybrid variation of the hyphenated multiplex artist-curator-critic-theorist-activist-historian-model-actor. While it might seem easy to account for this as the triumph of inter-disciplinarity over the modernist doctrine of specialization, the rise of hyphenated identifiers has been matched by the equally ubiquitous multiplication of new forms of specialised critical discourse. Nowhere is this more evident than in the emergence since the late 1980s of curatorship as an independent field of critical inquiry.(3)

1. Statement attributed to Robert Storr in an article entitled 'Everybody's a Curator' by Christopher Borrelli that appeared in the *Chicago Tribune* October 4, 2013. The article's title and Storr's position are resonant of a wider journalistic dismissiveness with respect to a change in the professional self-presentation of the curatorial role. http://articles.chicagotribune.com/2013-10-04/entertainment/ct-ae-1006-borrelli-curation-20131004_1_curator-fake-shore-drive-kristin-cavallari/3
2. Sam Thorne evaluating new publications on contemporary curating in the book review section of Frieze Magazine Issue 152 January-February 2013. http://www.frieze.com/issue/category/issue-152/
3. From a blog by Henry Francis Skerritt, a doctoral researcher at the University of Pittsburgh, in a post under the sub-heading 'The Curator as Fall Guy'. http://henryfskerritt.com/2013/07/01/book-review-paul-oneill-the-culture-of-curating-and-the-curating-of-cultures/

These citations may be contrasted with more expansive accounts of the professional and ideological stakes of curating that are also widespread in contemporary art discourse. Some of these accounts of the curatorial have looked to the margins of practice, resisting categorical resolution and instead proposing the curatorial as a constellation of activities whose precise definitions and objectives are intentionally allowed to remain somewhat elusive. In a similar manner, the role of the curator's discourse within these expanded conceptions of the curatorial is understood as something other than a literal disclosure of intended 'effects' or a script for full realisation in actual practice. This is evidenced for example in Maria Lind's and Beatrice von Bismarck's different elaborations of 'the curatorial':

> Can we speak of the curatorial beyond curating in the expanded field: as a multidimensional role that includes critique, editing, education, and fund raising? The curatorial can contain all these varied dimensions as a loose methodology applied by different people in various capacities. [...] I imagine curating as a way of thinking in terms of interconnections: linking objects, images, processes, people, locations, histories, and discourses in physical space like an active catalyst, generating twists, turns and tensions [...](4)

> The political potential of the curatorial [...] represents a continual process of negotiation in which the positions taken vary in relation to the other subjects or objects involved in exhibitions, take on new directions, and appear in various constellations. It is quite fundamentally about processing the curatorial role in addition to other processes of 'becoming'.(5)

Clearly, as practitioners, educators and editors of this volume, we are much more orientated towards an expanded notion of the curatorial than a narrower conception of the curator as the impresario of 'the show' or

4. Maria Lind, *Performing the curatorial within and beyond Art*, Sternberg Press, 2012.

5. Beatrice von Bismarck, 'Curatorial Criticality: On the Role of Freelance Curators in the Field of Contemporary Art' in Marianne Eigenheer (ed.), *Curating Critique*, Revolver, 2007. Other examples of this expanded reading of the curatorial include Irit Rogoff's articulation of the curatorial as critical thought that does not rush to embody itself, but instead raises questions that are to be unfolded over time; and Emily Pethick's proposal that the curatorial presupposes an unbounded framework, allowing for things, ideas, and outcomes to emerge in the process of being realised. See Irit Rogoff, 'Smuggling – A Curatorial Model' in Vanessa Joan Müller and Nicolaus Schafhausen (eds.), *Under Construction: Perspectives on Institutional Practice*, Walther König, 2006; and Emily Pethick, 'The Dog that Barked at the Elephant in the Room', *The Exhibitionist*, issue 4, June 2011.

the crafter of display. While remaining deeply committed to the specificities and critical potentials of exhibition practices, we are also engaged by the extended curatorial field and by the attempt to realise curating as an entanglement of actors, rather than exclusively a matter of presenting discretely authored, clearly bounded 'works'. This might enable us to move past an impatient reflex that seeks to dismiss curatorial discourse as just so much special-pleading and self-promotion for particular professional cadres and to take some time to give consideration to the discursive work of emergence and enquiry.

Research, in some informal and mostly un-problematised sense, seems to be generally recognised as a prerogative of curators – both with respect to the narrow sense of the curator as exhibition-maker, working with works that are construed as self-sufficient, and to the extended sense of the curator as (variously) co-producer, auteur, critic or agent provocateur, working with a range of different art practices which unfold in ways that are imbricated with each other within the curatorial process. Given the widely accepted role of research within curatorial practices, it is interesting to note that, while there has been a lively discussion around research in-and-through art practice – motivated by a range of different factors – research has not been sufficiently problematised in relation to the curatorial field. This would seem to indicate that the constructs 'curatorial research', 'curatorial knowledge' and 'curatorial enquiry' already have some tacit standing, even for the champions of more conservative understandings of professional roles and norms. Reading this volume and taking account of the location of debates on *artistic research* suggests that curating has an accepted, relatively uncontested epistemic dimension, while the making-of-art appears deeply contested as a research domain that might claim intrinsic epistemic content. Of course, things are not quite as simple as this; however, it is worth considering the overall pattern of debates here.

Arguably, the debate on artistic research, particularly as it has unfolded in the orbit of European higher arts education, has been largely structured around the rhetorical persistence of the paradigm of the artist as a radically self-determining agent and the autonomous work of art as the normative index of properly 'artistic' work. This has engendered a problematic of 'artistic research' that most often pivots on the question of the purportedly radical alterity of artistic agency and artistic subjectivities, constantly refracted through the identity of the authentically 'artistic'. By contrast, the heteronomous practices of the curatorial field have given rise to very different discussions of research, whereby the contingent agency of the curatorial is posited as always already caught in fields of tension across multiple actors and apparatuses. This opening of the curatorial to co-production, collaboration and dialogical production practices is, of course, also present in (indeed inseparable from) a wide range of artistic practices; however, the artistic research debate has arguably not been paradigmatically structured by these modes of artistic practice. Herein lies the key differentiator when considering how the debate on research plays out in the distinct rhetorical fields of the artistic and the curatorial. One might also wish to point to differences between the predominant institutional forms within which these debates unfold – between the academy and the gallery; the studio and the exhibition; the university and the museum; education and infotainment; and between formally accredited academic fields and informal reputational economies. However, it should be acknowledged that the artistic research debate has managed to operate across a much wider institutional terrain than just the academy, and it has, in many respects, managed to escape the procedurally focused orbit of higher arts education. Therefore, is it still possible to see a very different productive potential in the discussion of curating and research? More precisely, do discussions proceed from discursive bases that are distinct from the exclusive rhetoric of the autonomous work of art, which may be seen to hamper the development of the artistic research debate? These are some of the questions that require further enquiry within and beyond the pages of this book.

Exhibition projects, construed within the expanded frame of the curatorial, have employed a wide range of methods, models and modalities that may be seen as generative of new knowledge or as implicit or explicit research activities. Prominent examples of this include *If I Can't Dance...*, *Contemporary Arab Representations*, *Homeworks*, *Making Things Public*, *Collective Creativity*, *Projekt Migration*, *Governmentality*, *Laboratorium*, the last four incarnations of *Documenta*, *Altermodern*, *This is a Show* and the *Show is Many Things*, *Cities on the Move*, *Animism*, *Mining the Museum*, and many others. While these curatorial projects might be seen to share a broadly process-based character in their modi operandi, they differ greatly in form and content, and are geographically dispersed. Furthermore they span a period of almost four decades from the 1980s through to the present day. These examples indicate that curatorial practices have developed multiply, as active forms of knowledge production; as ways of contesting established epistemic schemata; and as research actions and epistemic practices in their own right.

In inviting contributors to explore the interaction between the fraught definition of curating and the question of research, we anticipated that different lines of development might be possible. In turn, we proposed that this could open paths beyond a potentially disabling, and internally focused, contest over professional formation and legitimation within contemporary art systems. Moreover, we believe that such new lines of development – thinking through the twin constructs of curating and research – may extend the critical energies that are so prominent across the wide spectrum of curatorial practices that have reshaped the terrain of contemporary art. (It is something of these energies that we sought to identify in our previous two edited volumes in this series, *Curating Subjects* and *Curating and the Educational Turn*.)

Integral to the expanded conception of the curatorial, there has been renewed recognition of the exhibition itself as a potential mode of research action, which exceeds the familiar (but nonetheless noteworthy) idea of research activities being conducted in order to generate exhibitions. Several of the contributions to this volume explore the exhibition as research action. These cover a geographically and chronologically dispersed set of references, ranging from the layered historical reconstructions of exhibitionary agency and enquiry, in Jelena Vesić's treatment of projects by Prelom Kolektiv and DeLVe, to the survey of recent interrogative formats framing international platform exhibitions by Georgina Jackson; from the identification of a non-serious and inauthentic gesturing at enquiry in Maja and Reuben Fowkes's commentary on the Budapest Kunsthalle's 2012 *What is Hungarian?* exhibition as part of their treatment of the theme of 'translocality' to the description of the Hong Kong-based Asia Art Archive's expanded curatorial practice via interconnecting archival and exhibitionary practices.

These widely differing examples are disclosed in different voices, ranging from the close-questioning tone of the activist engagé to the confident, surveying voice of the somewhat detached observer. However, rather than developing a shared paradigm of the curatorial, what unites these disparate voices (in what we conceive as a productive tension) is a widespread – and, importantly, longstanding (i.e. predating the putative ascendancy of curatorial discourse in the 1990s) – recognition of exhibition-making, and of the wider institutional frames that condition and enable it, as a fundamentally dynamic process of co-production, structure of experience and extended space of meaning-making. This is very different from implicitly construing the exhibition as a unitary system of unequivocal 'utterance' or finalised display, mirroring, in its fixity, the imagined self-sufficiency of the autonomous work of art that the exhibition is presumed to mediate.

In *Curating and the Educational Turn*, the framing of a discussion on the 'educational turn' precipitated a very lively debate around the commodifying impact that a discussion of counter-hegemonic educational projects might effect by imposing a unifying rubric or brand upon these different practices. This was especially pronounced when questions of self-consciously 'critical' art practices intersected with themes of cognitive capital, immaterial labour and the structural exploitation of precarious creative and intellectual labour. This anxiety, with respect to commodification of intellectual work, may be taken as indicative of the necessary caution among many practitioners with respect to the dynamics of reputational economies and the institutional/market co-optation of critical practice. It is clear that shifting focus onto the conjunction between curating and research again activates this need to exercise caution against any mere valorising of cognitive labour in the art field.

In putting together the present volume, we have sought to create multiple fields of tension in the interaction between the two themes of the curatorial and research. These two themes could perhaps be more appropriately identified as two *refusals* – on the one hand, a refusal to reduce the essential idea of curating to the crafting of display practices for autonomous art works; on the other hand, a refusal to faddishly cast the question of curatorial practice in terms of a fantasmatic idea of 'knowledge production' or a fetishised cliché of academic/professional expertise. The contributions assembled here construct this open field of tension by disclosing the different ways in which curating can enact situated enquiries and construct multi-layered platforms of questioning, experience and production – platforms that fold sense, reference and meaning together rather than positing a fundamental opposition between aesthetic and cognitive concerns in the art field.

Inevitably, the archive looms large in many of these discussions, and the archive-on-display might risk appearing as the new orthodoxy, seeking to displace the autonomous-artwork-on-display. It has been identified above that exhibition projects can, on occasion, manifest inauthentic – merely rhetorical – forms of questioning (the Fowkeses' critique of *What is Hungarian?*), and this is confirmed in the opening section of Jackson's text, surveying the vogue for question-titles in various exhibition projects of the 2000s. Recognising the challenge of enquiry as more than the adoption of interrogative formats, many of the contributors here seek to move from discrete curatorial research actions and questions, and from particular strategies of archival and discursive presentation, to construe some curatorial practices as potentially embodying an extended enquiry that exceeds the duration and terms of any one particular project, of any one exhibitionary moment or of any one mode of public address.

The Texts

This first four texts that open the volume, each address a general aspect of the intersection between curating and research. Liam Gillick begins his reflections on the figure of 'the complete curator' by positing a disappointment with most contemporary art and a new 'desire system that now points towards its own yearning for ethical social change'. In the course of his unfolding of the current moment of apparent artistic underachievement and curatorial over-reaching, Gillick concisely rehearses the changing dialectic of exhibition and work in contemporary art. His conclusion sounds a note of caution that may be taken to contextualise all that follows when he asserts that research 'cannot build better systems or structures, yet it can point out how far away they still appear to be'. Operating as a counterpoint to Gillick's scene-setting rehearsal of the curatorial field, Simon Sheikh critically unpacks the construal of the curatorial as intrinsically research-based by exploring a definitional conundrum through opposing constructions of research (*forschung and recherché*), concretising the discussion by turning to two examples: *All That Fits: The Aesthetics of Journalism* (2011) and *Unauthorized* (2012). Maja and Reuben Fowkes establish a broad historical characterisation of the current context, proposing that 'curatorial research is not only channelled by the strategic interests of art institutions but also constrained by the compulsion to incorporate the relentless search for innovative forms, methods and outcomes in order to best capture the present moment within the flux of contemporary art'. However, this critique also opens onto other possibilities, as the authors note that 'the inclination to spread across several formats allows curators [...] a more nuanced perspective than purely academic or discourse-based research'.

Georgina Jackson further elaborates on these critical potentials in her examination of the emergence of the exhibition as a space of critical enquiry into the nature of the 'political'. These four opening essays combine to establish a framework of issues that the subsequent series of focused case studies serve to refract through specific projects and local curatorial agendas.

Henk Slager's treatment of the 'Academy as Exhibition' bridges the earlier discussion of the educational turn with the current focus on the question of research. With respect to the interchange between curatorial enquiry and what he describes, in a phrase borrowed from Peter Lamborn Wilson, as the 'temporary autonomous zone' of artistic research, Slager gives a different reading (from that provided by Gillick, Sheikh and the Fowkeses, for example) of the potentials of exhibitionary practices in unfolding moments of collective enquiry through the networked relations of the exhibition site, citing a series of academy-as-exhibition projects that culminate in the 2012 *Offside Effect*. Olga Fernández López takes as her focus the specific case of the Madrid-based institution, Intermediae, and describes an expanded curatorial institutional project as an 'institutional hypothesis', in a line of argument that may be read in critical dialogue with Sheikh's earlier question of the role of 'thesis' in exhibition-making. Vesić's closely argued consideration of the dilemma of self-organisation and co-optation is an exposition of the practical working-through of some of the problems identified by Gillick and the Fowkeses in their description of the deployment of post-Fordist logics in contemporary art. Vesić's discussion of two experimental exhibition projects, which attempt to address different traditions of self-organisation in the arts in former Yugoslavia, demonstrates both the critical acuity of curatorial research and the importance of concretising the terms of the debate through consideration of individual cases and situations. In a similar way, Marion von Osten's 'Movements That Matter: The Projekt Migration (2003–2006)' provides a detailed account of a curatorial project examining the multiplicity of perspectives on the highly contested construct of 'migration', which concretises the claims for curatorial work as a differentiated form of epistemic production. Von Osten argues for the epistemological importance of the curatorial position adopted in this project, asserting that it 'differs from the representation of history in museums, which tries to recall the past with artefacts and documents and, at the same time, claims an objective view on history'. Importantly, her tactic of differentiation of the curatorial position is not simply to set up an opposition of objective–subjective poles in knowledge claims, but rather to focus on the agonistic constitution of the project itself: 'All the partners, artists and researchers involved either took part in investigative activities or commissioned artistic works. *Projekt Migration* was a locus of antagonism, self-empowerment and ceaseless struggle for representation and citizenship'.

Kate Fowle's text, 'Action Research: Generative Curatorial Practices', returns us to the level of an overarching historical reflection, echoing the themes set in play by Jackson's essay on the exhibition and the political, as Fowle seeks to identify the specificity of curatorial research as it has emerged over the past twenty-five years. In this, she indicates a broadly pluralist way beyond the professional dichotomies identified earlier, when she argues that, with respect to an emerging division in the field, 'between those who think of curating as a means to an end and those who want to refine the practice for the sake of its form', there is room for both approaches. Pursuing this inclusive approach, Fowle declares that the important challenge in the knowledge work of contemporary exhibition forms is to provide 'the tools with which an audience can ask questions and draw independent conclusions'.

Slager, Vesić, Fernández López, Von Osten and Fowle provide a range of different cases in which the exhibition functions as a research context by bringing together different moments: research in preparation for the event of exhibition; the exhibition as disclosure of research activities; and the exhibition institution as a research event in its own right, an occasion for the public performance of enquiry. In the following contributions, we see further extensions of these strategies, in which the curatorial process arguably prioritises the epistemic work of knowledge-making, rather than the specific production of the exhibitionary moment. This is not to propose a categorical difference, but more a matter of a distinction of degree. Sidsel Nelund's description of the Beirut-based *Home Works* series, operating since 2002, is an interesting case in point, in which the role of a collaborative and iterative curatorial process in developing an extensive shared knowledge base is profiled. Nelund's treatment focuses on the practical strategies of balancing programmatic curatorial direction and the conditioning of open contexts for emergent artistic agency by operating in a way that is responsive to political cultural urgencies. This is followed by Hyunjoo Byeon's essay on Asia Art Archive which gives an account of another durational project, where the production of a knowledge infrastructure is a key curatorial action, one that clearly draws out the practical interchange between the exhibitionary and the archival.

The cumulative project of Asia Art Archive is followed by Vivian Ziherl's detailed treatment of the extended curatorial platform project *If I Can't Dance...* (2004–14), which operates a different research logic of accretive commissioning of broadly performative works. Ziherl's essay indicates a way beyond the autonomous artwork problematic referenced earlier, when she describes *If I Can't Dance...*'s 'disinterest in the curatorial mastery and authorial mode' as 'accompanied by a re-focusing upon deep investment in the singularity of artistic practice'. Ziherl's analysis of the operational logics of *If I Can't Dance...* provides another model of curatorial research, clearly differentiated from a positivist hypothesis-testing model, and elaborated with reference to an 'experimental disposition' that is tuned to the processes of commissioning new performative works. Again, the anchoring of the question of curatorial research within a concrete project situation makes the themes in the wider debate more amenable to critical and practical development. This can also be seen in Chris Fite-Wassilak's treatment of Eastside Projects which may be read as a partner text to Ziherl's in that it provides an analysis of operational logics of Eastside that enact an experimental disposition but refuse the positivistic reductions of hypothesis-testing, enacting instead a radical layering, cross-referencing and entanglement of practices. Fite-Wassilak's text may also be seen as a contribution to research methodology, both in terms of the text's recapitulation of Eastside's operational logics in its own construction, and in terms of the description of Eastside's own disclosure of its operational logic through the iterations of the *Eastside Projects User's Manual*. The volume closes with two key contributions. The penultimate text comprises a dialogue between Carson Chan and Joanna Warsza, stemming from their experiences in different curatorial collaborations: the 4th Marrakech Biennale and the 7th Berlin Biennale respectively. Their dialogue functions as a reprise of many of the themes traced through the preceding texts.

The final text in this collection *The Curatorial Dictionary*, a collaborative project initiated by tranzit.hu that seeks to provide interpretations of some of the keywords that circulate in contemporary curatorial discourse. The entries from this dictionary explore some of the terminological points upon which many of the earlier contributions rest. *The Curatorial Dictionary* is itself an exemplar of a collaborative enquiry into the terms of current practice and as such seems a fitting text on which to conclude the volume.

The Subtext

In closing this introduction, we should underline that our intention in commissioning and assembling these texts for the reader has not been to construct a fixed taxonomy of curatorial research practices, but rather to suggest the ways in which the different conjunctions of curating and research might open up a pathway through what has been presented above as the current impasse in curatorial and critical debate. The obstruction that we propose to navigate here is a reduction of the curatorial experimentation and discourse of the past two decades to the status of a secondary relay (a superstructural consequence) of the primary political economic realities of the biennial explosion (as determining base). Opening up the theme of research in relation to recent curatorial practices enables us to see a differentiated field of cultural research actions that draws upon many different operational logics, temporal framings and exhibitionary modes, instantiating many different accumulations and dispersions of knowledge and enquiry. This is a matter of practical strategies and tactics for working within the complex and uncertain terrain of the contemporary while maintaining an openness to knowing things other than those that are currently known without simply reproducing an uncritical valorisation of the new.

24 – 31

THE COMPLETE CURATOR

Liam Gillick

Over the past 25 years, the complete curator has emerged as an agent within cultural practice. This heightened individual or group demonstrates varied responses to ethical demands, exceeding those being produced by artists, and posits new models in advance of art being made today. The complete curator bypasses the complexities and dead ends produced by attempting to match theories to forms – curatorial conceptualisation runs ahead – dragging desire for new structures into direct confrontation with theoretical [philosophical, sociological and psychological] constructions. The complete curator voices a disappointment with current art, in its glossier, petulant and uninhibited forms, and weariness with art's inability to produce new societies and new relationships. It does so alongside a revived critical community, bolstered by the academy and the rise of contemporary art as an area of advanced study. The complete curator desires a world – expressed and realised by art, artists and themselves – which expels the present domination of capital via the machinations of neoliberalism. The use of the word 'complete' here does not imply 'finished' but rather 'full' or 'having all the necessary parts'. The complete curator exists as a manifestation of an art object's lack in terms of its fundamental incompatibility with free-floating social constructions. At best, the complete curator defines themselves by expressing discontent with art's weakness, and gains some solace by describing heightened potentials that are always hampered by the subsequent deployment of diminished structures. This disappointment takes place within frameworks that reach out into the social and political sphere in order to describe art's failure to escape from capital's rapacious reach. The complete curator is fully aware that cultural workers are part of a precarious class, terminally alienated from the parallel insecurity of zero-hour casual workers. For, while it is comforting to suggest that precarity could be redirected towards solidarity across class and professional specialisation, there are fundamental differences in regard to the potential of the complete curator and the potential of artists. The curator may be able to see potential connections that the artist's delusions must override. It is not that the complete curator muddles the fast-food worker and the bad painter; rather that the complete curator can identify the artist's isolation in their specific forms of precarity. The complete curator is not a problem; it is the epitome of a process that began in 1987 when the first curators graduated from Le Magasin in Grenoble. The complete curator is met by the incomplete artist who both aids and resists, resists and aids, the curator in their attempt to load expectations onto art, artworks and art contexts – expectations that art can provide new worlds and demonstrate, in articulate form, the failure of the varied constructions of society that surround us today. The complete curator begins by questioning the validity/content of exhibitions and quickly moves on to challenging the notion of a constructed society being capable of resistance and stability.

Three dominant contextual structures appear to have determined the growth, interpretation and flow of art and created this context of extended expectations on the part of the complete curator. Each of them applies pressures that have moderated yet, perversely, enabled the expansion of contemporary art alongside a continued fragmentation of critical processes. The first of these bounding structures is simply termed the art market. The contemporary art market is an apparently straightforward, barely regulated process of exchange that appears to be firewalled from its more self-consciously critical others – those who lay claim to the potential of critical cultural practice to operate outside orthodox forms of exchange, i.e. the complete curator and their extended demands. The second is the general area of concern known as the curatorial – the complete curator's area of focus. If the curatorial has a bounding model at all, it increasingly derives its structural validation from the academy, the re-imagined institution and various self-organised, self-conscious structures. The third is the positing of art as a paradigm of potential – a space of human action and interaction that could, and should, propose models which function outside the capitalisation of every moment and every exchange. Where it cannot achieve this – due to the churning effect of the art world's unique forms of labour division – the ideal is to produce work that at least exposes new potentialities for curatorial practice by default and, in doing so, avoids all contact with established forms of commercial art exchange. These three contextual models provide varying degrees of self-awareness within a regime of continued submission to the phantom of art's potential to operate as a non-criticable sphere that runs just ahead of its analysis or a secretion of ever-more-specific accounts of the world. It would appear, therefore, that we face a simple dichotomy in relation to the ways in which art should be developed, interpreted and exchanged. One option is to give in to a market model, in which art flows through a commercial funnel into the hands of a small group of people while being temporarily shown off to larger groups of people. The other option is to thoroughly engage with the complete curator and their attendant processes – critical, in advance of and in parallel to fragmented self-consciousness and projected desires for the potential of art as a vehicle from which to both recognise and reject the current deployment of people, objects and forms of exchange throughout societies and without limit.

Twenty years ago, I wrote a short, rather journalistic text for *Art Monthly* magazine.(1) In 1992, the Royal College of Art had begun offering an MA course called Curating Contemporary Art. At that point, the idea of an advanced degree in curatorial practice did not necessarily imply the development of the complete curator, new forms of curatorial consciousness or even success. In the subsequent period, it has become clear that, by focusing on the struggle to deal with research and various, apparently contradictory, modes of activity within exhibitions, the best of such courses to have proliferated since the early 1990s have made broader claims about the potential of revised curatorial structures. Most importantly, the Royal College course and others have functioned to structure critique in response to the needs of the curatorial rather than those of art. It might be assumed that the abundance of curatorial thinking would have been accompanied by new critical models that offered revised ways of addressing the problem of contemporary art. In some sense, this has been the case; yet, this has mainly produced critical processes that have tended to overlook one key aspect - namely the ethically Western Judeo-Christian language at the centre of the complete curator. Further, it might be argued that a specific connection can be made to the history of Protestantism - with its particular adherence to the text, good works and a universal priesthood of believers - locked into an ever-more-pious set of schemes facing thwarted desires.

Some observers have suggested that this sense of projected piety is revealed in the somewhat tortured language deployed by the complete curator in their places of display and interpretation - a process

1. Liam Gillick, 'Curating for Pleasure and Profit'. *Art Monthly*. June 1993. p. 15-18. A short note on the original title of the *Art Monthly* text. Founded in 1976, *Art Monthly* had originally been intended to fill a gap. Sitting somewhere between the *New Statesman* and *The Nation* in terms of format - it had been designed to be cheap - it offered listings and news, as well as reviews, in advance of most other magazines at the time. By 1993, while retaining its format, the magazine had settled into a niche that was moving towards a more polemical style while retaining the mixture of reviews, news and opinion specifically focused on the endless battle to retain government subsidy for art. The editorial tone was intended to be sceptical and accessible. The title of my original article reflected this tendency. On reflection, I might prefer to disown the title. But it was my own - intended to form an association in the reader's mind with a cheap self-help book and offer a warning about the potential pitfalls of a course such as this becoming a finishing school for aimless, but culturally curious, people.

that does not exclude the writing of some artists. But loose language is not the root cause of the critical deficit here; it is merely a symptom of something more deeply embedded in the communication and approval structures that lie at the core of a developed curatorial sphere. The complete curator has moved beyond the disappointment and partial quality of most contemporary art and has engaged a desire system that now points towards its own yearning for ethical social change. The complete curator has no need to build new critical models restricted to art in object or structural form, for they gain momentum from art's lack and the increasingly precise description of societies' needs. It is not that the complete curator is incapable of deconstructing art's often wry and self-abasing engagements; rather, such an exercise has become pointless in the face of a new conversation with the academy and its own self-conscious institutions.

If the complete curator increasingly finds validatory models in the academy and revised institutions, they have reduced their speculative role and conceded, reaching forward to other structures. The discursive has become formalised within a frame that simultaneously engulfs and diminishes critique. Whole territories have now been abandoned in favour of reiteration and recuperation. Serious work is being done to reconfigure the distant past and leave the recent past and near future to artists and their degraded speculative structures. The structural premise of the exhibition has become a series of conceits, floating free of that which is being produced. It is hard to find a curatorial strategy that could reflect the evasive techniques of artists in the face of a renewed dialectics between rocks and slate. The exhibition as a form has shifted from being a neglected aspect of curatorial practice to becoming the central focus of the complete curator. The artwork, in sullen response, has become resistant to the exhibition or only significant within the exhibition as form. The exhibition is no longer restricted to a moment or a set period. It exceeds all temporal constraints and extends beyond any singular deployment of work which would only have meaning in the context of the exhibition. The potential of discourse and filtration has given way to illustrations of accretion. The discursive cannot be accurately reproduced within a regime of didactics. Within this frame, research becomes any reading and could include any work. Any reading and any work, gridded by didactics, does not reproduce more than the content with which it started, combined with the excessive framing that results. Research as an act of semi-autonomy cannot be critically accessed within the regime of the complete curator; the process of research is a type of work that remains *just alongside* and is only sustained by the artworks' supporting role or perceived relegation to the market. This is where research finds its strength and indefatigability – via its endlessness and its unlimited purview.

Alongside these developments, the art fair has remained a place of exhibitions arranged by gallerists, which exists in sympathy with some curatorial consciousness but only within a retarded set of references that attempts to empty out all significance from the dominance of the exhibition as form. The essential relationality of the art fair actually diminishes the autonomous potential of the work – not due to processes of valuation and exchange, but due to its echo of the exhibition prior to the complete curator. Navigation of the art fair only makes sense in relation to the exhibition as a historical experience. The art school cubicle is perfect training for the future art fair booth – lacking both exhibition and curatorial consciousness. The two are analogous architectures that are both phantoms of a pre-curatorial gallery. The contemporary mega artist's compound of various production stages and workshops is the museum space of the pre-curatorial. The *products* of such luxurious sites of limited production are no longer shipped out to become part of a mega work authored under the comforting regulations of the curatorial – neither the work nor the interpretation of the work can compete with the contextual drive of the exhibition as a form reified by the complete curator. Discursivity is excessively verifiable and forms a partnership with research within domains that appear to resist the reach of capital or at least to keep precisely priced exchange moments at a distance. Discursivity and research ex nihilio are the strategies of the complete curator. They feed into each other and provide a push into and pull out of precisely determined roles towards a continual identity in motion. While incapable of offering a complete break, this creates an image sequence of roles in motion, which dazzles the insatiable desire of art structures that seek to possess and exchange the products of the complete curator.

The complete curator no longer locates him/herself in a tense standoff with specific institutional frameworks. The curatorial and institutional have meshed, melded and reformed. The arrangement of structures has become the deployment of exhibitions. The institutional lays down a history of exhibitions and not a history of art or artists. At the same time, the complete curator focuses upon a history of yearning exhibitions and structures and no longer a history of artists and particular institutional mechanisms. The notion of a work undertaken in advance of any other work has become subsumed within the strategic demonstration of the exhibition as a form. The projection of potential through the discursive, or the work of the artist filtered by the curatorial, has been replaced by a verifiable sequence of steps that furthers the history of exhibitions over and above the potential of any given development. Once an overlooked terrain of understanding, the exhibition as form, with its own histories and meanings, has completely transformed the curatorial and the work of some artists now. We should not look towards individual artworks – unless we are completely ignorant of, and smitten with, value as cost – but rather towards the way objects and ideas are performed within the setting of the exhibition with all the new complexities that this might imply. Within this terrain, the developed artist offers self-curatorship as a demonstration of fidelity towards the exhibitionistic aspect of the complete curator.

The arrangement of ideas in space is, nevertheless, still mediated. Object combinations are no longer sufficient to function in relation to each other by troubling the complete curator who, in turn, does not agitate the limited sufficiency of the object, action or intent. In this arrangement, the critical posture is permitted to float free from that which is arranged and from the arranger of those things. This means that a given set of objects or ideas, in combination in any place or form, cannot trouble or distress or override the complete curator. At the same time, the complete curator's disinterest with this lack allows a 'cloud' of ideas and potentials to float around any contingent display of things or ideas in any given exhibition structure that might be imagined. This is neither fully conceptual nor conceptualistic. It is a set of parallels in which the space between the artwork's lack (however 'conceptual' the work might claim or appear to be) is matched by the complete curator's sense that it is not worth agitating to replace the lack; instead, it might be more productive to accept that an unseen potential within an exhibition now points away from the work and towards something that cannot be made and cannot be fully imagined without the transformative conditions of a completely new model of human relations. A permanent exchange of absences has developed – an absent logic meeting an absence of regard. Each deployed work is offset by an increasing sequence of contextually interpretative structures. In this constant flow of control between varied points, the primacy of 'art' is only visible when it resists the codes of the complete curator. The diminished status of art operates in direct correlation with its utility for the curatorial and its potential as a straightforward commodity signifier – an irresolvable doubling.

Research is at the basis of certain artistic practices and some methodologies deployed by the complete curator. However, research cannot be independently verified. Unless enacted within the frame of the exhibition, research may suggest lengthy engagement while the actual intensity of 'finding out' is impossible to gauge. The gathering of material without judgment may be research, as might the detailed investigation of one minor object. Research carries a scientistic authority. Research implies an evacuation from zones of commodified exchange and directs us towards the apparent authority of the institutional library or laboratory. Alone, it cannot build better systems or structures, yet it can point out how far away they still appear to be.

32 – 46

TOWARDS THE EXHIBITION AS RESEARCH

Simon Sheikh

The current codification of the term 'the curatorial' indicates an expansion of the notion of curating, of curatorial processes - its practices and histories, the role of the curator and its potentialities. It signifies an emerging field of education, which has to do with curating as a field for, and possibly of, research. One can now, for instance, research curatorial histories, whether via the figure of the curator or in terms of single exhibitions - research that has both canonical and non-canonical form and that takes place both within and outside of academia. Although there are no clear divisions between these endeavours, certain oppositions are beginning to emerge between the academic and the anecdotal, the historical and the practical, the hagiographic and the critical. As with all new terms, its very definition is a battleground for ideological struggles, as well as for territorialisations from individual authors and players, as well as institutions and disciplines. For instance, are exhibition histories the remit of an art history department of a curatorial studies programme or, even, a discussion to be had outside academic structures among practitioners (i.e. curators) themselves, for themselves? Alas, curatorial conferences and publications are now so numerous that it is easy to forget that the literature, and even knowledge, about curating as a separate entity within art production was more than scarce just a decade ago. The same timeframe has also seen the proliferation of curating as an object of study - not just theoretically and historically but practically, with many educational programmes in curating now available worldwide, which means, if nothing else, that there is a certain scholarly market for books and debates around curating.

Researching the Curatorial

In all of these employments of the term, the curatorial has to do with research, in terms of art history and the (brief) history of the concept and practice of curating. However, perhaps, and more intriguingly, the curatorial could now be posited as a form of research, not just into exhibition-making, but a specific mode of research that may or may not take on the spatial and temporal form of an exhibition. After the advent of the curatorial and post-research, the exhibition would, so to speak, simply be the designation for any project realised through curating and all that this implies in terms of addressees and research methods. The curatorial is, in this sense, not necessarily something that takes on the form and eventual character of the exhibition, but something that employs the thinking involved in exhibition-making and researching. So, on the one hand, we are witnessing a period of historicisation - through exhibition histories and canons of curating, in which research is understood in terms of excavation, (re)evaluation and contextualisation of particular exhibitions and curators - slowly but surely making a new history of art through the curatorial rather than through artists' works, oeuvres and contexts.[1] Although histories of exhibitions and exhibition-making tend to be located in a specific period, namely the European post-war period - the prolonged moment of art as contemporary - they must, by definition, also reconsider the very definition of periodisation, whether in the sense of art history or within the methodological debates on periodisation within the broader discipline of history.[2] On the other hand, research not only takes place within a tendency towards historicisation, and, perhaps, re-enactment, but also through a mode of expansion - what we could call the expanded field of curating.

In the expanded field of curating, the curatorial is itself an activity of research; although there is no consensual definition of research, it would seem to encompass varying, and sometimes divergent, ideas of the exhibition as a form of research. The curatorial project is a vehicle for researching into something specific - into a particular field of interest or topic, into a particular cultural location or local artistic practice - or for cultural research understood as experimenting with various forms of public address and congregation, building or even antagonising communities, whether designated and located or universal and unknown, inoperative or becoming. Within exhibitions or otherwise, the curatorial is that which can research into, and onto, an object of study that does not necessarily stem from artistic production and development per se. Rather, the aesthetic and, to a large degree, the art world are here seen as tools for investigating something other than art, for presenting ideas, research results and project outcomes in a different discourse from other forms such as politics proper, sociology, science, journalism, etc. What is implied here, and also what is at stake in a more general and political

1. These days, many conferences are dedicated to exhibition histories, as is a book series, three volumes and counting, published by the journal, *Afterall*, and several books are emerging about the careers of particular curators (at least six books have so far been published on the work of the late Harald Szeeman, for example).

2. I am here thinking of critical and conceptual approaches to history-writing, as in the figures of Reinhart Koselleck and Hayden White. For more on post/modern debates on the discipline of history, see: Keith Jenkins (ed.), *The Postmodern History Reader*. Routledge. 1997.

sense, is the curatorial as a specific system of knowledge production and its relation to other forms of research and an overall research culture – and thus to the relationship between knowledge and power – and, moreover, between knowing and unknowing and what this means in relation to empowering subjects, groups and movements.

Two Notions of Research

However, before making such claims for curating as research based and capable of contributing – negatively or positively, critically or affirmatively – to a general research culture and broader issues of power and knowledge relations, it is pertinent to define what exactly is meant by curatorial research – a notion easily bandied about, particularly in the current debates, denigrations and celebrations of so-called artistic research. Surely artistic research, whatever we might mean by that or think about that, would be the first cousin of any notion of curatorial research we can possibly think up. Would the idea of curating research have any momentum or relevance were it not for the now decade-long discussion on the merits and methods, trials and tribulations of artistic research as an entity, whether discussed in the academy as practice-based PhDs or used as the main reference point for something as hegemonic as documenta? Without becoming immersed, or even lost, in that particular discussion and its trajectories, it might be useful to simply recall two very different translations of the English word 'research' that we find in other languages (being fully aware of the irony of translating anything from English, the *lingua franca* of the art world, into one of the languages that provides English with its roots). Whereas, in English, research covers very different types of researching – which can then be distinguished through various prefixes such as 'artistic' – one would translate research into French or German as either *recherché* or *forschung.*

The first term, *recherché*, indicates looking into something, as when a reporter looks for sources, witnesses and stories, but also in terms of checking these for accuracy. In this sense, research is not only about getting your facts straight but also about finding a story and an angle on this story, a sort of framing of the real. This notion of research is obviously also found in other production processes, ranging from consumer research to location scouting. Within artistic practice, it also always has a place, as when an artist researches a topic, looks into an archive, finds and experiments with materials etc., in ways not fundamentally different to those of a journalist or fact checker in a news agency, which is why this work is often not the work of the artist him or herself but rather delegated to the studio assistant. The same goes for curatorial work, in which there is always research about possible artists and artworks within a given frame: who are the artists working in this vein or in this region and are such and such pre-existing works relevant to this particular survey, and so on. Although rarely celebrated in contemporary debates on artistic research, this is the most widespread form of curatorial research, to the point of being presupposed as an almost unquestioned tradition, which is perhaps precisely why it receives so little attention.

At the same time, *recherché* is absolutely vital to any understanding of the curatorial as research-based – or, for that matter, research-led – in acknowledging that we are thinking of the curatorial as historical or expanded, in the terms outlined above. The seriousness, depth and rigour of this factual type of research is highly pertinent to the curating of exhibitions, even if it is placed lower in the hierarchy of creative work and not usually understood as authored. In the first instance – that of the historical – *recherché* is paramount in revisiting an exhibition, when, not unlike an investigative journalist or diligent biographer, one needs to check the facts and compare them to the myth. What is most often needed when considering exhibition histories is, perhaps ironically, that one looks beyond an exhibition's historicisation, particularly when dealing with famous or notorious exhibitions that have come to symbolise certain tendencies and breakthroughs over time.(3) How did the exhibition actually look, what was included and how and what has been highlighted or downplayed in the subsequent historicisation? Theoretically, we could think of an exhibition's after-life in a Benjaminian sense (but that would, of course, lead us straight into the realm of the not-yet-discussed notion of *forschung*). The process of recherché is equally useful when discussing a less well-known, or even unknown or forgotten, exhibition, since it is this very process of looking for facts and evidence that, presumably, led the researcher to this exhibition in the first place. Similarly, with curating as an expanded field – as a particular

3. A case in point is the historicisation of *This is Tomorrow*, held at the ICA in London in 1956, as a pop art exhibition. While what was subsequently named pop art has been represented in exhibitions, notably the work of Richard Hamilton, the exhibition actually consisted of a number of collaborations between architects and artists, and by far the majority of them actually highlighted a functionalist and constructivist modernism instead.

mode of investigating subjects, objects and their relations - we again find the need to collect materials, data, sources, which, in turn, can form constellations, leading to both speclation, presumption and the positing of a thesis, i.e. moving from recherché towards *forschung*.

Research As Science

Whereas *recherché* is to be understood mainly in terms of journalistic research, *forschung* implies a scientific model of research, and thus an entirely different relation to subjects and objects. If journalism understands itself as an endeavour that uncovers the truth by looking at the facts, and thus constructing a story, or what we can call a discourse, from what it finds, then science works, principally and traditionally, in the opposite direction - that is, from the discourse to the objects. Science implies a specific way of looking, through apparatuses of knowledge, as exemplified by the microscope and the laboratory, which also goes for ethnographic and sociological models of field research. *Forschung* is thus the translation of research in the scientific sense, meaning that it not only uses specific methods of investigation but, moreover, that it operates with hypotheses and propositions which - contra to journalism - can then be tested against the behaviour of its objects of study. A thesis may be proven, discarded or modified depending on the results of research. So, unlike *recherché*, which treats its findings as facts, *forschung* treats them as uncertainties and concepts that need to be defined and may contradict the pre-emptive thesis about them. If, according to the method of *recherché*, a certain story turns out to be untrue or, for that matter, not interesting enough to be newsworthy, this does not, in itself, lead to a modification of journalistic methods, just as the inability to find a proper location for a shoot does not undo the idea of location scouting, but rather simply moves the gaze somewhere else, onto something else. In science, however, a thesis will have be forsaken if it transpires that molecules do not act as expected under the specific experimental conditions. The procedures for research in the sciences thus constantly undergo transformations which, in turn, transform science itself and its paradigms of truth - at least in principle. In order for science to be scientific, it always needs to have a theory about its object of study and thus a different claim to authenticity in relation to the production of truth than that implied by the notion of *recherché*.

There is a grey area between research that is scientific, or makes claims for scientificity, and research that is not - that is, between what has been described as *forschung* and *recherché* respectively - namely the social sciences, which seem to operate between the two. Sociology can be accused of only finding what it looks for - that its methods of sourcing and surveilling always already inscribe its objects within the remit of its existing knowledge system. But, in its quest and claim for scientificity, sociology must always try to repress, or make invisible, its moments of *recherché* and heighten and insist upon its framing as *forschung*. This is important on two counts - partly because it speaks of a hierarchical relationship between the two notions of research, and partly because the curatorial, insofar as it is a part of the social sciences, faces similar methodological questions as sociology in terms of defining its research culture in relation to the hierarchy of knowledge. As sanctified production of knowledge, science is part of the academy, and, as such, an elevated form of knowledge. It receives official support and requires public respect, and is, for those very reasons, also viewed with suspicion in certain quarters. Conversely, journalism may be regarded a more lowly form of investigation, seedy even, and simultaneously as not only manipulative but also truthful and brave, when exposing the dishonesty of those in power at all costs, or going where no one else dares to go, providing images and testimonies in spite of everything (such as in the much fêted figure of the war correspondent). In this sense, while we can view *recherché* and *forschung* as two different regimes of truth, they nonetheless share a virtual monopoly on the production of truth in the public realm.

The location of research is not only a matter of hierarchy, however, but also indicative of its methodology. Whereas *recherché* could take place in the archive or out in the field, *forschung* implies the spatial production of specific sites for research - such as the laboratory and clinic - antiseptic spaces in which things can be isolated and thus studied and examined. Moreover, the formulation and execution of the thesis indicates a notion of time, of a project contained within a certain timeframe. Scientific research must not only provide a working thesis but also do so within a given timeframe. It requires a research plan that specifies not only goals and how to achieve them but also how long this will take, be it three months or three years. Research funding is never provided in a continuous stream, but always limited to specific timeframes, and success in achieving formulated goals will determine whether a research team will be able to have its next project funded. The parallels with curatorial research are only too obvious – the historical similarities between the laboratory and the white cube of the gallery as spaces for isolated viewing and experimenting with objects are self-evident. But the notion of a hand-picked specialist project team is nowadays also all-pervasive in the making of exhibitions, particularly those with clear research objectives. While it is obvious that almost any exhibition employs *recherché* to a lesser or greater extent, not all exhibitions can truly be thought of as *forschung* – lacking a thesis, proposition or laboratory. We must, then, ask which curatorial research projects and exhibitions are built upon a thesis that is to be proven or disproven.

The Exhibition As Research

This proposition can be radicalised further. Let us presume that a curatorial project did have a thesis, which it set out to investigate through its research and present in an exhibition, proving or disproving the thesis; could this lead to the exhibition presenting its own failure? Furthermore, would this lead to a questioning of its research method and to the transformation of curatorial processes and institutional practices? Adopting the most ambitious notion of research, this question should be asked both within the historical and the expanded sense of the curatorial field. When looking at exhibition histories, we must thus not ask how they produced discourse, added to it and/or transformed it, but instead consider their negative space. How could the writing of exhibition history be negated, and negate, the very idea of curatorial history as linear and isolated from other forms of public display, other forms of exhibition-making, from markets and fairs to science expositions and world exhibitions? Besides looking into exhibition practices as a form of research, can one also think of the exhibition itself as researching? In other words, can the exhibition be a site for research and, if so, can one, then, also think of it as a type: the research exhibition? We would then have to understand the exhibition as a proposition, which may be exactly how we can understand *forschung*, in terms not only of exhibition history but also contemporary curatorial practice, and thus what we should take it to task for as a so-called expanded practice (implying the curatorial as not just exhibitions but also other forms of assemblage and assembly).

By now, it should be evident that an art-historical exhibition requires research, but that does not tell us what research is. Rather, research here has multiple meanings; there is, in certain cases, the research of tracking and registering all the works of a certain artist, period or genre, then research into the availability of such works for a given exhibition, and so on. There is also a more scientific notion of research involved, partly in techniques of preservation, but also in the claims for art-historical methods as scientific – in terms of making a new analysis of the given works, constellations, and all the rest of it. But what are the moments and notions of research in exhibitions of contemporary works and positions? Again, they might differ according to the type and scope of the exhibition – a regional exhibition, for example, requires research in terms of reading, study visits, consultancy with important players in the local place, etc., which may differ drastically from the research involved in the formulation of a thesis or even a proposition. Whereas the thesis can be proven or disproven, the proposition advances its claims along a different rationale, namely positing its ideas as claims which, if followed, would then make certain things possible, not only logically and philosophically, but also, in our case, aesthetically and politically. In this way, invoking the proposition allows for speculation, for the curatorial as political imaginary.

The curatorial project – including its most dominant form, the exhibition – should thus not only be thought of as a form of mediation of research but also as a site for carrying out this research, as a place for enacted research. Research here is not only that which comes before realisation but also that which is realised throughout actualisation. That which would otherwise be thought of as formal means of transmitting knowledge – such as design structures, display models and perceptual experiments – is here an integral part of the curatorial mode of address, its content production, its proposition. The idea of the research exhibition – in which the exhibition is not only a vehicle for the presentation of research results (in both senses) but also a site for ongoing research around the formats and thematic concerns of the exhibition – lies behind the conceptualisation of two exhibitions, which will be analysed in some detail below.

Case Study 1: Enacting Research

The exhibitions in question are *All That Fits: The Aesthetics of Journalism*, realised in 2011 at QUAD in Derby, curated by myself and Alfredo Cramerotti, and *Unauthorized*, which I put together as part of a PhD thesis at Inter Arts Center in Malmö, Sweden, in 2012. In *All That Fits*, research was not only undertaken in an exploration of the thematics of the show but also enacted in the very form of the exhibition, unfolding the intricacies of the topic in spatial terms and in experiments with modes of (possible) viewership. Presenting seemingly incompatible components – such as aesthetic experience and political activism, community events and private investigations – Alfredo Cramerotti and I tried, perhaps provocatively, to advance the idea that art and journalism are not separate forms of communication, but rather two sides of the production and distribution of images and information. In communicating this nexus between imaging and informing, the exhibition brought to the surface the aesthetic principles used in such acts of transmission. The artworks, many of which were time-based, were presented in three groupings, or chapters, that followed each other throughout the exhibition period, although with some works displayed continuously.[4] This change of scenery and topicality was made visible through a special exhibition design, consisting of a different colour scheme for each group – red, blue and green, mirroring the RGB colour code and the cathode ray – as well as through a specifically designed modular system of display, consisting of small adjustable cubes that could be reconfigured in various ways to accommodate the different works, simultaneously *reflecting* the rotation of the news cycle, albeit at a different, slowed-down speed. Simultaneously, the cubes were fairly simply and cheaply made, which heightened the sense of pragmatics and changeability; it would be easy to imagine more or less of them, in different configurations, and it was hopefully feasible to make them oneself. We believed that modulation of the cubes and colour scheme would not only make our curatorial editing more visible but also make the material more user-friendly – with the works not just one after another in an endless row of images and information, but a juxtaposition of different approaches each dialoguing with each other, the media and the overall theme in various ways and combinations. Since 16 out of the 24 total works were time-based, mostly videos, we wanted to give the audience a proper chance to watch, and

4. The 'permanent' installations were the works of Eric Baudelaire, Graziela Kunsch, Walid Raad/The Atlas Group, Michael Takeo Magruder and SLUM-TV, although Kunsch's selection of short videos was remixed according to each chapter and the position of Raad's piece was shifted. As for the other three pieces, they were kept unchanged due to their relevance to all three chapters in the case of Baudelaire's staged photographs, whereas the other two – including Magruder's commissioned work on the news-breaking phenomenon of Wikileaks, realised quickly to comment on current events – were both placed in the lobby outside the exhibition space proper as a kind of commentary. SLUM-TV's work is a short, pseudo commercial, advertising the possibility of winning an artists' residency in Mathare, a slum in Nairobi, Kenya.

even re-watch, each piece, which would be feasible as QUAD does not charge any entrance fee.[5]

All three chapters in the exhibition - *The Speaker, The Image* and *The Militant* - related to the notion of truth production, as implied by the genres of art and journalism. As aesthetic regimes, both journalism and art make claims for the truth, albeit of a different kind. One is a coded system that speaks for the truth (or so it claims); the other a set of activities that questions itself at every step (or so it claims), thus *making* truth. Whereas journalism provides a view on the world 'out there', as it 'really' is, art often presents a view on the view - truth posited as acts of (self)reflection. *All That Fits* examined both types of truth production, as systems of information that define truth in terms of the visible - producing not only what can be seen but also what can be imagined, and thus imaged. As such, the exhibition was centred on what we called the aesthetics of journalism - how images are produced to appear as truthful. Referring to Foucault's concept of *parrhésia*, the question of the truth-sayer was examined; who can speak the truth, and does this require certain types of speaking as well as certain subject positions?[6] As singular figures throughout modernity, both the reporter and the artist have been viewed as authentic voices and heroic figures. Simultaneously, they have been vilified as complicit and corrupt. What we wanted to investigate was the aesthetic means of representation and rhetoric that makes these figures - journalist and artists as truth-sayers - become visible, as such, in discourse.

In this way, *The Speaker* concerned itself with a specific figure - the speaking subject, or author, its figures of authority and figures of speech, as well as its framings of the real in terms of editorial processes and camera angles. How does this figure emerge through discourse, and what are its functions? What can be said and not said in order for a speaking subject to appear real, authentic, authoritative and/or truthful.

5. QUAD also houses a BFI archive, which can be accessed free of charge, as well as a commercial cinema. The cinema was used for the screening of Douglas Fishbone's feature film, and we worked with a curator from the BFI to make a special selection from the archive relating to the theme of our exhibition, to be available in the BFI space for the duration of *All That Fits*. The full list of artists participating in *All That Fits* was: Sammy Baloji, Yael Bartana, Eric Baudelaire, Ursula Biemann, Ross Birrell, Michael Blum, Broomberg & Charain, Abraham Cruzvillegas, Anita Di Blanco, Marcelo Exposito, Douglas Fishbone, Zachary Formwalt, Tamar Guimaraes, K8 Hardy & Wynne Greenwood, Lamia Joreige, Graziela Kunsch, Renzo Martens, Walid Raad / The Atlas Group, Oliver Ressler, Katya Sander, Hito Steyerl, SLUM-TV, Michael Takeo Magruder and Alejandro Vidal.

6. Michel Foucault, *The Courage of Truth - Lectures at College de France 1983-1984*. Palgrave Macmillan. 2011.

What is implied in certain speech acts and subject positions, such as the figure of 'the reporter' and 'the artist, as well as the 'witness' and the 'source'? *The Image* examined how images are ideologically produced, not only through the framings and positionings of the above-mentioned categories but also through counter-images being created. Here, the making and politics of image production was reflected, discussed and deconstructed, proposing an aesthetics of journalism and documentary as that which can get to the truth of the ideology of mass-media images, in opposition to their claims to neutrality and pragmatism. Finally, *The Militant* continued the strand of counter-images and counter-information, but through the artistic employment of journalistic traits such as exposé and research. However, the practices highlighted here tended to function in the place of the media, and uncover what media does not, going where it does not go, thus returning to some of reportage's initial claims, which have been left behind in an increasingly commercialised industry.

The chapters had the potential for a dual function. On the one hand, they had the potential for broadening the issues the exhibition tried to discuss - namely, how does one frame the truth, how does one make it appear truthful through framing and staging? This multidimensional approach was meant to supply several entry points into the topic, as well as possible exit routes. On the other hand, the chapters served a reflective function, making the possible forms of a show visible through the transformation of the same installed elements, re-arranged and repainted for each constellation. The changeability of the cubes served as a metaphor for, if not the production of truth, the formation of discourse. In a positive sense, the exhibition was less modernist than a model, seemingly less clinical and more a suggestion for the exhibition as a try-out or mock-up. As truth production, the exhibition tried to pose a principal question, namely whether it is possible to work with both aesthetics *and* informatics, to be both reflexive and meditative, all the while asking viewers to query how reality is presented as real and thus engage in a politics of truth.

Case Study 2: Research and Authority

The second example of a research exhibition, *Unauthorized*, was a showcase for various archival artefacts and works of art, organised around the notion of unauthorised cultural practices and initiatives that may or may not go against sanctified cultural policies. This outlined the contours of a vast field of positions and possibilities, ranging from historical forms of alternative culture to current strategies of political exodus, as well as artistic positions such as the secretive, even elitist, underground ethos, or such figures as the amateur and the outsider. In each of these very different instances, there is a shared concern – namely, the attempt to establish a separate system of value and meaning, a system or discourse which does not require institutional validation, which does not suppose institutionalisation, as such, but rather its own, often private, forms of circulation and authorisation. Here, two contradictory notions of research, different from those outlined above, are at play simultaneously – not historically, but within the form of the exhibition itself. On the one hand, research is required in order to excavate and represent these artistic positions, while the positions themselves are a form of artistic research into representation, circulation and validation. And, since these practices are somewhat outside, perhaps even oppositional to, the remit of institutional, cultural and curatorial practice, a tension existed at the heart of the exhibition that was unresolvable but nevertheless productive of a critical space between institution, anti-institutionalisation and self-institutionalisation. The exhibition must, then, become a place for a discussion about the status of its objects of study, asking what the role of authorisation is within artistic practices of self-organisation and self-publishing. How is something authorised, and, indeed, authored, outside of hegemonic cultural institutions? And how do such efforts relate to, as well as alter, their positions and articulations when confronted with institutional inscription and initiation, as presented in this exhibition?

In contrast to *All That Fits*, only four projects were presented in *Unauthorized*, precisely to steer clear of any notion of a survey. The institutional setting was also quite different, Inter Arts Center being a university gallery and a research centre for the arts, with all that entails in relation to academia and a scientific model of research at the expense of its public side (by default, if not design, university galleries generally tend to have less publicity). Moreover, each of the four projects was not necessarily a singular artwork or installation, but rather bodies of work and research materials that attested to a specific mode of archiving and collecting. Exhibited thus were objects and artefacts that had to do with artistic production, research and autonomy, each referring to its own system of production, ordering and circulation but comparable through the system of the exhibition itself. The exhibition was employed here as a mode of organisation of objects and discourses, and the artistic positions represented were, in this sense, to be viewed as *exemplary.* These collections were displayed through and around a reconstruction of George Nelson's Struc-tube display system – a light, transportable module envisaged for exhibitions at trade fairs in 1947, at the height of architecture and design being thought of as social forms of aesthetic production. The easily constructible and moveable Struc-tube was never actually put into production, and has been appropriated by the artist Martin Beck, questioning both authorship, authenticity and authorisation.

On show in and around the Struc-tube were a number of mail art objects from the artist Niels Lomholt's large collection from the 1970s and '80s. The representation of this informal and anti-institutional global network took the form of a single project from 1976, entitled *Two-Circle Formular.* This was a formula designed by Lomholt and sent out to all in the network, to which he received 224 responses, making sender and receiver one and the same. A formula can be viewed as a tool for collecting and organising data, for undertaking research, although, in this case, there was no apparent function for these data, circumventing the very idea of a formula. Rather, they functioned as a type of MacGuffin, a template for possible artistic responses and rejections. The mail art network itself is highly instructive to the discussion of authorisation, and especially the notion of working outside authorisation, refuting and even refusing it. The network was open to everyone, on the condition that everyone took active part in it. Everyone had to send and respond in order to receive – one could not, crucially, participate only as a consumer or collector, simply subscribing and paying for the reception of objects. Rather, mail art operated on the basis of a gift economy, with all participants giving each other their labour. As a network, it existed in and for itself, not for institutional recognition or financial gain but as an exchange of something not yet commodified – the circulation of thoughts and ideas.

In addition to this historical material, there was a collection of even earlier self-published magazines, edited and drawn between 1918 and 1922, by a teenage Otto Melchior when he was a young communist. Three magazines, *Quick, World Echo* and *The Free Review*, have been excavated by the artist, Eva la Cour, forming the basis of a series of works and reflections, as seen in a video accompanying the display of the archive. Also on show was the self-described 'eccentric archive' of Ines Doujak, who has collected artefacts and textiles from Bolivia and Peru that escape easy classification as either art or craft, lying outside such hegemonic Western concepts and modes of understanding. They have their own system not only of signification but also of use, having both a practical and symbolic function. In turn, these artefacts and their stories and storytelling inform Doujak's collages, presented in Malmö through a number of posters, the surface of which became a place for multiple inscriptions of meaning within a transcultural transfer. Doujak's collection is not ethnographic in any sense, but immersed in artistic practices of research and representation. Finally, a collection of album covers, mostly from the 1980s, by the reclusive Texan outsider, Jandek, were on display, alongside a documentary on his enigmatic work. Jandek is the pseudonym of a cultural producer whose 'real' name, or even life world, has so far never been revealed. His albums are all self-produced and released, through the label Corwood Industries, and they bear no credits apart from the song titles and a PO box number. They simply exist in themselves, as conceptual objects, without any participation in the circulation of discourse – interviews, promotion, concerts etc. – that usually characterises the music industry.

The works and objects were presented in the form of an archive, with internal, and perhaps uncertain, rules, while shedding light on the processes of researching, collecting and exhibiting. The exhibition was thus used as a site for both presentation and representation, in which forms of display were interwoven into the discursive formation of marginalia and authority, not least in the sense of a politics of autonomy in the act of self-instituting. As cultural production, the four positions represented in *Unauthorized* all attempted to sidestep institutionalisation through self-instituting production, circulation and reception, whereas the exhibition, as such, was inevitably placed between various forms of authorisation – artistic, institutional and academic. This raises questions not only about what research is – and about possible hierarchies between its various forms and modes – but also about who has the authority to designate theirs and others' practice as research and call themselves or someone else a researcher. As the positions represented in *Unauthorized* hopefully demonstrated, artistic research is not necessarily concerned with authorisation, despite ongoing efforts to institutionalise it within art educational facilities. On a more positive note, the exhibition as research can challenge the monolithic and populist tendencies of exhibition-making and history-writing and contribute to the overall culture of research, altering what is understood as either *recherché* or *forschung* and their virtual monopoly on truth production. But it can only do so by avoiding solidification and codification, remaining unwieldy, uncertain and unfinished.

47 – 59

RENEWING THE CURATORIAL REFRAIN: SUSTAINABLE RESEARCH IN CONTEMPORARY ART

Maja & Reuben Fowkes

The overwhelming sense of crisis - which has become a global leitmotif over the past few years, manifested in politics and the media as a seemingly intractable economic emergency - is also being felt in the cultural field. Within the curatorial nexus, the tremors of the crisis are apparent in the first place in a decline in public funding for culture and a drought of collectors for all except the bluest chip galleries. They have, though, also led to concerns about the lack of contemporary relevance of the activities of art institutions, whose failure to explore radical alternatives reflects their implication in the structures that engendered the crisis in the first place. The institutional art world colludes in the maintenance of retrograde social hierarchies - a tendency that is also expressed through the wholesale adoption of business models and the readiness of art institutions to accommodate themselves to the needs of power.

Curatorial research is not only channelled by the strategic interests of art institutions; it is also constrained by the compulsion to incorporate the relentless search for innovative forms, methods and outcomes in order to best capture the present moment within the flux of contemporary art. Exhibition themes and lists of artists spread like wildfire in today's hyperlinked art world. No sooner has an idea, personality or cultural reference tweeted its way to the surface of global awareness than a string of curatorial projects has arisen to capitalise on the trend. Curatorial research is driven by a manic quest for the next big idea before it goes viral, the next up-and-coming artist before he or she is snapped up by the museum-gallery double act of commercialisation and the most radical theorist before they are charmed into writing opinion pieces for profit-orientated art magazines.

The task facing curatorial researchers is, in fact, not unlike the scenario proposed by Paris-based duo, Société Réaliste, in their 2006 project, *Transitioners* - a trend design agency that predicts the colour schemes and logotypes of future revolutions[1] - in that curators, operating under the nerve-wracking conditions of the cultural entrepreneur, face constant pressure to be at least six months to a year ahead of the curve. The short-termism of mainstream art institutions, combined with the continuous demand for the manufacture of novelty, raises the question of sustainability, not in the sense commandeered by economics, but in its original, wide-ranging ecological meaning.

1. See the website of Société Réaliste: http://www.societerealiste.net/#TRANS

Camouflaged by the global economic downturn, the ecological crisis looms at an unprecedented scale, from the rapid melting of the Polar icecap to the pollution that has spread to the outer orbits of the Earth, with spacecraft and satellite debris floating in space. At the same time, green capitalism has spectacularly failed to solve the energy crisis, with research into renewables overtaken by the rush for Arctic oil and the expansion of nuclear power, regardless of Fukushima. All the while, deepening economic inequalities and the unrelenting infiltration of capitalist logic into social relations have corroded the landscape of human subjectivities, which are endangered as much as the species disappearing daily.

The ecological crisis is best apprehended in terms of what Félix Guattari conceived of as the interlinked environmental, social and mental domains in his seminal study of the *Three Ecologies*. Any attempt to think about sustainability in the curatorial sphere needs, therefore, to take into consideration all three registers of ecology, by being aware of the environmental, social and mental impact of the practice of exhibition-making. In other words, the extent to which consideration of the environmental footprint is an integral part of the creative processes of curating, whether exhibitions are conceived and realised according to egalitarian and democratic principles and the degree to which they succeed in clearing the fog of consumerism, could provide the elements for a sustainable 'mood board' of curating. Further considerations could be the affirmative aspects of collaboration, translocal insights and autonomous thinking, which could add up to an 'antidote', in the Guattarian sense of reconstituting human subjectivities. The most optimistic outcomes of such practice could be a curatorial 'refrain' – akin to Guattari's concept of the 'existential refrain' – which, like the famous 'taste of the madeleine' in Proust, has the catalytic power to transform.[2]

The formidable obstacles on the route to more sustainable curating include the spread of post-Fordist business practices to the art world and the influence of pernicious ideologies, such as resurgent nationalism, on curatorial positions. The influence of managerial thinking on contemporary art is manifested in the increasingly hierarchical organisation of institutions, as well as in the widespread adoption of outsourcing as a strategy for curating major art events such as biennials. Within large-scale exhibition projects, the top-down model of appointing a chief

2. Félix Guattari, *The Three Ecologies*. The Athalone Press. 2000. p. 36.

curator with a team of subordinate curators, each of whom is responsible for a particular geographical or thematic area but has no ownership of the overall concept, has much in common with the practice of sub-contracting in the business world, which, according to an online dictionary, is 'very useful in situations where the range of required capabilities for a project is too diverse to be possessed by a single general contractor' and 'may assist in keeping costs under control and mitigate overall project risk'. In short, there is a clear difference between 'sub-curating' and genuinely collaborative models in which authorship and responsibility are shared and power structures are horizontal rather than vertical.

The infiltration of capitalist practices into the realm of contemporary art has come about as an almost accidental consequence of developments in the profession of curating. Enthusiasm for an ultra-expanded notion of the curatorial – which encompasses a multi-functional remit, incorporating most, if not all, of the activities associated with the realisation of art projects – may end up being tempered by the realisation that such changes to the division of artistic labour play into the hands of semio-capitalism. The fluidity of the concept of the curatorial may even be viewed as an instrument of de-skilling, since, once you move away from the integrated figure of the curator to a more fragmented and abstract notion of curatorial activity which can be broken up into ever smaller parts, the sense of individual responsibility for curating exhibitions based on intimate knowledge is diminished.(3)

The influence of the post-Fordist schema on curatorial practice opens up the possibility for anomalous situations in which art programmes are curated by committees or by even more abstract entities that would, under normal circumstances, be restricted to ancillary roles such as funding art projects or buying finished artworks. Accordingly, finance capital is no longer restricted to providing the funds for, and benefiting from the publicity from, contemporary art; it may also take the opportunity to participate in the core activities of curating. The 2012 exhibition, *At Your Service – Art and Labour*, at the Technical Museum of Vienna may be considered an innovative form of cooperation between a public museum and the charitable wing of an Austrian bank. The latter appointed two in-house curators – one from the advisory board of its art collection and one from its cultural programme – while three members of the museum

3. For the relation of deskilling to the legacies of conceptual art, see John Roberts, *The Intangibilities of Form: Skill and Deskilling in Art After the Readymade*. Verso. 2007.

staff were deemed 'responsible for project management and scientific aspects'.[4] In a topsy-turvy world order, it seems strangely appropriate that a financial institution would choose to curate an exhibition examining the flexibility of labour in a post-Fordist art world.

On the other end of the spectrum are curatorial projects that are played out through ideology and an appeal to mono-histories, claiming to offer a panacea for the ill effects of economic globalisation. A glaring example of this approach could be recognised in an exhibition curated by the director of the Budapest Kunsthalle in the summer of 2012. Rhetorically entitled *What is Hungarian?,* this was ostensibly a thematic exhibition containing many of the elements typical of a research-based exhibition, taking literary texts that posed the same question on the eve of World War II as its historical starting point and featuring extensive interviews with contemporary Hungarian writers and philosophers to flesh out the concept. Notably these exchanges were conducted by the curator and prominently displayed as a quasi artwork within the exhibition.

Deeper scrutiny of *What is Hungarian?* reveals a blatant intention to harmonise with the nationalist agenda of the current Hungarian government, with the curator failing to open up the reading of identity to include transnational migrant flows, let alone including artists whose work addressed questions of nationality from a critical perspective. Furthermore, artworks were deployed within the single-track layout of the show as part of a 'game of cultural-political legitimacy', as a result of which it was impossible for any individual work to 'preserve its original intention, critical character or even aesthetic autonomy'.[5] There are parallels here with what Guattari described as 'nationalitary schisms that suddenly flip into reactionary closure', which, for him, suggest a danger that lies in wait if we fail to see a 'rearticulation of the three fundamental types of ecology'.[6]

Countering such instances of retrograde 'nationalitarian' thinking offers a position from which to critique dominant ideological and social systems. It arises from the existential situation of living and belonging in different places, combining a comparative experience of the global with a sense of rootedness in multiple localities. Translocality, it is argued, 'deliberately confuses the boundaries of the local in an attempt to capture

4. See exhibition press release on: http://www.erstestiftung.org/factory/at-your-service-art-and-labour/
5. Review of 'What is Hungarian?' by G.M Tamás and Emese Kürti in *Magyar Narancs* 34/2012 (23 August 2012).
6. Guattari, op cit. p. 35.

the increasingly complicated nature of spatial processes and identities'.[7] Recent research in human geography also suggests that 'localities need not necessarily be limited to the shared social relations of local histories, experiences and relations, but can connect to wider geographical histories and processes', invoking the importance of local-local relations across spatial and temporal divides.[8]

Understood as 'simultaneous situatedness across different locales', translocality sounds like a rallying cry for those curators and artists who are trying to carve out a niche in Berlin, London or Prague while maintaining a presence in the place from which their transnational adventure started. In Eastern Europe, where multi-ethnicity is the more common form of transnational identity, translocality is a newer phenomenon that reflects the post-Cold War importance of counter-flows across Europe, with non-native artists, art historians and curators able to play a role in articulating and reimagining the post-national landscape of the region.

This was the axis of an exhibition, curated by the authors of this text, which brought to light the contribution of foreign artists to Hungarian contemporary art since 1989, entailing extensive archival research and interviews with art professionals, the organisation of a conference alongside the exhibition and the editing of an accompanying publication. The combination of all these elements increased the visibility of often-overlooked aspects of translocal exchange in the Hungarian art world.[9] In that sense, the many successful instances of curatorial research which aim to explore and foster connections between different localities short-circuit the monocultural orientation of particular art scenes and ground them in translocal realities.

The question of the renewal of the curatorial refrain can also be approached from the angle of the changing notion of curatorial research, which increasingly fails to lend itself to being sharply delimited but could rather be characterised as operating in a plural and cohabited space that overlaps with art historical practices and exists in parallel with artistic research. While much has been written about the tension between the curator as meta-author and the traditional figure of the artist, there are also problematic overlaps between the work of the curator and that of art historians, although the latter have been less outspoken than artists

7. Katherine Brickell and Ayona Datta, *Translocal Geographies: Spaces, Places, Connections*. Ashgate. 2011. p. 1-2.
8. Ibid, p. 2.
9. Maja and Reuben Fowkes, *Revolutionary Decadence: Foreign Artists in Budapest since 1989*. Kiscell Museum. 2009.

in defending their patch. References to art history on conference panels organised by curators are often couched in a conspiratorial snigger, as if to say that art historians belong in the archives while curators bring a uniquely contemporary perspective to the past. In their turn, art historians are irked by what they see as the superficial approach to art history taken by curators, who have a tendency to ransack the past for examples to illustrate their concepts while deselecting artists and phenomena that do not.

In addition to the distraction of territorial infighting with other art professionals, curatorial research is frequently hampered by time constraints; with a project timeline of a year or two at the most and the need to multi-task on numerous aspects of exhibition production, curators tend to cut straight to the chase rather than pursuing the careful, scholarly excavation of a topic. After an exhibition is completed, the curator will typically move on, falling foul of the 'what's your next project' mantra and leaving art historians to pick up the pieces of their high-profile interventions. At the same time, the characteristic curatorial approach to researching an idea can be distinguished from the practice of most art historians. This can be felt, for example, in the outcomes of curatorial research, which rarely ends in the writing of a text but rather tends to spread irresistibly into multiple forms – from a film screening to an exhibition, from a panel discussion to a full-blown conference.

The inclination to spread across several formats allows curators to approach problems from myriad directions, offering a more nuanced perspective than purely academic or discourse-based research. Expanding beyond the exhibition frame also enables contemporary curatorial research to be contextualised through wider discursive perspectives and understood as a work-in-progress, with each new element – a text commissioned for a publication, a series of interviews or a symposium – providing an opportunity to generate fresh knowledge. However, there is a fine line between the curatorial desire to experiment across several platforms and the tendency towards the over-production of ancillary events on the part of art institutions. When supplementary events are organised to fulfil a quota, balance sheet or venue brochure, and when there is no meaningful feedback from, or contribution to, the curatorial project, such events may fall into the category of unsustainable exercises in cultural consumerism.

In addition to the tendency towards multiple formats and approaches, curatorial research frequently turns out to be more collaborative than art historical investigations, not least because, unlike the writing of a singly authored art historical text, the realisation of an exhibition or event depends on an extended process of communication and exchange. While the primary exchange is often that between the curator and the artist(s), it may also involve the input of others with a shared interest in the project. There are, of course, different forms of collaboration – those that are based on more egalitarian, horizontal power structures and those that are closer to the business model of teamwork, as well as instances in which the declarative mode of collaboration is egalitarian; but, in reality, a top-down model of authorial control operates and collaboration is little more than a code word for the redistribution of public funding. On the one hand, more spontaneous and intimate forms of collaboration may occur in workshop situations, in which all the participants feel motivated to let their ideas flow freely, in a spirit of solidarity. Such situations of collaborative exchange could be perceived as contributing to a 'reconstruction of the modalities of group being', which refers to Guattari's second register of the social dimension of ecology.[10] On the other hand, collaboration is enacted at stage-managed meetings, periodically organised by corporate-style multinational art institutions or the new breed of transnational foundations with global or regional interests, to instil an esprit de corps in their team, at which curators on short-term contracts vie for the eye of the director.

A sustainable sensibility in curatorial research may also involve being reflective about different contexts and attuned to the ways in which topics or artworks function in particular environments. Organisation of the SocialEast Seminars on the Art and Visual Culture of Eastern Europe was based on the principle of alternating between venues in the UK and Eastern Europe and including, on equal terms, speakers from the region and non-native scholars, as well as a range of presentations by artists, curators, theorists and art historians.[11] More generally, the practice of alternating between different geographical contexts enables the overturning of unreconstructed assumptions about, for example, the relationship between what art history had assumed were 'centres' and 'peripheries' but now, and most vividly within a contemporary curatorial context, appear to be more complex sites that coexist on a levelled global field based on equal and simultaneous access to information.

10. Guattari, op cit. p. 34.
11. http://www.translocal.org/socialeast

Curatorial research does not necessarily stop when an exhibition is installed, especially if a show is destined to move to another venue. Despite the added transport costs, an exhibition that reincarnates may, in some senses, be more sustainable than one that has a short run in a single location, because more visitors have a chance to be touched by the work and because the artists and artworks have the opportunity to respond to different physical, institutional and geographical contexts. Arguably, there is a difference between the model of the 'travelling show' as an exhibition bought in by a major institution to fill space, frequently with little curatorial attention being paid to the specificities of the site, and a living, evolving exhibition that takes on a new form when migrated to a new venue.

The curatorial researcher, going on location in search of emerging artists and exhibition concepts, may follow one of at least two contrasting trajectories. Curators from well-funded, mainstream art institutions are more likely to jet in for an intensively organised trip, visiting a select list of pre-arranged destinations – from the studios of internationally profiled artists to meetings with the directors of local institutions – departing, more often than not, with their preconceptions intact, leaving behind them an extensive carbon footprint but little trace in the local art scene beyond a glamorous apparition. This can be contrasted with the more grassroots opportunities for research available to less corporate curators, who, following in the footsteps of the informal artistic networks of the neo-avant-garde, are in a position to make more meaningful connections.

Another important aspect of curatorial research, related in terms of social impact to the ways in which curators conduct themselves in their interactions with local informants on research trips, is the way that artists and participants involved in the realisation of art projects are treated. The Berlin Biennale of 2012 provided many examples of questionable curatorial practice, including the treatment of several dozen activists from new social movements, who were invited to occupy the ground floor of the main exhibition venue for the duration of the biennial. Only a couple of weeks into the exhibition, the activists began to agitate over the situation in which they had been placed by the curators, with their indoor protest camp resembling a 'human zoo' that visitors could voyeuristically observe from a raised viewing platform. Significantly, the activists' complaints not only related to the physical conditions at the camp – including poor quality food and the lack of bathrooms – but also addressed the impression that they were being exploited and objectified as part of a social experiment initiated by the curators.[12]

Returning to the Guattarian categorisation of ecology, issues of environmental sustainability related to curatorial practice arise from concerns over the impact of excessive travel – either from research trips or flying in speakers for an educational event – and may add significantly to the ecological impact of a research project. Corresponding to Guattari's second register, the social aspects of sustainability also come to the fore when considering the organisation of conferences as part of curatorial research. Compared to most of the conferences organised within academia, symposia realised alongside contemporary art projects tend to be, perhaps surprisingly, less exploitative of participants. While the organisers of art historical conferences typically expect speakers to cover their own travel, accommodation and dining costs and rarely offer a fee, events in the world of contemporary art (even on very similar themes) are generally much more hospitable. Academic conferences also have a propensity to create unnecessary hierarchies between keynote and panel speakers, and often seem designed to minimise audience participation by pre-selecting a reliable academic as the primary respondent to each paper. However radical a conference may sound in terms of content, if this fails to be reflected in the way the event is organised at a more social level then something is usually amiss, and the chances of encountering the conference equivalent of the curatorial refrain – a lively discussion, involving everyone, at which something new or important is voiced – are significantly reduced.

The notion of the curatorial refrain imports the Guattarian idea of 'enunciative assemblage' into an art context. This implies a situation in which the curator articulates a project by incisively collecting together individual elements while also referring to those precious moments of enlightenment within contemporary curatorial practice that provide a rewarding experience of renewal. Curatorial refrains may take the form of inventive models that spring up unexpectedly – moments of solidarity that can occur anywhere – but they are most likely to be encountered in circumstances that are less dominated by the faceless processes of capitalism. In more concrete terms, such regenerative encounters often arise in liberated zones or loopholes, independent of public and private

12. See this blog account of life in the 'human zoo' on the occupy museums website: http://occupymuseums.org/index.php/actions/43-occupy-museums-and-the-7th-berlin-biennale

funding agendas, as part of the practice of curators who operate collaboratively, rather than competitively, with artists and art historians.

The hostile backdrop against which such attempts to renew the curatorial refrain are taking place is incisively analysed by Franco 'Bifo' Berardi, who condemns the financial markets for 'changing the destiny of the living body of society, destroying resources, and like a draining pump, swallowing the energies of the collective body'.[13] The alternative to this soul-destroying system is described by Bifo's theoretical forerunner, Guattari, in terms of visions of 'artistic creation liberated from the market system'. In line with Guattari's third ecological register of the mental domain, he considered such forms of creation to be intimately connected to a multi-layered understanding of ecology and essential for the production of human existence in new historical circumstances.[14]

Working within the crisis of neoliberal global capitalism, artists and curators from Eastern Europe are revisiting the persistent paradigm of non-market critical art practice, which flourished during socialism, and recycle tactics such as the evasion of power, grassroots self-organisation and expressions of solidarity. In that sense, Tibor Horváth's solo show, *No Dominance*, held at Budapest's ACB Gallery in 2012, directly confronted the problem of chauvinism in Hungarian public life with works which radically questioned the dominance of nationalism, offering a radically different take on issues of identity to the official survey, *What is Hungarian?*' Horváth's exhibition was also exemplary of the potential of self-curated projects to suggest curatorial approaches that are more resistant to the corrosive influence of power and the market. Unbeknown to the gallerist, the artist also created a false wall with a secret door to another space containing an unofficial exhibition of works by his friends.[15] This sub-show within a solo show – which was also, in a way, a metaphor for the present situation in Hungary, in which political interference in culture calls forth innovative strategies of resistance – also pointed to the necessity for a more fearless attitude on the part of curators.

The search for new spaces for showing art that restores a sense of radical autonomy, by removing dependence on financial backers of all kinds, is an increasing global tendency, which can be related to the search for solutions to the economic and ecological crisis. In 2008, the

13. Franco 'Bifo' Berardi and Alessandro Sarti, RUN Morphogenesis. dOCUMENTA 13. 2012. p. 8.
14. Guattari, op cit. p. 34.
15. Review in *Time Out Budapest*. February 2012.

desire to be free from market influences led a group of friends from Kraków to set up Goldex Poldex - an art space that declared itself to be 'independent and 100% self-funded'. The decision not to seek support from public or private sources reflected a conscious rejection of both the trade-offs involved in modifying curatorial concepts to suit the criteria of funders and the 'horrible' role model of the 'cultural entrepreneur'[16], which was in the process of being introduced to the region. The desire to resist the imposition of this model was felt all the more strongly in light of the informal and collectivist mentality that had characterised the art scenes of Eastern Europe in the socialist era.

A singular artistic event, held at the Georg Lukács Archive in Budapest in May 2010, offers an example of one of those transitory moments in contemporary art that engender solidarity among those present. Within the archive - uniquely preserved in the flat in which the famous philosopher spent the final third of his life - several artists, curators and philosophers were invited to collectively reflect on Lukács's legacy.[17] The actions ranged from the gesture of making small repairs to the doors and windows of the archive to the spraying of conceptual graffiti behind a painting in the philosopher's office. The shooting of a film, relating to a controversial episode in Lukács's life, involved members of the audience, who were also invited to meditate on a pile of the neo-Marxist author's books. Furthermore, a climax of performative acts entailed a ghostly Lukács lookalike walking into the flat in the middle of discussions, led by his famous disciple, Agnes Heller, fumbling around for a moment at his desk and then disappearing. The fleeting sense of community that arose among the diverse participants was aided by the fact this was a completely self-organised and self-funded assemblage of interventions underpinned by an altruistic desire for shared knowledge.

Caught up in the chaotic reality of interlinked crises in an economic order that, whilst famously adaptable, is crashing against the ecological limits of the planet, curatorial practice is severely affected. As tremors on the global stage are instantly transmitted to the sensitive systems of the art world, the orientation of curatorial research has the potential to provide both a quick fire response to the social and ecological implications of systemic crisis and intimations of escape. Drawing on aspects of

16. See the interview with Janek Sowa, Janek Simon, Kuba de Barbaro and Agnieszka Klepacka on http://www.designingeconomiccultures.net/goldex-poldex/
17. Maja and Reuben Fowkes, 'Reclaiming Lukács: Interventions in the Archive of a Marxist Philosopher'. *IDEA Arts + Society* 35 (2010).

collaboration, translocal existence and a revitalised sense of autonomy, the renewal of the curatorial refrain could be experienced through forms that invoke gestures of human solidarity. Strikingly, attempts to curate a way out of the crisis are most likely to be grounded in a multi-layered understanding of ecology and its implications for contemporary artistic practice.

60 – 78

AND THE QUESTION IS...

Georgina Jackson

In an advertisement for a new US game show, Bob Goen slowly rolls down the tinted window of his large car at the security gates of the Game Show Network (GSN) television studios in Los Angeles, and announces himself as the host of *That's the Question.*[(1)] The voice at the end of the intercom demands to know the name of the game show and Goen promptly repeats '*That's the Question*'. The agitated voice quips, 'Don't answer my question with a question'. Goen frustratedly responds, 'the answer to the question is That's the Question', but confusion ensues.

The temporary suspension of knowledge that is necessary to prioritise a question, rather than a singular specific answer, resonates within recent curatorial practices. In the early 2000s, Roger Buergel and Ruth Noack curated a series of exhibitions and projects exploring conceptions of governmentality including *Com volem ser governats?* [How do we want to be governed?] (2004) across a number of venues in Barcelona.[(2)] Between 2006-08 Charles Esche and Annie Fletcher realised a series of discussions and events in and around the Van Abbemuseum under the title of *Be(com)ing Dutch*, which explored 'Dutch-ness' and the formation of cultural identity in the increasingly antagonistic socio-political landscape that defines the purportedly open Netherlands.[(3)] For the 11th Istanbul Biennial (2009), the curatorial collective, What/How and for Whom posed the question, 'What Keeps Mankind Alive?', signalling their intention to provide a thoroughgoing consideration of collective coexistence by interrogating contemporary social and political formations in the context of the recent global economic turmoil. In 2010, Kathrin Rhomberg asked 'What is waiting out there?'[(4)]

1. The show ran on GSN between 2006 and 2007.
2. *Com volem ser governats?* [How do we want to be governed?] was organised with Museu d'Art Contemporani de Barcelona [Museum of Contemporary Art Barcelona (MACBA)] and *How do we want to be governed? (Figure and Ground)* (2005) took place at Miami Art Central, Miami. The series of projects curated by Roger Buergel and Ruth Noack began in 2004.
3. The project had partnerships with Basis voor Actuele Kunst [Foundation for Contemporary Art (BAK)], Utrecht; the New Museum of Contemporary Art, New York; Goldsmiths College, London; Kosmose, Eindhoven; Gate Archive, Eindhoven; Kungl. Konsthögskolan [Royal Institute of Art], Stockholm; National Sculpture Factory, Cork; and the Interart Foundation, Arnhem.
4. The original title of the exhibition was *Was Draussen wartet auf?* Rhomberg posits that this title 'specifies the direction of its view: from within the art realm outward, at reality – a reality which simple explanatory models of the world no longer suffice to describe' K. Rhomberg, 'What is waiting out there', http://bb6.berlinbiennial.de/index.php?option=com_content&task=blogcategory&id=141&Itemid=99&lang=en, 2010. She further states that: Technological developments as well as global economic, political and social crises of the present have caused cracks in our reality, widened the gap between the world we talk about and the world that is really there. The works presented in the show reject the tendency – increasingly observable in art – to turn away from reality and toward art-immanent and formal problems. They counter this tendency by insisting on a stringent view of our present and its reality (Loc. cit.).

for the 6th Berlin Biennale, insisting upon the necessity of engaging with 'reality', while the 13th Istanbul Biennial, in 2013, demanded a rethinking of the not-so-innocuous concept of 'progress' and the public domain as political forum by demanding 'Mom, Am I Barbarian?'[5] This array of multi-faceted research and exhibition projects bears witness to the increased prioritisation of the exhibition space and curatorial projects as a site of questioning and enquiry of the socio-political present and future.

In their introduction to *Cultures of the Curatorial,*[6] Beatrice von Bismarck, Jörn Schafaff and Thomas Weski delineate a 'curatorial turn' in contemporary cultural practices and discourses, widening the scope of curating 'beyond showing or presenting to include enabling, making public, educating, analysing, criticizing, theorizing, editing and staging'.[7] In the context of this broader shift, the role of the curator has altered since the 1990s, from a position of authority about artistic practices and their contexts to encompass a significant expansion of the concerns and knowledge bases of curators through the incorporation of multiple disciplines within exhibition projects and a surge of large-scale and durational curatorial projects. From Catherine David's integration of diverse experts in the '100 Days - 100 Guests' programme at *documenta X* (1997), explored later, to the mobilisation of post-colonial theories in the development and realisation of Documenta11 (2001-2) and its multiple global platforms, there has been an increasing incorporation of disciplines beyond art into the field of curating. In fact, one might even argue that curating, as a field, engages with multiple disciplines not in an interdisciplinary or adisciplinary way but in a mode identified by Jacques Rancière as 'indisciplinary',[8] as 'not only a matter of going beside the disciplines but of breaking them'.[9]

Research and exhibition projects attest to an intensifying link between curating and knowledge production; however, since the late 1990s, there has been an increasing tendency towards mobilisation of the exhibition as the location, form and medium for distinct enquiries into

5. Curated by Fulya Erdermci.
6. This book emerged from a symposium entitled '*Cultures of the Curatorial*' at the Hochschule für Grafik und Buchkunst, Academy of Visual Arts Leipzig between 22-24 January 2010. The symposium emerged within the context of the Cultures of the Curatorial postgraduate programme, which started in October 2009 at the Hochschule.
7. Beatrice Von Bismarck, Jörn Schafaff and Thomas Weski (eds.), *Cultures of the Curatorial*. Berlin. Sternberg Press. 2012. p. 8.
8. Jacques Rancière, 'Jacques Rancière and Indisciplinarity', *Art & Research: A Journal of Ideas, Context and Methods*. Volume 2. No. 1. Summer 2008. http://www.artandresearch.org.uk/v2n1/jrinterview.html
9. Loc. cit.

the state of the world today. While the examples cited above explicitly deploy a question in their title, other exhibitions - such as *Making Things Public: Atmospheres of Democracy* (2005), curated by Bruno Latour and Peter Weibel at Zentrum für Kunst und Medientechnologie [Centre for Art and Media (ZKM)] in Karlsruhe - called into question the very notion of representation that is central to democracy and utilised the exhibition as a representative space, in order to engage with this problem. Similarly, *Rethinking Dissent: on the limitations of politics and the possibilities of resistance*, the 2007 Göteburg Biennial, curated by Joa Ljungberg and Edi Muka, explored the potential for dissent and radical change in the absence of a political alternative. Solvej Helweg Ovesen acknowledges the expanded remit of curating and exhibition-making when she outlines that 'to make an exhibition is to create a structure through which you can look at the world, look through to the other side of conventions, and experience and develop alternative models of being in the world'.(10) As she continues:

> Curating exhibitions is part of creating cultural, aesthetic, and historical transformation. Today one of the primal social and cultural necessities is to direct and create exhibitions or events - where processes of consumption are turned into an activity. Our task as art producers, exhibition producers, and art consumers/users is to find ways of using discourse, history, aesthetic and cultural formats in a socially and politically responsible way.(11)

This assertion of social and political responsibility has manifested itself in the emergence of a swathe of exhibitions that explicitly invoke, and emphasise the necessity of engaging with, contemporary global political and social issues. For example, *Ausgeträumt...* [Disillusionment...] at Secession, Vienna (2001-2)(12) referenced the political disenchantment which followed 11 September 2001, displacing post-1989 optimism. In describing the genesis of the exhibition, its curator, Kathrin Rhomberg, stated that 'Ausgeträumt... tried to address something more than the paradigm of disillusionment. It also attempted to emphasize the new productive conditions that might be seen as resulting from the experience

10. Solveig Helweg Ovenson, 'How productive are curatorial collaborations with artists? Who owns the copyright for exhibitions' in Christoph Tannert and Ute Tischler (eds.), *Men In Black: Handbook in Curatorial Practice.* Künstlerhaus Bethanien and Revolver. 2004. p. 225.
11. Loc. cit.
12. Curated by Kathrin Rhomberg.

of disillusionment. This includes the questioning of criticism, resistance, art and culture, in the light of the economic and political structures in which they are embedded'.[13]

Also indicative of this shift towards the space of the exhibition as a laboratory in which to explore the crisis of democracy or the potential of dissent are more recent examples, such as *Vectors of the Possible,*[14] curated by Simon Sheikh at Basis voor Actuele Kunst [Foundation for Contemporary Art (BAK)], Utrecht (2010), which reconsidered the horizon as a means of testing the boundaries of realising an alternative to neoliberal capitalism. In the foreword to the exhibition pamphlet, artistic director of BAK, Maria Hlavajova, asserted that 'this notion of the horizon - as a motivating and emancipatory tool that might inspire us to overcome the limitations of the present - seems to belong to what art can offer to society for an examination of the options beyond the dominant ideology'.[15] This differentiation between what already exists and the potential for radical change echoes the distinction between 'politics' (consensus orientated business-as-usual in the existing systems of liberal democracies) and *'the political'*[16] (dissensus-based modes of contestation, leading to radical political reorganisation and social renewal). While this distinction originates from political theory, with reference to the work of Carl Schmitt in the early twentieth century and political theorists such as Ernesto Laclau and Chantal Mouffe, the term *'the political'* has increasingly been used within contemporary art and curatorial discourses as a broad conceptualisation of the potential for socio-political change. Increasingly, the proposal of dissent and the assertion of the potential to think through political and social transformation, the political, have been made within exhibitions.

The disruption of disciplines, or extending beyond what is present, is echoed in Maria Lind's differentiation between 'curating' and 'the curatorial'. Lind proposes using Chantal Mouffe's distinction between 'politics', or 'the formal side of practice that reproduces certain orders',[17]

13. Kathrin Rhomberg, 'Ausgeträumt...'. *Manifesta Journal.* No 3. Summer 2004. p. 283.
14. The exhibition is one of a series of 'research exhibitions' as part of the project Former West (2008-2014). Exhibiting artists included Mathew Buckingham, chto delat/What is to be done?, Freee, Sharon Hayes, Runo Lagosmarsino, Elske Rosenfeld, Hito Steyerl and Ultra-red.
15. Simon Sheikh and Jill Winder (eds.), *Vectors of the Possible Newsletter.* BAK basis voor actuele kunst. 2010. p. 5.
16. The term *the political* denotes a broad conceptualisation of the potential for socio-political change (radical political reorganisation and social renewal). Italicisation of the term is used to differentiate it from Mouffe's specificity of 'the political'.
17. Maria Lind, 'The Curatorial' in Brian Kuan Wood (ed.), *Selected Maria Lind Writing.* Sternberg Press. 2011. p. 64.

and the 'political', or the 'antithesis of consensus'.[18] In adopting this logic, Lind defines 'the curatorial' as 'a more viral presence consisting of signification processes and relationships between processes and relationships between objects, people, places, ideas, and so forth, a presence that strives to create friction and push new ideas'.[19] Crucially, underlining the scope and ambition of the projects cited above, and many others since the late 1990s, is an explicit engagement with the world-at-large, the processes of globalisation, the crisis of democracy and critical enquiry into real socio-political change. This essay will explore a number of key examples including: *documenta X* (1997), Documenta11 (2001–2) and *Making Things Public: Atmospheres of Democracy* (2005) in order to elaborate on these significant developments within exhibitions since 1997.

'Documenta can't ignore the state of the world'[20]

documenta X (1997) marked a radical shift in both the function of the exhibition and the institution of documenta. Previous editions of this quinquennial exhibition had been characterised by the prioritisation of artwork and specifically new media (D7) and the experiential (D9). By contrast, for its tenth iteration, Catherine David deliberately focused on the intellectual function of the exhibition, calling for critical engagement with the political, social, economic and cultural problems of the day. In advance of the exhibition opening, David argued that '[t]he art world, at the moment, is becoming a little autistic, because it has no real connection to the outside world. So it was very important for us to reposition contemporary art within contemporary cultural practices as a whole'.[21] David explicitly cited the global shifts that had taken place since 1989 and the politics of representation,[22] underlined by the acknowledgement of the role of documenta in post-war politics. During the press conference, she stated that 'These days, documenta is both an exhibition and a cultural event [...] *Documenta X* continues the

18. Loc. cit.
19. Loc. cit.
20. As Catherine David stated to Robert Storr in an interview before the opening of *documenta X* (1997). Robert Storr, 'Kassel Rock: Interview with curator Catherine David'. *Artforum* 35. No. 9 (May). p. 129.
21. Ibid. p. 131.
22. Thereby incorporating the criticisms made against exhibitions such as *Primitivism in the 20th Century* (1984) and *Les Magiciens de la Terre* (1989) as well as the acknowledgement of the global-ness of representation exacerbated by the proliferation of the biennial.

tradition of innovation, but sees itself as a prospective (forward-looking) and not retrospective (backward-looking) definition of position [...] the tenth Documenta is thus intended to be rather a place for experiment, for conflict, for controversy, a type of laboratory'.[23]

Acknowledging the limits of the museum as a space for today's creative practices, David extended Arnold Bode's designation of documenta as a 'Museum of 100 Days' to '100 Days - 100 Guests',[24] devising a daily programme of lectures and discussions,[25] inviting architects, urbanists, economists, philosophers, scientists, writers, artists, filmmakers, stage directors and musicians to debate 'the great ethical and aesthetic questions of the century's close: the urban realm, territory, identity, new forms of citizenship, the national and social state and its disappearance, racism and the states, the globalization of markets and national policy, universalism and culturalism, poetics and politics'.[26] As the press release asserted, '[t]he state of culture has always been an indicator of the state of the world, art a unique language for talking about this state. How do others speak, and about what?'[27] During the one hundred days of the exhibition, political philosophers, such as Etienne Balibar and Giorgio Agamben, discussed the opposition between state and nation as well as the future of society; sociologist, Saskia Sassen, considered the effects of globalisation on urban spaces; psychoanalyst, Fethi Benslama, considered the psychological effects of immigration; writer and literary critic, Edouard Glissant, cultural critic, Edward Saïd, curator, Okwui Enwezor, curator, Carlos Basualdo, architect, Rem Koolhaas, exhibiting artist, Michelangelo Pistoletto, and filmmaker, Harun Farocki, presented and engaged in discussions.

As Thomas Köhler wrote in *dx short guide*, David 'considers it urgent to work against a deficit in public confrontation with the content of social, cultural and economic issues. Thus the concept of "cultural

23. Cited in Michael Glasmeier and Karin Stengel (eds.), *50 Years documenta 1955–2005: Archive in Motion: Documenta Manual*. Kunsthalle Fridericianum Kassel and Steidl. 2005. p. 352.

24. In 1964, Arnold Bode argued that documenta should not just be the display of contemporary art; it 'should be a place of encounter, [...]it should regularly become a laboratory for artistic work, the artists' very workshop'. Justin Hoffmann, 'documenta 3' in Glasmeier and Stengel, op cit. p. 214.

25. These events took place in the Documenta Halle every evening at 7pm during the hundred-day run of the exhibition.

26. Documenta and Museum Fridericianum (eds.), *documenta X short guide/* kurzführer. Hatje Cantz. 1997. p. 12.

27. Universe in universe, 'Press information <<110 Days - 100 Guests>>'. Universe in universe. 1997. http://universes-in-universe.de/doc/e_press2.htm

event" includes political discourse as well as aesthetic apprehension'.[28] This broadening of the spectrum of the exhibition to include multiple disciplines outside of art,[29] as well as the discussion of issues such as immigration, Rwandan genocide,[30] globalisation, cultural theory and more, was a significant shift in the exhibition's relationship to contemporary politics and political issues. Furthermore, each presentation was documented and uploaded onto a website for worldwide access, fittingly available until the beginning of the next century - the year 2000.[31]

It is significant that the main accompanying publication, *Poetics/ Politics documenta X - the book*, did not catalogue the works in the exhibition but re-examined the historico-cultural condition of modernity. David focused on four politically emblematic dates from recent history - 1945, 1967, 1978 and 1989 - through texts by past and present critical theorists, writers, philosophers and sociologists, and posited a survey of the 20th century as a means with which to consider the present - the issues of globalisation and beyond. Everything from discussions on Italian political architecture to the state of Algeria in 1956 - via texts on Samuel Beckett, Vietnam, African/Black American cinema, Japan, punk, the USSR and a recurring reflection on Antigone - was present within the book against a backdrop of stills from films by Jean-Luc Godard, works by Hans Haacke and a multitude of other images. Texts were reproduced by geographer and theorist, David Harvey, cultural theorist, Paul Virilio, literary critic and poet, Edouard Glissant, Saskia Sassen, philosopher

28. Documenta and Museum Fridericianum, op cit. p. 258.

29. Including Catherine David, artistic director; Edward Saïd, philosopher, USA; Rem Koolhaas, architect, Netherlands; Raoul Peck, filmmaker, Haïti; Cabelo, Tunga, Lilian Zaremba, artist, Brazil; Valentin Yves Mudimbe, writer, Zaire/USA; Okwui Enwezor, artistic director Johannesburg Biennale 1997, Nigeria/USA; Fethi Benslama, psychoanalyst, Tunisia/France; Suely Rolnik, psychoanalyst, Brazil; Abderrahmane Sissako, filmmaker, Mauritania/Mali/France; Ackbar Abbas, culture critic, Hong Kong/China; Etienne Balibar, philosopher, France; Ariella Azoulay, art critic, Israel; Carlos Basualdo, art critic, Argentina/USA; Gayatri Chakravorty Spivak, culture critic, India/USA; Geeta Kapur, art historian, India; Paulo Mendes da Rocha, Sophia Telles Silva, architect/archit. historian, Brazil; Paulo Herckenhoff, director Biennial of São Paulo, Brazil; Yang Lian, Dichter, China/UK; Michael Oppitz, anthropologist, Germany/Switzerland; Johan Grimonprez, artist, born in Trinidad, USA/Belgium; Ery Camara, art critic, Senegal/Mexico; Colette Braeckman, journalist, Belgium; Masao Miyoshi, culture critic, Japan/USA; Tierno Monénembo, writer, Guinea/France; Ea Sola, choreographer, Vietnam/France; Sarat Maharaj, art historian, South Africa/UK; Matthew Ngui, artist, Singapore/Australia; Wole Soyinka, writer, Nigeria.

30. Belgian journalist Colette Braeckman spoke on the genocide in Rwanda under the title of 'the evolution of the problems of the refugees and the analysis of their return'.

31. The address was http://www.mediaweb-tv.com, but videos can now be viewed at http://documentaarchiv-mediencluster.stadt-kassel.de/R/H522L4KCA3K-15I1F4EJPHSIHXNAEAPE88Q4P4HDVQK4MDXU821-00875?func=collections-result&collection_id=1653

and social theorist, Michel Foucault, writers and theorists, Frantz Fanon and Maurice Blanchot, political philosophers, Hannah Arendt and Jacques Rancière, writer and film director, Marguerite Duras, filmmakers, Pier Paolo Pasolini and Rainer Werner Fassbinder, sociologists, Theodor W. Adorno and Jürgen Habermas, among many others, with little art criticism or aesthetic theory. In 2005, Lutz Jahre wrote that *documenta X* (dX) 'marked a paradigm shift'; looking 'far beyond (Western) art, [it] entered the debate on globalization, and in doing so took up sociopolitical and philosophical themes. The plurality of perspectives, disciplines and media not only affected the exhibition, which was criticized as insufficiently sensuous; it also had an impact in the catalogue'.(32)

In the development and realisation of '100 Days - 100 Guests', David acknowledged the deficit of the public sphere as a space for the debate of political and social issues politically, and proposed documenta, an exhibition, as a space for the vital discussion of topical issues. While theorists had previously written catalogue essays - or, in the case of French philosopher and literature theorist, Jean-Francois Lyotard, curated an exhibition that garnered significant critical attention (*Les Immatériaux*, Centre Pompidou, Paris, 1985) - the incorporation of diverse experts, theorists and practitioners was a significant development in the realm of exhibition-making and the exhibition's relationship to social and political issues. The exhibition and the practice of exhibition-making was asserted as a location of enquiry. Donna de Salvo states that 'an exhibition is a discursive space. Each time an exhibition is staged, different narratives can be elicited, as in a play. At its best, an exhibition is a beginning, a catalyst for critical enquiry'.(33) As David stated in the introduction to the *short guide*, facing global complexities and neoliberalism's domination necessitates 'seeking out the current manifestations and underlying conditions of a critical art which does not fall into a precut academic mold or let itself be summed up in a facile label'.(34) Emphasising the prioritisation of enquiry over authority, David disclosed in an earlier interview that 'The question is: What are the conditions of possibility for critical aesthetic practices today? Where are

32. Lutz Jahre, 'Curators and Catalogues' in Glasmeier and Stengel, op cit. p. 58.
33. Donna De Salvo, 'Notes on Curating' in Carin Kuoni (ed.), *Words of Wisdom: A Curator's Vade Mecum on Contemporary Art*. Independent Curators International. 2001. p. 47.
34. Documenta and Museum Fridericianum, op cit. p. 7.

the homogenizing forces and where are the areas of resistance – formally, culturally, intellectually, and politically?'[35]

documenta X's explicit engagement with the state of the world echoes Von Bismarck, Schafaff and Weski's assertion that, '[e]mbedded in the globalization of the art field, on the one hand, and the conditions of labor in the twenty-first century, on the other, the curatorial has also gained a specific socio-political relevance within contemporary society'.[36] Furthermore, the prioritisation of engagement with 'reality' in exhibitions resonates in Hlavajova's question, 'How does one refer to an artistic practice that undertakes a responsibility for society and participates in the production of a new reality – a practice that strives for a better world and embraces the poetics and the politics of such endeavour?'[37] However, Hlavajova problematises previous avant-garde tendencies towards utopia, arguing that 'ideal social, political, and moral constructions, have been invoked in (too) many exhibitions recently. But the unattainable aspect of utopia, its *not-to-be-realized* characteristics, seems once again to enclose art in an ivory tower'.[38] By contrast, she expressed a preference for advocating 'the idea, however abstract it may seem, that art creates a particular mental environment in which creative thoughts with political relevance can be mediated, presented, and experimented with, and that such thoughts can even be tried out and implemented within a broader social context as real proposals for positive change'.[39]

'[C]onceived not as an exhibition but as a constellation of public spheres' [40]

The increasing link between enquiry and socio-political change is highlighted in the example of Documenta11 (D11) (2001–2), in which the public sphere – as a space to debate political, social and cultural issues linked to the very functioning of democracy – was asserted with the proposal of the exhibition as multiple global public spheres. Artistic director, Okwui Enwezor, signalled the shift of documenta from the

35. Robert Storr, 'Kassel Rock: Interview with Curator Catherine David'. *Artforum* 35, No. 9 (May). p. 142.
36. Von Bismarck, Schafaff and Weski, op cit. p. 8.
37. Maria Hlavajova, 'For Lack of a Better World'. *Manifesta Journal,* No. 3 (Spring/Summer 2004). p. 232.
38. Loc. cit.
39. Loc. cit.
40. Okwui Enwezor, 'The Black Box' in Okwui Enwezor, Carlos Basualdo, Ute Meta Bauer, Susanne Ghez, Sarat Maharaj, Mark Nash and Octavio Zaya (eds.), *Documenta 11_Platform5: The Exhibition. Catalogue.* Hatje Cantz. 2002. p. 54.

museological - framing a singular perspective in order to engage with the world - to the discursive - positing discussion and the multidisciplinary debate as a mechanism for tackling contemporary global social and political issues.[41] D11 was decentralised from its historical location in Kassel and expanded into five global platforms in Europe, Asia, the Americas and Africa. There was an extension of 'the locus of the disciplinary models that constitute and define the project's intellectual and cultural interest'.[42] As Enwezor outlined, 'Documenta11's paradigm is shaped by forces that seek to enact the multidisciplinary direction through which artistic practices and processes come most alive, in those circuits of knowledge produced outside the predetermined institutional domain of Westernism, or those situated solely in the sphere of artistic canons'.[43]

Enwezor argued for the necessity of thinking beyond the status quo to the 'location of culture today and the spaces in which culture intersects with the domains of complex global knowledge circuits'.[44] One of the first steps in engaging with the world as a whole was the assertion of post-colonial[45] discourse as a toolbox to engage with intensifying capitalist globalisation[46] and indicative of an ambition to shift beyond Western hegemonic notions of the universal - beyond modernism and the assertion of Euro-centrism that had occupied documenta since its inception.[47] As Enwezor outlined, 'the post-colonial space is the site where experimental cultures emerge to articulate modalities that define the new meaning-and memory-making systems of later modernity'.[48] Unlike postmodernism and its relativisms, the post-colonial made ethical demands on historical interpretation.[49]

41. This shift can, in part, be considered as a continuation and elaboration of the work begun in the second Johannesburg Biennale curated by Okwui Enwezor in 1997.
42. Ibid. p. 42.
43. Loc. cit.
44. Acknowledging the task of this role, he states that 'the prospects for contemporary art and its position in producing and explicating critical models of interpreting the features of the contemporary imagination could not be more demanding or daunting'. Documenta and Museum Fridericianum, op cit. p. 6.
45. Post-colonialism in the context of Documenta11 refers to theories outlined by Gayatri Spivak as 'the contemporary global condition' contrasting European colonialisms from the mid-eighteenth to mid-twentieth centuries and inclusive of neo-colonialism, with their uneven economic, cultural and political power structures.
46. Documenta and Museum Fridericianum, op cit. p. 6.
47. As he states, 'Postcoloniality, in its demand for full inclusion within the global system and by contesting existing epistemological structures, shatters the narrow focus of Western global optics and fixes its gaze on the wider sphere of the new political, social, and cultural relations that emerged after World War II'. Enwezor, op cit. p. 44.
48. Ibid. p. 44.
49. Ibid. p. 45.

Asserting the necessity to think critically about the world in which we live, Enwezor stated 'in fact, if the larger intellectual and curatorial scope of Documenta11 is to be placed in proper perspective it is in the idea that there are no overarching conclusions to be reached'.[50] Contrary to the grand narratives represented within other large-scale exhibitions, there was an assertion of the role of documenta in intra-disciplinary knowledge production.[51] As Enwezor stated, 'Traversing continents and cities, locations and disciplines, practices and institutions, formats and publics, Documenta11's proposition to open up new spaces for critical reflection on contemporary artistic and cultural situations, creates for us – in dialectical interaction with heterogeneous, transnational audiences – a public sphere through which to think and analyze seriously the complex network of global knowledge circuits on which interpretations of all cultural processes and research today depend'.[52]

Underlining this ambition to consider the global – rather than the local, European, African or American – perspective was an assertion of the potential of the global public sphere:

> The framework within which this takes place has both political and aesthetic objectives. But rather than subsume the concerns of art and artists into the narrow terrain of Western institutional aesthetic discourses that are part of the current crisis, we have conceived of this project as part of the production of a common public sphere. Such a public sphere, we believe, creates a space whereby the critical models of artists, theorists, philosophers, historians, activists, urbanists, writers, and others working within other intellectual traditions and artistic positions could productively be represented and discussed.[53]

But, whereas David had acknowledged a deficit of public confrontation with social, political and economic contemporary issues and developed the '100 Days – 100 Guests' programme as an integral part of dX, Documenta11 was proposed to operate as critical global public

50. Ibid. p. 42.
51. It is notable that, rather than working solely on the development of Documenta11, Enwezor appointed a team of curators, including Carlos Basualdo, Ute Meta Bauer, Susanne Ghez, Sarat Maharaj, Mark Nash and Octavio Zaya, thus expanding the role of artistic director and undermining the notion of the single author or worldview.
52. Enwezor, op cit. p. 53.
53. Okwui Enwezor, 'Introduction' in Okwui Enwezor, Carlos Basualdo, Ute Meta Bauer, Suzanne Ghez, Sarat Maharaj, Mark Nash and Octavio Zaya (eds.), *Documenta 11_Platform1: Democracy Unrealized.* Hatje Cantz. 2002. p. 11.

spheres. Enwezor and the curatorial team expanded upon the notion of debate and political discourse, with the realisation of a series of 'platforms'. The platforms were posited as 'an open encyclopedia for the analysis of late modernity; a network of relationships; an open form for organizing knowledge; a non-hierarchical model of representation; a compendium of voices, cultural, artistic, and knowledge circuits'.(54) In their preface to *Documenta11_Platform1: Democracy Unrealized,* Okwui Enwezor, Boris Groys, Hans-Georg Knapp and Ulrich Podewils described how 11 September 2001 had launched worldwide debates 'on themes of fundamentalism (religious and secular), concepts of governance and political participation, juridical interpretations of civil society, ethical principles of terrorism as a tool of radical political struggle, peace, security, and other secular and theocratic themes'.(55) They further claimed that '[n] ot since the end of World War II and then the collapse of communism in the Soviet Union have there been such demands for such radical rearticulations and reinterpretations of the basic principles of political rights'.(56) In response to this perceived state of affairs, each platform had a particular focus; Platform 1, 'Democracy Unrealized', Academy of Fine Arts, Vienna, 15-20 April 2001 and House of World Cultures, Berlin, 9-30 October 2001; Platform 2, 'Experiments with Truth: Transitional Justice and the Processes of Truth and Reconciliation', New Delhi, 7-21 May 2001; Platform 3, 'Créolité and Creolization', St. Lucia, 13-15 January 2002; Platform 4, 'Under Siege: Four African Cities: Freetown, Johannesburg, Kinshasa, Lagos, 16-20 March 2002; and finally, Platform 5, the 'Exhibition,' Kassel, 8 June-15 September 2002. Within this, 'the continuity and circularity of the nodes of discursivity and debate, location and translation, cultural situations and their localities that are transmitted and perceived through the five Platforms, Documenta11's spaces are to be seen as forums of committed ethical and intellectual reflection on the possibilities of rethinking the historical procedures that are part of its contradictory heritage of grand conclusions'.(57) The variety of subjects, as well as the diversity of participants, was asserted as a 'critical interdisciplinary methodology' distinguished, by Enwezor, from what he referred to as interdisciplinary as 'a form of exhibitionism'.(58)

54. Enwezor, op cit. p. 49.
55. Ibid. p. 9.
56. Loc. cit.
57. Ibid. p. 43.
58. As a criticism of other large-scale exhibitions and the increasing tendency to incorporate other discourses and disciplines, see ibid. p. 10.

Enwezor envisaged D11 not as an exhibition or 'cultural event' but as a 'constellation of public spheres'. In this, he evinced a re-conceptualisation of Habermas' singular 'bourgeois public sphere', emphasising the exhibition as a 'plurality of voices'.[59] Enwezor outlined the role that contemporary art could play within global discourses, recalling the role of art practices and institutions in the 1980s in struggles of visibility for multiculturalism, feminism and representation of minorities, further iterating that 'contemporary art institutions have often been defined as the most enlightened and liberal of all cultural institutions working on the global stage.'[60] Enwezor argued against 'the inadequacy of spaces of agency to interrogate the uneven conditions of global development and governance today, the scope of Documenta11's intellectual and exhibition project needed redefinition and enlargement – that is if we are to understand the contribution contemporary art and artists can make in shaping the future'.[61] In prioritising the discursive, there was also an attempt to address the proposed autonomy of art and its tendency to disable the potential to 'engage critically with all domains of socio-political life without being integrated within their mechanism'.[62] In D11's linking of the public sphere as a critical space in a functioning democracy with the reconceptualisation of Habermas' bourgeois public sphere into multiple spaces across the globe, there was an assertion of the potential role of the spaces of art, of documenta and the exhibition, with thinking through critical questions of our time and effecting change.

'It is a Gedankenaustellung [thought exhibition] in the sense that it tries to present a problem'[63]

As this exploration shows, the proposition of the exhibition as a potential space of critical enquiry, interlinked to the political, has become increasingly evident since 1997. The prioritisation of the exhibition as the location of such enquiries was further highlighted in the exhibition and catalogue project, *Making Things Public: Atmospheres of Democracy*

59. Ibid. p. 53.
60. Loc. cit.
61. Loc. cit.
62. Ibid. p. 54.
63. Bruno Latour and Tomás Sánchez-Criado, 'Making the *Res* public'. *Ephemera Theory & Politics in Organization*. Volume 7(2) 2007. p. 370.

(2005),[64] which was curated at ZKM by philosopher, sociologist and anthropologist, Bruno Latour, and artist, curator and director of ZKM, Peter Weibel. As outlined in the introduction, *Making Things Public* addressed the proclaimed crisis of politics and called into question the notion of representation central to democracy, but crucially, it was the form of the exhibition that was mobilised as a method with which to think through the problem of contemporary politics and actually existing democracy.

In rethinking politics, Latour and Weibel revived the German concept of *Ding* [thing], as both archaic assembly and object, to question what is at stake when we come together. In considering the role of objects, or things, politics shifts from operating in a defined space, between a given number of people, to being something which draws out the complexities of how we live together. Or, 'In other words, objects - taken as so many issues - bind us all in ways that map out a public space profoundly different from what is usually recognized under the label of the "political." It is this space, this hidden geography that we wish to explore through this catalog and exhibition'.[65]

The scope and ambition of the exhibition was limited neither historically nor geographically, and it contained certain resonances with Habermas' endeavour within *The Structural Transformation of the Public Sphere* to chart a philosophical and empirical (historical and sociological) account of the emergence (and decline) of the 'bourgeois public sphere'. Presented across 3,000 square metres of ZKM, interactive projects, models, sculptures, drawings by Honoré Daumier, reproductions of Ambrogio Lorezetti's *The Allegory of Good Government and Bad Government* (1337-9) and Diego Rivera's *The Detroit Industry Murals* (1932-3), films, videos and documentaries were juxtaposed with books including two first editions of Thomas Hobbes' *Leviathan* (1651), shopping trolleys and other objects. The exhibition was divided into a number of thematic spaces, negotiated via a circular route that assimilated different viewpoints, beginning with 'No Politics Please', which examined the spaces of assembly in multiple cultures and the objects that brought them together. The spaces were divided by large, transparent polycarbonate panels on a visible aluminium structure, designed by architects,

64. This exhibition and catalogue project was the second in a series curated by Weibel and Latour and developed from the exhibition *ICONOCLASH. Beyond the Image Wars in Science, Religion and Art*, which took place at ZKM in 2002.
65. Bruno Latour, 'From Realpolitik to Dingpolitik or How to Make Things Public' in Bruno Latour and Peter Weibel (eds.), *Making Things Public: Atmospheres of Democracy*. The MIT Press. 2005. p. 15.

Nikolaus Hirsch and Michel Müller, echoing an illusion of structure as well as its permeable nature. In gathering politics in its historical formations, from agora or assemblies to the pneumatic parliament proposed by Peter Sloterdijk, the location of politics and the issues of concern were prioritised. From examples of Otto Neurath's Isotype – an international system of typographic picture education – and research in communication theory to Bureau d'études's re-presentation of capitalism in *World Government: A Synoptic Outline* (2005), the issue of representation in politics, art, science and elsewhere was highlighted. One of the omnipresent works within the exhibition was Michel Jaffrenou and Thierry Cody's invisible *Phantom Public* (2005), in which the activities of visitors were inputted into a complex computer system to create adjustments in the lighting, sound and other forms of action within the exhibition space. There was a spectre-like presence of the 'phantom public', their action illuminating or obscuring the exhibition, and in the juxtaposition of forms of assembly with objects, layering historical reference with contemporary issues and an underlining questioning of representation, the exhibition manoeuvred the viewer from being subject- to object-orientated. In this way, the exhibition was not only a space of representation but also an acknowledgement of the exhibition space as a space of assembly. As Weibel discussed in his essay, 'Art and Democracy: People Making Art Making Democracy':

> The exhibition shows quite manifestly and renders quite transparently what essentially constitutes every public assembly that is 'thing-base: a complex set of technologies, interfaces, platforms, networks, media and 'things,' which give to a public sphere. Precisely in this way, the exhibition itself becomes the model of an 'object-oriented democracy'; ' a gathering,' 'a things' in itself. The visitors' behavior triggers influence, responses and changes at every moment, repeatedly creating new public spheres. To this extent, the exhibition and its design are not only an image of an 'object-oriented' democracy and not only the model of the res publica but are themselves a democratic 'gathering'.[66]

While a number of other exhibitions from this time explored forms of democracy, social systems or critiques of political mechanisms – such

66. Ibid. p.1026.

as *Whatever Happened to Social Democracy?* at Rooseum (2005)(67) - *Making Things Public* offered a critical space in which to consider the constitution of politics and extend the laboratory of democracy. As Latour stated in an interview at the time of the exhibition, 'I call this show a *Gedankenaustellung* [thought exhibition] in the same way people talk about *Gedankenexperiment* [thought experiment]. It is a *Gedankenaustellung* in the sense that it tries to present a problem. It's a conceptual point: can we think of politics in other terms than usual ones, by turning to things? In what would politics turn into without centering on human opinions?'(68)

Weibel and Latour have described both *Making Things Public* (2005) and their earlier project *ICONOCLASH: Beyond the Image Wars in Science, Religion and Art* (2002) as 'exhibition experiments'.(69) As they outline, 'the usual constraints of time, space and realism are suspended'(70) in an exhibition, translating into it into an ideal space of experimentation. Delineated, multi-faceted research and exhibition projects ask questions, sometimes demanding answers, but they crucially propose the space of the exhibition, or the space of curatorial activities, as spaces of enquiry, spaces of questioning, in which enquiry is prioritised over a thesis.

With the increasing manifestations of critical enquiry through exhibition-making, there has, more recently, been a prioritisation of the associations between artistic practice and research, from the burgeoning practice-based PhD to 'artistic research' as a key focus of dOCUMENTA (13) (2012). The prevalence of research within both contemporary art and curatorial discourses - and its use as a suffix in relation to terms such as 'artistic' or 'curating' - appropriates a language that is dominant within academic and industrial discourses. In part, this situates 'artistic research' as a form of knowledge production between methodologies and disciplines. More recently, the term 'research exhibition' has increased in prominence in relation to a number of exhibition projects associated

67. Others include; *Die Regierung/The Government,* Secesssion, Vienna, MACBA, Barcelona, Witte de With, Rotterdam, curated by Roger Buergel and Ruth Noack, 2003-2005; *Social Democracy* Revisited, Apexart, New York, curated by Jonas Ekeberg, all 2005; or a series of projects and exhibitions which engaged ideas on democracy around the 2008 US presidential elections such as Creative Time's year-long programme *Democracy in America: The National Campaign* culminating in the exhibition Convergence Center, Park Avenue Armory, New York, curated by Nato Thompson, 2008, and *OURS: Democracy in the Age of Branding,* Parsons The New School for Design, New York, curated by Carin Kuoni, 2008.

68. Latour and Sánchez-Criado, op cit. p. 370.

69. Peter Weibel and Bruno Latour, 'Experimenting with Representation: Iconoclash and *Making Things Public*' in Sharon McDonald and Paul Basu (eds.), *Exhibition Experiments*. Blackwell Publishing, 2007. p. 95.

70. 'Ibid. p. 94.

with Former West.[71] The juxtaposition of 'research' and 'exhibition' could be taken to imply that research did not occur prior to such exhibitions - although this is obviously not the case - or that such exhibitions mobilise the exhibition as a form of research. However, rather than focusing on curating as research or another form of knowledge production, curating may be asserted as a field of activity which engages with critical enquiry through diverse means, interlinking practice in which research is central. Latour and Weibel contend that '[E]xhibition experiments cannot, of course, be accomplished without long preparation and an intense collaboration between curators and the "experimentalists" (a term we prefer to "artists"). The main point is that neither artists, nor academics, nor curators are putting their sacrosanct autonomy first. Rather, in the experimental exhibition process, everyone submits to the risks and interests of heteronomy'.[72]

documenta X, Documenta11, and *Making Things Public* as well as many other exhibition projects, attest to the expansion of the exhibition and the practice of exhibition-making as a location of enquiry or 'thought experiments'. This development is paralleled by the multiplication of large-scale exhibitions, biennials and triennials as well as the incorporation of numerous disciplines highlighted by the examples explored previously. Dorothea von Hantelmann argues that:

> The contemporary art exhibition has become a sort of meeting place for different kinds of specialized discourses. As such, it is specialized in the sense that it produces a specific meaning or knowledge, yet at the same time it is (or at least claims to be) expected to be accessible to a general public - unlike the university, for instance, which is not required to open its discourse to a broader public.[73]

71. 'Former West is a long-term international research, education, publishing and exhibition project (2008–2014), which from within the field of contemporary art and theory: 1) reflects upon the changes introduced to the world (and thus to [the] so-called West) by the political, cultural artistic and economic events of 1989; 2) [is] engaged in rethinking global histories of the last two decade[s] in dialogue with post-communist and post-colonial thought; and 3) speculates about a 'post-bloc' future that recognizes differences yet evolves through the political imperative of equality and the notion of "one world".' Former West, http://www.formerwest.org/

72. Weibel and Latour, 2007. op cit. p. 94.

73. Dorothea von Hantelmann, 'On the Socio-economic Role of the Art Exhibition' in Juan A. Gaitán, Nicholaus Schafhausen and Monika Szewczyk (eds.), *Cornerstones*. Sternberg Press and Witte de With. 2011. p. 268.

It is the location of the exhibition as both space of enquiry, the production of knowledge, and meeting place between artistic practices and publics which is crucial in thinking through the relationship between curating, enquiry and public-ness. However, as von Hantelmann cautions, attaining 'this combination of specificity and openness might be the biggest challenge for producers and mediators of art today'.[74]

Are There Any Questions?

In 2008, artist, Sarah Pierce/The Metropolitan Complex, realised a performance after a 1979 work by artist Kevin Atherton.[75] Sitting in front of an eager audience, Pierce commenced with the question 'are there any questions?' Responding to questions from the audience, she finished each answer with the same question – 'are there any questions?' As the performance progressed, there was an increasing anxiety among the audience in the room, expecting a performance rather than being questioned. The spectator became participant, respondent and agent. However, this cycle of answering a question and then demanding another question resonates with the exhibition examples cited. *documenta X*, Documenta11 and *Making Things Public: Atmospheres of Democracy*, among many other exhibitions, signalled the prioritisation of the practice of curating as an enquiry and the exhibition as a location of debate conducted through diverse research and knowledge bases. Rather than concentrating on the multifarious distinctions made between 'what is the curatorial?', 'what is curating?' and 'what is the difference between these two terms or modalities?', there is the potential for exhibition-making, as well as other forms of curatorial activities, to function as spaces for the emergence of questions about the world in which we live, gathering multiple disciplines in an 'indisciplinary' way. In this way, exhibitions become spaces in which the suspension between question and answer permits the continued proposition of meaningful ways of thinking and realising the world anew. The necessity for such spaces is as acute as ever.

74. Loc. cit.

75. Performance by Kevin Atherton, 1979. Frascati, Amsterdam 2008. Commissioned by If I Can't Dance | Project, Dublin 2009. Commissioned by If I Can't Dance | Ludlow 38 Wyoming Building, New York 2009. Commissioned by The European Kunsthalle.

79 – 87

ACADEMY AS EXHIBITION

Henk Slager

The Educational Turn

Over the past decade, art education has repeatedly been confronted with neoliberal attitudes. As a result, It has been gradually turned into a product, focused on quantifiable and verifiable results, legitimised by the rhetoric of marketing and efficiency. In most programmes, only a tiny amount of time and space - if any - is reserved for exploring higher, emancipatory values such as engaging in experimental, speculative thinking or critical processes of self-enlightenment. This dwindling of Humboldtian values, combined with an attempt to overcome advancing bureaucratisation and instrumentalisation, has served as the backdrop to a series of thought-provoking curatorial projects. For example, Manifesta 6: *Notes for an Art School* (2006) departed from an approach that could be labelled the 'educational turn in curating' to draw attention to discursive practices and the ways in which these tend to be coloured by an interaction between curatorial strategies, educational praxis and artistic research. The ways in which reflections on the entanglement of these three constituents has manifested themselves over the past decade will be critically addressed in the following text.

Academy

During the panel discussion, *Art Education Today* - a project organised as part of the 2007 Frieze Art Fair - one of the curators of Manifesta 6, Anton Vidokle, proposed that the educational turn was related to the way in which visual art was transforming the relationship between spectator and public space. The paradigm of an exhibition being visited by a public was formulated in the days of the French Revolution. For the first time, such a public could offer artists, such as Courbet and Manet, the possibility of transforming their community through art and its critical function. Since then, exhibitions have been obliged to contribute to a critical, social awareness and a conscious sense of citizenship. But, as Vidokle argued - and as US artist, Martha Rosler, has consistently demonstrated in her work - the traditional art spectator has disappeared over the past two centuries.[1]

At the same time, art seems to have adopted the role of entertaining the masses ('audiences') in their leisure time. This makes it increasingly difficult for art to have an impact upon society. Yet, in spite of

1. Cf. Anton Vidokle, Exhibition to School: *unitednationsplaza* in Paul O'Neill and Mick Wilson (eds.), Curating and the Educational Turn. Open Editions/De Appel. 2010.

the end of a consensus around the function of public space, both artists and curators would like to see a return to the 19th-century sovereignty of art. In stressing a desire for (restoring) political agency, they develop exhibitions that draw attention to more effective curatorial strategies while including the concepts of education and participation in the form of experimental academies that could offer spaces for speculative thinking.

Not Yet Known Knowledge

Much has been published about these developments by the UK theorist, Irit Rogoff. Rogoff considers curatorial focus on the academy to be a consequence not only of the emergence of technocratic reason in education but also to the fear accompanying this development:

> The fear that is repeatedly expressed around this process is that all individuality and possibility for a longer term, more processual, reflective and less outcome-bound model of education will be lost through these developments. Certainly the spectre of the extreme bureaucratization and increasingly result-oriented culture overtaking higher education is hardly an encouraging one for the fearful "Bologna sceptics" in Europe.(2)

That is why Rogoff proposes that, in a world dominated by knowledge production – or, better put, cognitive capitalism – the academy should radically revise its epistemological perspective:

> I would argue that the questions in art education, the questions that we have not yet begun to deal with, are not that of specifying what we need to know and how we need to know it, of who determines this and who benefits from it; instead it is a question as to how we might know what we don't yet know how to know.(3)

It is here, with the aim of addressing this complex aspiration, that we need to change our vocabulary. Rogoff suggests that the concept of 'academy' should no longer be connected with cognitive-capitalist concepts such as knowledge transfer, knowledge assessment, professionalisation, quantifiable outcomes and marketability. Instead, a dedicated space should be claimed

2. Irit Rogoff, Academy as Potentiality in Angelika Nollert, Irit Rogoff et al. (eds.), A.C.A.D.E.M.Y. Revolver. 2006. p.14.
3. Ibid. p.14.

for another set of terms and aspirations – a space no longer characterised by regulatory knowledge protocols or predictable outcomes of investigative processes, but one that provides room for another attitude, welcoming both the impossibility of knowing in advance and procrastination around the issue of where an enveloping thought-and-practice might ultimately lead. In this way, the academy would be rehabilitated as a field of possibilities, an environment for non-instrumental, indirect, experimental, speculative thought processes that depart from the 'contemporary moment' and focus on enabling the analysis a certain number of crucial issues and urgencies in a performative sense.

The Curatorial

More or less parallel to Rogoff's reflection on the art academy, another debate has developed around what has been designated 'the curatorial'. Maria Lind defines this as an activity with greater scope than a mere technical modality connected to organising exhibitions. Lind argues that the curatorial involves thinking in terms of interconnections – linking objects, images, processes, people, locations, histories and discourses. In her view, curatorial thinking is, therefore, able to adopt various roles in critique, editing and educating. Thus, the curatorial is multidimensional and could be characterised as rhizomatic – in other words, a form of thought capable of erasing the Cartesian, hierarchical tree (of knowledge) that gave rise to linear thought and binary logic in the Western world and replacing it with a continuous process of connectivity.

Lind relates the dynamic character of 'the curatorial' to the work of Chantal Mouffe. In *On the Political,* Mouffe introduces an agonistic worldview characterised by the tension between politics (the formal side of practices that reproduce certain orders) and the political (an event-present potential that cannot be precisely located or defined). In much the same way that Mouffe frames 'the political', Lind considers 'the curatorial' to be a qualitative term, 'a more viral presence consisting of signification processes and relationships between objects, people, ideas, and so forth, a presence that strives to create friction and to push new ideas'.(4)

4. Maria Lind, 'The Curatorial' in Brian Kuan Wood (ed.), *Selected Maria Lind Writings*. Sternberg Press. 2010. p. 64.

Artistic Thinking

Both the educational and the curatorial discussion are characterised by thinking in post-identitarian terms such as agency and performativity. At the same time, as reflective practices, they also focus on the conditions and potentials of presenting art. In that sense, they seamlessly connect, and also partly overlap, with a possibly even more dominant discourse - that on artistic research. This discourse, which emerged in the 1990s, initially focused on the emancipated artist, capable of contextualising her/his own practice and contributing to the presentation of knowledge production - in other words, artists who related to the domain of the curatorial. The current debate on artistic research - as a specific mode of operation initially described as a radical, experimental practice, but currently threatened with being formatted through increasing academicisation - shows considerable parallels with the 1970s debate on semiotics, as exemplified by Roland Barthes in *The Pleasure of the Text.*[5] In this publication, Barthes sketched a continuous movement between disciplining academic semiotics and a dynamic process of boundless signification ('textuality').

Does artistic research create a similar oscillation between disciplinary knowledge production and a boundless process of artistic thinking? Artistic research, viewed as a specific mode of operation, necessitates a focus on what makes artistic knowledge possible. That focus includes the investigation of modes of artistic thought, forms of differential thought and thinking in a multitude of connections. There is a need for a form of thought that concentrates on artistic knowledge production, but which is simultaneously capable of manifesting itself as research within an institutional environment.[6] However, such a form of thought must also include possibilities for deformation, deconstruction or de-territorialisation of conceptual frameworks if thinking in terms of knowledge production becomes too limiting.

5. On the present situation of Artistic Research, see also Henk Slager, The Pleasure of Research. Finnish Academy of Fine Arts. 2012.
6. See also Henk Slager, 'The Institutional Conscience of Art' in Angela Vettese (ed.), *Art as a Thinking Process.* Sternberg Press. 2013. p. 210–221.

Temporary Autonomous Research

But how do the processes of thinking in art connect to institutions dealing with models of research? Could these institutions provide room for extra-national, interconnecting, transforming and fluent ways of thinking beyond the traditional frame of modern or modernist histories? These issues are put forward by Simon Sheikh in Spaces for Thinking, which asks: 'is it possible to think of education as a process of thinking, of unlearning certain modes of knowledge and production and subjectivity, of questioning these very structures rather than embracing them. Is it possible to think of educational spaces that are produced through subjectivities rather than merely producers of them'?[7] The project, *Temporary Autonomous Research*, in the Amsterdam Pavilion at the 2012 Shanghai Biennale,[8] intended to further interrogate these questions through a number of sub-questions related to an institutional interpretation of the concept of temporary autonomy. What does thinking in terms of temporary autonomy actually mean for topical art practices immersed in research-based forms and perspectives of knowledge production? Can we chart moments of deconstruction and de-territorialisation, moments of resistance to the managerial domain and moments of refusal of instrumental reason? Does the current society of spectacles, the world of marketing and commodity, actually allow an outside? Is there a direct link between a temporary autonomous situation and the generation of critical artistic research?[9]

Since time immemorial, a research environment has existed by virtue of a form of autonomous awareness as a place of non-dogmatic knowledge, of the public sharing of knowledge. As Franco 'Bifo' Berardi observes in *Cognitarian Subjectivation,* 'Research should not be subjected to any restraining criterion of functionality, because its very function is to explore solutions that, although dysfunctional in the present paradigm, may reveal new paradigmatic landscapes'.[10]

7. Simon Sheikh, 'Spaces for Thinking'. *Texte zur Kunst*. No. 62. June 2006. p. 191.
8. The Amsterdam Pavilion at the 9th Shanghai Biennale (2012) included work and texts by Nicoline van Harskamp, Falke Pisano and Jeremiah Day (Publication: *Temporary Autonomous Research*. Metropolis M Books. 2012).
9. This question was at the core of the symposium, Doing Research, dOCUMENTA 13 (Kassel, September 2012) and in the Doing Research publication (eds. Annette W. Balkema, Jan Kaila and Henk Slager), Finnish Academy of Fine Arts, 2012.
10. Franco Berardi Bifo, *Cognitarian Subjectivation*. e-flux Journal. November 2010. p. 5.

Offside Effect

In addition to the institution-based discussion on research as a paragon of the capacity to generate a free, artistic space for thought, the conformist dangers of neoliberal instrumentalisation prompt us to be alert and engage in dialogues on the specificity of art education with those academies and platforms that are outside the Bologna Process and its sphere of influence. After all, in such a confrontation, the awareness of one's own institutional identity is not only accentuated but also expanded in a continuous process of reassessment.

In order to underscore anew the process of decentralisation, the 1st Tbilisi Triennial in 2012[(11)] concentrated on the theme of the Offside Effect, asking: How could educative platforms beyond the influence of the Bologna Process articulate their 'exterior' awareness as a surplus value? In a forum-like display system, a number of keynote artists (among them Anton Vidokle, Stephan Dillemuth and Marion von Osten) and lecturers, in collaboration with their students from a dozen experimental academies from all over the world, presented their strategic ways of working. This was inspired by art academies reacting against the managerial turn while searching for an experimental room for education. All the presentations showed how, in unexpected and fascinating ways, forms of resistance could emerge against the powers that discipline artistic knowledge, serving as a reminder of the ever-present desire to escape fixed and fixing models of thought.

Performative Research

The 1st Tbilisi Triennial showed many processional activities and presentations that, from the perspective of collective agency, focused on unlearning preconceptions while including a performative dimension together with the generation of a counter public space. Annette Krauss organised a test site in the form of a para-educational department, directed at the significance of 'unlearning' when engaged in artistic (research) practices. For this, she employed a 'diffractive methodology': an ethical mode of working which articulates the kind of differences

11. The various participants contextualise their contributions to the Tbilisi Triennial in the publication *Offside Effect*. Metropolis M Books. 2013. René Francisco, 'The Fourth Pragmatic' in Henk Slager (ed.), Offside Effect. Metropolis M Books. 2013. p. 57.

that matter. In a workshop environment, the ways in which institutional structures and normative processes shape our bodies came to the fore, suggesting ways in which a de-disciplining academy could critically counterattack those phenomena.

René Francisco showed documentary work related to his *Pedagogia Pragmatica* workshops, which take place outside the art academy at unexpected locations in Havana's urban landscape such as a deserted house or a posh swimming pool. The workshops deal with artistic group processes, awareness of communicative action, reinterpreting relations between doing, seeing and saying: 'Although the professor was addressed by the individual student, the field of actions created as a group produced a multiple, educational effect in showing behaviors, forms of life, and symbolic production. The borders between author, artist, spectator and also those of professor-student diluted, because of similitudes to be acknowledged, novel forms of knowledge to come into being'.(12)

Tiong Ang's *Pavilion of Distance* was initiated and presented as an experimental platform in which to pursue collective artistic production and to develop an educational methodology of co-creation: 'It offers a perspective on the academy's function to be a discontinuation of sorts, providing a shelter for experiment, a conceptual hub of converging ambitions within a sense of shared learning, organic cultural distance and performative mediation'.

Academy As Exhibition

In conclusion, one could argue that the 1st Tbilisi Triennial generated a novel perspective on the relationship between curatorial strategies, educational praxis and artistic research - a novel perspective based on both the curatorial starting point and the dynamism of participatory educational and research projects. Thus, in presenting the academy as exhibition, *Offside Effect* contributed in a radical way to the promotion and understanding of ways in which 'artistic research', 'the curatorial' and 'educational praxis' could be manifested as an interlaced triad. In that framework, educational praxis is understood as an experimental space for the collective - a speculative and performative mode of reflection and presentation, contextualising connections between objects, images, processes, people, locations, histories and discourses. In that framework,

12. Tiong Ang, 'Pavilion of Distance, A Greek Tragedy' in Henk Slager (ed.), Offside Effect. Metropolis M Books. 2013. p. 53.

artistic research is considered a temporary, autonomous intellectual awareness of the ways in which educational praxis is institutionalised and artistic activity is directed towards the occupation of territory indicated by the notion of curatorial. In that framework, the curatorial equates to dynamic, continuously traversing spaces of learning in which the presentation of rhizomatic processes and transformations and a form of thinking directed to crucial issues and lingering forms of thought are instigated time and again.

88 - 113

WHAT IF AN INSTITUTION WAS CURATED? INTERMEDIAE AS AN INSTITUTIONAL HYPOTHESIS

Olga Fernández López

An Institutional Laboratory

In recent years, mediation and research have become key words within certain curatorial projects and debates. In Spain, this development has taken place against a backdrop of social unrest and a sense of dissatisfaction with the role that institutional culture has been playing. A quest for new cultural models has begun, intensified by the economic crisis while responding to a pre-existing context, which was already questioning the exhausted local institutional and curatorial framework. Several cultural projects have taken research as a guiding axis in an expanded version of curatorial practice in which knowledge production and cultural production go hand in hand, and in which the relation to the social fabric has proven fundamental.(1) In this text, I will look at a particular Madrilenian institution, Intermediae, examining the ways in which it has overcome the limitations of the so-called educational turn and new institutionalism, motivated by an idea of perpetual experimentation and a self-reflective questioning of cultural production, its social function and the role of the institution. This text attempts to make legible the curatorial challenges encountered by a team experimenting with horizontal institutional processes. In order to contextualise the significance of this initiative, I will begin with a brief mapping of the Spanish cultural field.

Spanish Exhibition Culture: Expectations and Discontents

The passage from Franco's dictatorship to a democratic political system in Spain, a process known as Transición [Transition] (1975–1992), was accompanied by the aspiration to be considered equal to other European countries and a politics of reconciliation, aimed at overcoming forty years of exceptionalism. The political parties agreed a consensus that sought to guarantee political and economic stability and social unity.(2) Under a recurring plea for normalisation, this agreement implied the suspension of the collective – and traumatic – memory of the Civil War and Francoism and the promotion of a culture of 'belonging', based on the neutralisation of past and present conflicts. In the 1980s, political decisions were accompanied by what the political journalist, Guillem Martínez, has coined the Culture of Transition, which implied a

1. One example could be Bulegoa: http://www.bulegoa.org/en
2. This consensus, known as the Moncloa Pact, was signed in 1977.

deactivation of the critical potential of cultural practices.[3] The smooth transition from dictatorship to neoliberalism was driven by an unstinting belief in modernisation, which implied the dismantling of local manufacturing industries and the promotion of cultural and tourism industries. The uncritical Culture of Transition continued into the 1990s, when Spain went through a promising period of economic growth that contributed to a widespread culture of money and a spectacularisation of cultural initiatives. However, since the democratic regime did not change the political habit of instrumentalising the arts, we can speak of an actual continuity between the two periods.[4]

In the specifically artistic field, during the 1980s and '90s, consecutive ruling parties attempted to implement policies to compensate for what they thought was lacking. This effort was orchestrated in a peculiar order – first through exhibitions and then through the creation of permanent venues (which were mostly established during the fifteen years following 1992).[5] During the 1980s, the majority of governmental energies in this area were put into the production of temporary exhibitions, thought to counteract the Francoist restrictions on showing avant-garde and neo-avant-garde movements, and into the presentation of the post-Francoist generation of artists at home and abroad. These exhibitions took place in the existing precarious and inadequate infrastructures.[6] In this decade, another main site in which contemporary art could be seen was at ARCO, an annual fair which began operating as

3. Guillem Martínez, *CT o la Cultura de la Transición. Crítica a 35 años de cultura española.* Debolsillo. 2012. The author states that left-wing parties in power, mainly the Socialist Party, played an important role in the de-activation of critical culture.

4. Whereas, during Franco's dictatorship, art had been used to present an image of modernity abroad, after Franco and until 2006, political intervention was also significant. For instance, the government chose the director of the most important museums, such as Museo del Prado or Museo Nacional Reina Sofía. See Jorge Luis Marzo and Tere Badia's, 'Las políticas culturales en el estado español (1985-2005)', 2006 found at http://soymenos.net/politica_espanya.pdf. About cultural industries in Spain, see Jaron Rowan, *Emprendizajes en cultura: Discursos, instituciones y contradicciones de la empresarialidad cultural. Traficantes de Sueños.* 2010.

5. In the scheme of things, 1992 stands out as an important year, due to the number of events taking place in Spain which proposed a modern image of the country. Among others, this included the Olympic Games (Barcelona), Expo'92 (Seville), European Cultural Capital (Madrid) and the Fifth Centenary of America Discovery.

6. See José Luis Brea, 'El desarrollo de la Institución-Arte en la democracia'. *Revista de Occidente* 273. 2004; Juan Antonio Ramírez (ed.), *El sistema del arte en España. Cátedra. 2010 and Nekane Aramburu, Luces y sombras de una cartografía fluctuante*, http//:cvc.cervantes.es/lengua/anuario/anuario_06-07/pdf/artes_01.pdf

early as 1982.[7] The popularity of the fair compensated for the scarcity of commercial galleries.

In the 1990s, as hinted at above, these policies were followed by the creation of new venues (art schools, museums, contemporary art centres) and of a public system for channelling funding, which subsidised the desired new image of Spanish art through official organisations, grants, awards and media coverage. At the same time, there was a growth in private initiatives (new art fairs and banks' cultural foundations). This development was facilitated by the consolidation of the seventeen regional governments, which not only decentralised the art system but also multiplied its institutions and agents. In trying to imitate the Guggenheim effect, the proliferation of art venues ran in parallel with the financial and construction 'bubble'. The growing number of museums needed both internal and independent curators to arrange the newly formed collections and to organise exhibitions with a wider perspective on art practices. This moment of abundance coincided, in the 1990s and early 2000s, with a new generation of artists and curators who performed a generational break, discernible in their thematics, artistic language and use of new media. This generation began to disseminate postmodern discussions in a reflection upon contemporaneity.[8] This renovation ushered in a different consideration of exhibitions, beyond the mere display of artists' works and towards discursivity. Individual figures with an authorial voice, bolstered by a prosperous environment, consolidated this curatorial turn in the Spanish scene.[9]

During this process, the artistic community imagined that the changing cultural landscape would give rise to a combination of good art schools, public institutions supporting free and challenging contemporary art, a regulated art market, cultivated collectors, an educated public, highly critical magazines and internationally recognised artists. In retrospect, there has been a sour acknowledgment that this conversion did not happen. Instead of the imagined model, cultural policy – with the support of corporate mass media – prioritised exhibitions that contributed to the *Transición* ideals of a new Spanish identity, the construction of

7. Alberto López Cuenca, 'El traje del emperador. La mercantilización del arte en la España de los años 80'. Revista de Occidente 273. 2004.

8. Gloria Picazo and Martí Perán (eds.), *Impasse 5. La década equívoca: el transfondo del arte contemporáneo español en los 90*. Ajuntament de Lleida / Centre d'art la Panera. 2005.

9. Gloria Picazo (ed.), *Impasse 4. Exposiciones de arte contemporáneo: importancia y repercusión en el arte español*. Ajuntament de Lleida / Centre d'art la Panera. 2004.

visually iconic museums, the conversion of huge buildings into art centres, the endorsement of a strong institutional and corporate collecting culture, some attempts to create biennials and a government-based promotion of Spanish artists abroad. Until recently, this systemic, uncritical approach to cultural production had been subject to little scrutiny by art critics and historians.

The institutional artistic model constructed in recent decades masked profound deficiencies. Dependence upon official policies generated an intricate network of institutionalised venues, practices and agents that monopolised most of the public and private funding. This situation especially affected independent spaces, medium-sized public galleries and artist-run spaces, whose network was never strong or had the possibility to become so.[10] This does not mean that there was no alternative scene whatsoever, but it was economically fragile and suffered from a considerable asymmetry in relation to the big institutions. This scenario engendered the lack of a diverse intermediate ground of and for action, capable of organically relating to the remaining artistic agents, institutions and social constituents. The possibilities for another kind of socio-artistic fabric were severely restricted, as was the development of an active public sphere.

The predominance of a powerful institutional culture made most of the existing alternatives deeply oppositional to it, provoking a distorted mirror effect, particularly in the quest for a critical public. This criticality ranged from attempts to connect art with a social constituency that had been alienated from it, to the activation of a dissenting public sphere or explicit cultural activism.[11] For a long time, official narratives - either cultural or artistic - overlooked these parallel stories. However, the dissatisfactions began to grow stronger, particularly in the early 2000s, coinciding with the peak of the economic bubble. Beneath the gleaming surface, certain artists, scholars, curators and cultural and civic movements were questioning the cultural consensus - a restlessness that was to develop into social unrest when the economic crisis hit.[12] In a context in which an entire model of cultural production was beginning

10. José Luis Brea, '(Re)construyendo un afuera'. 2007. arte-nuevo.blogspot.com.es/2007/02/reconstruyendo-un-afuera-jos-luis-brea.html and Nekane Aramburu (ed.), *Historia y situación actual de los espacios independientes y colectivos de artistas en el estado español (1980 - 2010).* allegrageler.bubok.com/ 2011.

11. For examples, see Jordi Claramonte, *Arte de contexto.* Nerea. 2011.

12. Among others, the series of readers about different topics, *Desacuerdos. Sobre arte, políticas y esfera pública en el arte español*, published between 2004 and 2012, or the ongoing critical project by José Luis Marzo at www.soymenos.net/

to be contested, a new generation of Spanish curators and institutions prompted a new cultural sensibility. This critical wave also brought about a major questioning of inherited modes of addressing the relationship between culture and society, politics or economics, and of the role that cultural representations have played in the legitimisation of hegemonic narratives. The various factors contributing to this mobilisation are beyond the scope of this text, but there seems to be an undeniable unrest coming from the generations that grew up against this backdrop.[13] More than being simply a 'return of the repressed', there is a conscious demand to discuss the assumptions constituting the political, social and cultural common ground. In this climate, the previous model of authorial curatorship was called into question, and various modes of curatorial practice, interested in mediation in the broadest sense, were researched and tested.

Madrid Cultural Politics: Gentrification and Other Contradictions

At the centre of these changes, Madrid was to play an important role, although not one exempt from contradictions. Madrid's cultural structure fully reflects its position as the capital of the country. The city has accumulated a large share of national museums, private artistic foundations and commercial galleries, various short-lived independent spaces and a permanently dissatisfied community of artists. However, until recently, the city and the wider region (Comunidad de Madrid) did not have a specific venue exclusively devoted to contemporary art.[14] With Barcelona and Bilbao as models, Madrid's conservative municipal and regional politicians resolved to transform the capital into a cultural/tourist 'branded' city.[15] This implied the visible alignment of the cultural infrastructure around an axis called Paseo del Arte [Art Walk], leading from the centre to the south of the city, in order to create an urban

13. Different social movements, ranging from 1990s anti-globalisation, to associations fighting for legal action against Francoist crimes and the recent 15-M movement, among many others, have created a climate of unrest and discomfort in relation to inherited political and social compromises.

14. With regard to this statement, authors are referring to venues devoted exclusively to contemporary art (kunsthalles), and not existing venues which also exhibit modern 20th-century art or which have a mixed exhibition politics. Tomás Ruiz-Rivas, 'De cómo Madrid llegó a ser una capital sin museos de arte contemporáneo'. El Huevo. 2004. accesible at www.antimuseo.org/teoria/teoria_textos2.html See also Manuel Ayllón, 'Madrid no crece, sólo engorda'. *Brumaria#3*. 2004.

15. Observatorio Metropolitano, *Manifiesto por Madrid. Crítica y crisis del modelo metropolitano.* Traficantes de Sueños. 2009.

'musealisation' capable of renewing the symbolic image of Madrid.[16] The Art Walk project, which began in 1995, entailed the extension of the museums Reina Sofía (2005) and El Prado (2007), the refurbishment of the Archeological Museum and their symbolic connection to other museums on the same axis, such as Thyssen-Bornemisza. In this scheme, the Reina Sofia served as a door to the 'creative' (and traditionally highly activist) part of the city (Lavapiés), which began to be filled with contemporary art venues and commercial galleries.[17] This extension to the south was advertised as a process of urban regeneration for an area filled with abandoned factories and populated with working class people and immigrants. This branch of the cultural axis ended at the old slaughterhouse [Matadero], a 150,000 m^2 industrial complex that had been abandoned for 25 years and lay ready for cultural re-use. The former abattoir was located at a natural frontier formed by the ring road and the soon-to-be-bridged Manzanares River.[18]

Matadero Madrid is the most visible manifestation of municipal policy of the past decade - a multifaceted project housing different venues involving multi-disciplinary programming and public and private agents.[19] In the visual arts realm, it accommodates the principal artists' association (AVAM), four artists' archives, a curatorial programme and Intermediae - the main subject of this text - a self-defined laboratory and experimental space.[20] Occupying 2,000 m2 of the former cold storage area of the slaughterhouse, Intermediae branched out of an earlier municipal project, MediaLabMadrid (founded in 2000), through which concern about the social value of artistic and cultural practices began to be raised by a city council team.[21] New to this context was an interrogation of the social significance of public cultural spaces, which

16. Most of the cultural venues and commercial galleries are located close to the same imaginary line (Paseo de la Castellana). This proximity has helped events such as PhotoEspaña (since 1998).

17. Different venues, usually renovated industrial buildings, have been opened as cultural sites in the neighbourhood, such as El Águila, La Casa Encendida, and the failed project of a moving image museum, now transformed into Tabacalera.

18. See Carles Guerra, 'Salir de Madrid'. *La Vanguardia*. 2 May 2007, for an account of Madrid Rio urban project.

19. See Jesús Carrillo, *Las nuevas fábricas de la cultura: los lugares de la creación y la producción cultural en la España contemporánea*. 2008. accesible at medialab-prado.es/mmedia/689

20. Matadero's programme includes three artistic lines: Abierto por obras, Nave 16 and El Ranchito.

21. The change of mayor in 2003 (Alberto Ruiz Gallardón) brought about a new Area de las Artes (Arts Area), with a new city councillor (Alicia Moreno). As Director of Projects, Juan Carrete was also the Director of MediaLab, between 2005 and 2012.

was contradictory to the city branding policy in which it was inscribed.[22] MediaLabMadrid aimed to explore these questions through the production, research and dissemination of digital culture (connecting art, science, technology and society).[23] Later on, Intermediae complemented these areas, expanding municipal interests into visual culture, social innovation and participation.

In the Spanish scenario, there were few precedents for projects that engaged with publics beyond the artistic community, which tried to connect art with social life or knowledge production or which considered curatorial practice to be something beyond the making of exhibitions. Adopting a situated approach to cultural production – which implied that solutions were not easily translatable – projects following this path needed to find their own ways of working. In the case of Intermediae, its director, Juan Carrete, and his team decided to adopt a self-reflexive research practice at the core of their expanded curatorial model.[24] As with all new institutions, Intermediae passed through an initial testing phase until it found its own specific working methodology.[25] Prior to the public opening, the first two years, from 2005 to 2006, were devoted to the planning of the programme and the preparation of projects to be launched during the first months of 2007. It is apparent, from preliminary documents, that proposals reacted to the existing cultural environment described earlier. The first two draft documents in which the institution was described insisted on three concepts: process, trans-disciplinarity and horizontality. This can be read as a reaction against art and exhibi-

22. In 2005, this concern was channelled through a series of meetings with local practitioners, activists and independent spaces and with the establishment of an open call for artistic production. See the conversations at *Prácticas artísticas independientes en Madrid.* www.medialabmadrid.org/medialab/medialab.php?l=0&a=a&i=251 In relation to the extension of the public, their first working text states: 'The institution is defined both by artists and the public or visitors who become involved in the processes occurring within. The institution itself will catalyse the activity, acting as an intermediary between artist and public'. 'Intermediae'. *Draft # 1.* 2005. p. 28. Some interviews that expose the institutional process held for The Future archive: archive.org/details/FutureArchiveZoeJuanFrank and archive.org/details/FutureArchiveCristinaConde

23. See medialab-prado.es/ Its name changed to Medialab Prado when it was placed in the Art Walk.

24. The team was formed by María Bella, José Miguel Medrano, Frank Buschmann, Suset Sánchez, Azucena Klett, Zoe López Mediero, Paqui Blanco and Pepa Vijuesca.

25. This analysis of Intermediae encompasses various sources: the assessment of the realised artistic projects, an examination of the internal documents that preceded the inauguration of the programme (2005 and 2007) and the first public report that summarised its first seven years (2011). Also, I have conducted interviews with several members of the team (María Bella, Suset Sánchez, Azucena Klett and Zoe López Mediero) and some external collaborators (Jaron Rowan and María Pérez Maestro).

tions being regarded as products, a reassertion of artistic autonomy and a critique of institutional verticality.

These initial documents were quite unclear about Intermediae's purpose beyond the establishment of a new kind of institution for contemporary art which fulfilled some of the needs of the city and its citizens. The most significant feature was that the institution posited itself as a host, a mediatory site between artists and public, evident in its name - Intermediae - which also responded to a post-media, collaborative and socially orientated approach. The main means for putting this into practice was the setting up of an annual call for applications in support of artistic projects (*Ayudas a la Creación*). Around 60 percent of the projects that have taken place at Intermediae have come to the institution through a selection made by the external selection committee for the Ayudas, in which Intermediae has a say but does not have the right to vote on the final choice.[26] This mode of operation raised important practical questions about the relationship between Intermediae, guest projects and the public. The team curates the remaining 40 percent of projects. The coexistence of different projects under the same roof generated questions about potential divergences between agendas, raising an issue about institutional porosity and its limits, which the team decided to actively explore.

In conceptual terms, the nature of projects did not represent too much of a conflict, since an element of consistency existed among the type of initiatives selected, which were carried out through exchange, participation, discussion and public intervention. Intermediae's guidelines included a specific concern about the connection with the immediate neighbourhood (Legazpi), although not all the projects needed to be linked to this. Along these lines, during the first three years (2007-9), a previously non-existent 'culture of collaboration' between different cultural agents and public in Madrid was engendered in Intermediae and Medialab. In addition to the social aspect, an experimental side was also present in the trans-disciplinarity of many projects and in the

26. The annual call funds different projects, such as independent spaces, mobility grants for artists or artistic production. The projects to be funded are selected by a board that changes every year, comprised by five individuals, three coming from the council and two of them voted in by art professionals (the call includes the option to propose jury members). See www.mataderomadrid.org/ficha/1670/convocatoria-ayudas-a-la-creacion-2012.html

interest manifested in sound, moving image and performance.[27] Both of these aspects informed the absence of conventional exhibitions. When different thematic lines, coming from the bottom up, began to give the institution a curatorial inclination, a number of tendencies became visible. As a result, four themes were determined to orientate the choice of future projects - utopia, permaculture, game and memory - themes that were to be developed through investigative processes.[28] The projects arising, associated, to varying degrees, with the fields of experimentation and social action, were extremely diverse in their aims, formats and duration, and relied upon a wide range of agents and publics, acting concurrently. This coexistence of projects, with sometimes conflicting agents, engendered multiple tensions. The significance of Intermediae can only be measured through a consideration of the way in which it has been able to confront these contradictions and speculate about them.

Intermediae: Inhabiting a Cultural Space

Contrary to many curatorial projects, the possibility of having a physical space has not always been an advantage for the team. Intermediae is located in the massive premises of Matadero, at the epicentre of the biggest urban regeneration plan in Madrid of recent decades. Intermediae was envisaged as a public space - a site which anyone (especially people from the local neighbourhood) could enter and spend some time in (reading newspapers, playing ping pong, using WiFi). In the beginning, the artistic 'aura' given to the premises conveyed a symbolic threshold, but the space was gradually occupied. The venue could be freely booked and utilised by other cultural initiatives. It was also used as an office for the staff, artists and collectives involved in projects and, since 2008, a part of it (called El Terrario) was employed for screenings related to the guiding themes.

27. In the first three years, projects took place such as *Neurotica: Bio III* (2007); *Todo sobre mi barrio* (2007), *Sinantena* (2007), *Dia-Logos* (2007); *In-Sonora* (2008), *La Intención* (2008), *FemeninoVisual 04: LesGay-Legal-Letal* (2009), among others. For a record of the initial years, see Suset Sánchez, Prácticas más allá y a pesar de la sospecha. Sobre las posibilidades de construcción de una institución pública, peripecias e intentos de gestión cultural. Intermediae Archive. 2008.

28. Some projects related to Utopia: *Utopias* (2007), *Alterpolis* (2008); Memory: *Procesos de archivo* (ongoing since 2007); Permaculture: *Avant-Garden* (2008-ongoing), *Spermöla* (2008); Games and Education: *CUE* (2008), *Hybrid Playground* (2008), *Al matadero sin miedo* (2009), *Free(k)* Culture (2009). All these lines are now under the labels Avant-Garden, Estación Futuro, Mundo Legazpi and Procesos de Archivo and are produced in collaboration with different agents and associations.

The unusual occupation of the space, along with the 'workshop look' of most of the artistic and trans-disciplinary processes, made it difficult to project an identifying image of what Intermediae was about. This provoked an impression of a curatorial 'emptying', which was very far from the expected authorial model. The broadening of the notion of art towards cultural production and its confluence with other disciplines was not easily understood by most artists working in the city. Some felt that the open call - an opportunity that had arisen for the first time with municipal funding - should have been devoted to production and exhibition. This was exacerbated by the fact that, during the early years, Intermediae was placed in the spotlight as the sole artistic programme within the huge Matadero premises. Yet, Intermediae was quite clear that it did not want to open a space for the 'cultural avant-garde elite'.[29] The absence of exhibitions, the funding of more experimental projects and the will to involve a non-specialised public would open a chasm between Intermediae and the artistic community. This resulted in an abiding difficulty in developing artistic legitimacy for the institution.

Apart from misunderstandings with the artistic community, the whole basis of Intermediae - process, trans-disciplinarity and horizontality - was considered by art critics to be rather hermetic and difficult to explain to the public. The indeterminacy conjured by the idea of experimentation created a latent conflict. This was compounded by the decision to operate with a low media profile and a resistance to the municipal demands of political and media profitability (especially given the working class and immigrant composition of the neighbourhood). The restrained communication strategy led to the conviction that Intermediae should not make catalogues, in order to avoid the celebratory tendency that had informed the 'catalogue culture' of previous decades. The most visible communication channel was its website, which was considered more of a repository for documentation and a dialogical tool (a blog of blogs) than a marketing medium.[30]

29. Tommaso Marzocchini, *Intermediæ: un laboratorio, no un museo. Algunas cuestiones sobre las prácticas en Intermediae* (Interview with Azucena Klett). Intermediae Archive. 2007.

30. See intermediae.es/project/intermediae/page/intermediae_virtual_blog_de_blogs

Producing and Testing Horizontality

The way in which Intermediae was conceived and run shaped the conflicts that needed to be faced. As we have seen, there was a mixed use of a space determined to be public, with plural, and sometimes antagonistic, agendas; a curatorial approach intended to mediate and catalyse; a range of artistic practices on the verge of becoming something else; a discontented artistic community; a low-profile communication strategy and a search for unspecialised audiences. These features prompted the questions: Should artistic projects maintain aesthetic distinction in a symbolic, legitimised space? Or should they try to dissolve beyond the closed walls of the institution? What is the difference between a sociocultural centre and an experimental centre for contemporary artistic production? How should the dialogue with the artistic community take place? To what extent should the institution be an accomplice of its own spectacularisation or neutralisation? Does mediation preserve or deny curatorial difference? Is it possible for institutions to interrogate their own power positions and become operative mediators? Intermediae needed to go beyond conventional wisdom about the social function of art and using art as social tool (which could easily be assimilated into the latest artistic tendencies). What needed to be addressed was the expansion of the notion of the institution as a tool, thereby transforming it into a laboratory in which to test institutional processes orientated towards a more democratic and public production of culture.

In this regard, Intermediae has tried to overcome the contradictions posed by so-called 'New Institutionalism'.(31) In Spain, the vitality of institutional debate over this period - which was also present in MACBA and Reina Sofia Museum - belied the supposed end of attempts to rethink the social function of art and artistic institutions.(32) The first decade of the 21st century in Spain was not characterised by a weakening of the

31. In 2003, Jonas Ekeberg put forward the possibility of applying the notion of 'New Institutionalism', a term coming from sociology, to art institutions. In his text he ended with an open question about its potentialities, still to be tested. See Jonas Ekeberg, 'Introduction'. Verksted#1. *New Institutionalism.* OCA. 2003. In the following years, the term was used and discarded. See Nina Möntmann, 'The Rise and Fall of New Institutionalism: Perspectives on a Possible Future' in Gerald Raunig and Gene Ray (eds.), *Art and Contemporary Critical Practice Reinventing Institutional Critique*. MayFlyBooks. 2009 and Jonas Ekeberg, 'Institutionalism Experiments Between Aesthetics and Activism' in Stine Hebert and Anne Szefer Karlsen (eds.), *Self-Organised.* Open Editions. 2013.

32. See http://www.macba.cat/PDFs/jorge_ribalta_colleccio_cas.pdf and http://www.museoreinasofia.es/sites/default/files/revista/pdf/carta2.pdf

welfare state, as happened in Northern Europe, but by the mirage of economic boom and the consolidation of national and regional artistic institutions. There was not an abandonment of the institution, but a reinforcement of it. It is in this context that Intermediae poses its institutional hypothesis. While process and trans-disciplinarity can easily be associated with research, horizontality is not usually related to this semantic field. Intermediae has made an extensive effort to research horizontality, as both the means and the ends of its practice, at the centre of the unpredictable effects and affects that all artistic projects generate. As one of their collaborators stated, public institutions generally work with an idea of producing culture *for* rather than *with* the people.[33] In this respect, for Intermediae, the notion of participation does not mean commissioning artworks that involve people, and mediation does not mean dissolving the boundaries between artists, curators, mediators, thinkers and producers, but making it possible for citizens to participate in decision-making processes related to art and culture.

This prospect has taken place in a variety of forms and has engendered a specific research field through which to test and assess institutional practices. In order to share its learning process, the team has explored concepts, taken from daily experience and theoretical approaches, which help them to think about their practice. Beyond the layer of dialogical artistic practices and social innovations which formed Intermediae's starting point, the team has strengthened the project with theoretical tools drawn from critical anthropology, sociology, pedagogy and philosophy. These disciplines build their praxis around power/knowledge positions in relation to social knowledge and around a situation in which one figure represents epistemological authority and disciplinary control. The questioning of power positions that comes from the critical development of these disciplines has served Intermediae as a field of reference against which to challenge its own institutional and curatorial authority. Along with this structural element, feminism, post structuralism and post-colonial thinking have informed inner debates, as methodologies dealing with domination and epistemological challenge.

In the case of critical anthropology, auto-ethnography has served as a possible model.[34] Auto-ethnography is a research methodology that

33. See archive.org/details/FutureArchive_Concha
34. See authors such as Eduardo Viveiros de Castro or Isaac Marrero for reference to critical anthropology, or Mary Louise Pratt, Carolyn Ellis or Patti Lather for auto-ethnography.

focuses on the construction of a point of view, based on the subjective experience of the researcher/writer in his/her relation with the others. In the process, always temporal and situated, the 'observer' is to be *affected* and transformed by the Other and his/her power position dissolved. This immersive positioning provokes a tension between an objective approach and a subjective experience, which is translated into a located, complex, self-questioning narrative. Applied to artistic and curatorial projects, this critical model challenges the contentious concept of 'artist as ethnographer', in which artists and institutions 'altericise' and exploit the communities involved. The comparative use of auto-ethnography as a methodological strategy for mediation-based institutions helps to erode the asymmetry between host and guest projects. Also emanating from this field, the notion of 'contact zone', coined by Mary Louise Pratt, has been useful in understanding the unequal relationships produced through the encounter of different communities, especially in colonial processes.(35)

Among the theoretical tools coming from beyond the cultural field, Actor-Network Theory (ANT) has worked as a possible reference model that studies interdependent social practices, helping Intermediae to think about the ways in which heterogeneous desires, beliefs, materialities, spaces, artefacts, actions, agents, influences and affects constitute a network of aligned interests.(36) Although ANT cannot be applied directly, it is interesting to observe how some of its concepts - such as the centrality of mediation, translation and delegation, the idea of becoming and change, the production of a network, the indeterminacy of the actor/actant, the importance of trajectories of creation or the conception of reality as transitional - help to situate the institution in a completely different dimension. This perspective implies more than a relativisation of the role of the institution as one possible actor. It actually transforms the notion of the institution into a temporal composite in which heterogeneous elements form an interdependent network of common interests.

35. For contact zones, see Mary Louise Pratt, *Imperial Eyes: Travel Writing and Transculturation*. Routledge. 1992.
36. Through the works of Bruno Latour, John Law and John Hassard or Annemarie Mol.

Institutional Learning

In the beginning of Intermediae's history, horizontality was more desired than achieved, and this was quickly pointed out by some of their earliest collaborators. One of these was Antígona Association, a consultancy specialising in the planning and assessment of participatory civil processes.[37] The first project that Intermediae commissioned was a study by Antígona Association of the Legazpi neighbourhood, as part of its method of documentation.[38] The assignment produced a number of misunderstandings; in the first place, Antígona did not think that a conventional sociological study would be helpful, but they made the report and started to collaborate with Intermediae, helping the team to reflect about the modes in which they were negotiating with agents involved in the projects, artists, members of the local community, public and administration. During this process, a member of Antígona began to be considered as another participating agent, with a say in the decision-making process.[39] Within this framework, Antígona was not considered an external advisor but part of the situated/temporal constituency of a variable curatorial team. The collaboration with Antígona ended in 2009, with a self-assessment of Intermediae's team, in which individual positions and roles were openly discussed. This served as a turning point that allowed the team to clarify their different working situations.

In the early moments, some disappointments punctuated the team's intentions. For instance, all the members interviewed agreed that one of their first experiences, called *Utopias* (2007), was a complete failure, although a successful failure, since it allowed the team to discard certain models and test different directions. *Utopias* was conceived as a collaborative project in which a group of artists and thinkers from different fields was invited to produce a common reflection on the topic of utopia, which demanded a research perspective.[40] However, the production and exchange of knowledge, through the sharing and archiving of information, documentation and reflection, did not bring the expected results.

37. See www.antigona.org.es/

38. Another initiative through which to understand more about the neighbourhood was carried out by Laboratorio Urbano for the collective memory project *Todo sobre mi barrio.*

39. For instance, Antígona participated in the meetings that derived from the open call, a programme that informed a large part of Intermediae's activities.

40. Natalie Bookchin, Heath Bunting, Santiago Cirugeda, Diego Díaz and Clara Boj, Luis o Miguel and Nils Norman, Néstor García Canclini, Charity Scribner, Ramón Fernández Durán, Derrick de Kerckhove, David Casacuberta, Antonio Lafuente and Brian Holmes.

With some distance, it is easy to point out that, behind all the good intentions and the apparently collective approach, traditional modes persisted at the core of the institution, including predictable incompatibilities between artists, considerations of the institution as a provider, relations with a possible public (thought of more as consumer than as collaborator) and the naivety of a 'beginner' organisation. All of these factors directly affected the expectations that the institution, artists and public had in relation to each other.

Operating under the same illusions, some of the collectives selected through the open call failed to understand that the institution wanted to participate in decisions involving the projects. Since the artists had gone through an open call, they assumed that the money they received was to be spent without institutional control, and asked: To what extent should the institution have a say about the way a collective spends a grant? How is public funding to be controlled? Should institutional expertise influence the outcome? On Intermediae's side, the team needed to make an effort to work with projects that were not necessarily related to their curatorial or institutional perspective, since they had been chosen by an external board, as mentioned above. On occasions, this brought about a mutual resistance, which made visible the stakes of practising in the public sphere. Once the institution was assumed to be public, by different cultural agents (not necessarily linked to the open call), the demand to use the physical site was read as a metonym of the space in which conflicts were being negotiated. This prompted further questions, such as: How could a balance be achieved between authority and autonomy? Or should this dialectic be disrupted? And how could the idea of a shared responsibility be constructed?

The year 2009 was significant because the self-assessment process coincided with a collaboration with The Future Archive - a platform that 'investigates how people and collectivities position themselves *vis à vis* the future, conceptually and practically'.(41) The Future Archive was invited as part of the memory strand, and participated in the first phase of the project, *Archive Processes*, along with with five other initiatives.(42) The Future Archive works with a specific methodology (complicit with radical pedagogy and militant research), based on interviews and dialogues in which 'two or more people performatively inhabit their proposed versions

41. See www.futurearchive.org/

42. See intermediae.es/project/procesos_de_archivo/page/procesos_de_archivo_2

of futurity'.[43] In the case of Intermediae, this took the form of a workshop and a series of the conversations (supposedly taking place in 2020), which aimed to decipher the desires of the different agents involved (artists, publics, collaborators, collectives, Intermediae's team and other cultural spaces). The aim was to share and confront past experiences as a means of imagining a possible future.[44] In its narrative dimension, the conversations also functioned as a kind of auto-ethnographic essay; as auto-ethnographers, Intermediae's members were able to construct an institutional, but subjective, point of view which revealed their enunciative position. This process proved fundamental to Intermediae, since it gave the team a complementary view of the self-assessment they had undertaken with Antígona and went beyond a social dynamics approach. The Future Archive opened them to a methodology based on imagination and fiction, closer to an artistic perspective.

Institutional Fading

Between 2009 and 2011, Intermediae pursued a thread between institution and imagination, both in their speculations and their projects. This led to an artistic/collaborative/learning environment, inhabited by projects dealing with tools of self-representation, in which fiction and meta-fiction, narrative and scenic strategies played an important part. In those years, Intermediae hosted a number of initiatives based on expanded film and theatre/plays/games –that can be characterised as collaborative projects for minor publics, based on the construction of individual and collective identities operating at the borders between reality and fiction.[45] It is interesting to mention that, among the large variety of projects, most of the interviewees, when asked to pick a successful project, chose one belonging to this approach. Beyond the usual formats - such as workshops and debates, which were common in the early years, in a bid to orientate and disseminate knowledge around the guiding themes - these projects merged artistic and educational aspects, compelling participants to re-imagine their identities, therefore

43. thefuturearchiveblog.wordpress.com/about-2/

44. The experience is described in Valeria Graziano, 'Instituyendo el futuro'. Zehar nº 66. Arteleku. 2009.

45. These projects include: *Corte Arganzuela* [Arganzuela Court], *Al matadero sin miedo* [To the Slaughterhouse without Fear], *Éxit: un corto a la carta* [Exit/ Sucess, a short a la carte film], *Las Historias Paralelas* [The Parallel Stories], *La fábrica del cine sin autor* [The Cinema Factory without Author], *La Gaseosa de Ácido Electrico* [The Electric Acid Soda Water].

working as an Other and through the others. Actually, the notion of role-playing in processes of subjectivation can be used as a metaphor for the working dynamics that Intermediae has tried to set in motion. The disclosure and questioning of its power position, beyond the relativisation of its authorial/authoritarian position, demanded that the institution became other: an institution that curates at the same time as it is curated.

This curatorial hollowing-out does not mean the substitution of the action field of art with a space occupied by social agents. The institution has not disappeared, but it has been transformed. Intermediae's team has started to use notions such as minor curating, *comisariado de la escucha* (translatable as *active listening curatorship*) or jaguar curating (after Viveiros de Castro) to qualify what it does.[46] In this respect, it is useful for the team to refer to modes of feminism that restore and vindicate affects, care and solidarity in the curatorial/mediation processes, trying to overcome the sexist ambivalence present in many areas of the art workers culture. As 'curators' who seek to blur the boundaries between artist, thinker, producer and mediator, in their own role playing and in relation to the various agents involved in the projects (the variable curating team), they 'withdraw' and try to become others through a process of contact and listening that enables them to be taught, to redistribute agencies and to share responsibilities in the construction of a cultural space.[47]

At the end of 2010, internal and external factors motivated the team to re-think and re-signify its cultural function in the city. The conclusion of Matadero's refurbishment situated Intermediae as one of six other significant cultural programmes. At the same time, other institutions in the city began exploring participation and/or institutional practices.[48] As part of

46. Azucena Klett, Zoe Mediero and Gerardo Tudurí, 'Curadorías jaguares, poéticas de lo múltiple. Una mirada decolonial en la producción de la nueva institucionalidad pública'. *Teknocultura* 10, 1. 2013. http://teknokultura.net/index.php/tk/article/view/94

47. Strategies and methodologies, such as feminist confessional narration, involvement/thinking in communities of affects and care have helped them to connect some speculative principles with an embodied practice. Other references coming from radical and critical pedagogy, theatrical teaching play, pedagogy of liberation and anarchist and communist pedagogy have deeply informed their discussions. In this regard, examples include Walter Benjamin, Bertolt Brecht, Antonio Gramsci, Georges Politzer (the theatrical teaching play), Paulo Freire, Celestin Freinet, Augusto Boal (pedagogy of liberation), Henry A. Giroux, Peter McLaren, Ira Shor, bell hooks (critical pedagogy) and other authors such as Grant Kester, Carmen Mörsch, Nora Sternfeld, Eva Stürm, Javier Rodrigo and Aida Sánchez de Serdio.

48. A new institutional approach is present at Museo Reina Sofia, via its 'Other institutionality' programme (see footnote 32 of this text), and in a more social and activist project at CSA Tabacalera.

its research methodology, Intermediae annually introduces a hypothesis-question that helps the team to speculate upon possible answers, such as: What if Intermediae was an extension of the street? What if it was an ecosystem? What if it was an archive? What if it was a living room for the city? Between 2011 and 2013, questions have included: What if there were more Intermediaes in the city? What if Intermediae was a school? The first question has evolved into an expansion of the project through so-called *Distributed Intermediae* (although the economic crisis implied a reduction of the team and the budget).[49] This dispersal is thought of as a kind of urban 'acupuncture' or 'seeding'. This modus operandi is consistent with the notion of dissolving the institution, since it listens to the demands of pre-existing communities or of cultural producers wanting to work outside of the institutional framework.[50] The second question has grown into a learning environment of/about/in cultural production, under the name of *Intermediae 404: school not found.*[51]

Since 2011, Madrilenian cultural circumstances have altered in response to the economic crisis and the *acampadas.*[52] This new context has generated a number of projects in which new public spaces are being co-produced through activism and citizenship, in the midst of a new wave of cuts.[53] While it is beyond the scope of this text to examine these changes, they do indicate the more recent concerns of Intermediae's team. In projects such as *CityKitchen*, the institution is used as an environment in which to interrogate municipal protocols for cultural, social and administrative agents in a moment of transformation. Behind such projects, we can discern an enquiry into the ways in which recent citizen movements have affected the social fabric, political activity and cultural field. In turn, this begs further questions about whether (and, if so, how) artistic institutions can still play a role in this changing landscape.

49. In 2009, the team involved eight full-time members and six collaborators, while, in 2012, it was reduced to five full-time members and three collaborators. Its budget has been also cut by nearly 50 percent.
50. Delocalised projects include: *La Gaseosa de Ácido Eléctrico or Vivero de Iniciativas Ciudadanas: Proyecto Greenvia.*
51. *Intermediae 404: school not found* has activated projects such as *Amar en tiempos Hipster* and *Euraca.*
52. The *acampadas* (public camping occupations), also known as the Spanish revolution, followed the social uprisings in Tunisia, Egypt and other Arab countries.
53. Among others, Campo de la Cebada, Esta es una plaza, Espacio Vecinal Montamarta, Basurama Autobarrios, Plan Cañada-Todo por la Praxis.

Eight artists initiated the contemporary art organisation Vector in 2001.[1] Being a fine art student in Iași at the time, I first started to work for Vector in 2003, and I became its director in June 2011, until May 2012, when I resigned to join tranzit.ro,[2] which is part of a transnational network of cultural institutions.[3] Looking back at the development of Vector, it is clear that it started out with shared authorship, where our work was characterised by experiment, dedication, and self-organisation. We developed new knowledge and new social spaces in our city, but that came accompanied with exhaustion caused by our dis-organisation. The gradual maturing of those involved made us embark on a process of transformation: from a group of invested professionals towards an institutional format. Or at least that is what we thought we were doing, but whether the institutional format was a real aim or something created out of a particular necessity and desire in our context remains to be determined.

'Becoming an Institution' and 'Being the Almost Institution' are two notions that sit at the centre of my reflections upon Vector today. The first includes a transformative process towards what I presume Vector's members understood it as, being an institution within the specific context of Iași. The latter describes a potentially static position that sums up the yet unfulfilled desires and projections of the same group of people on an image of the institution. Despite the fact that the becoming was embraced as a working method of our group, the almost seems to better encapsulate the way we actually functioned.

Since Vector's legal status was that of an association, it was an entity constituted and run by partners with equal powers and duties. This was the principle we tried to follow, although in reality we were actively heading towards an abstract structure characterised by hierarchy, a set of rules and practices, stability, archiving and institutional memory as well as continuity, all of which fulfilling the image of the institution for contemporary art that we could build in Iași. The 'Almost' was created by the intersection between the equity partners' visions, which in turn overlapped with a hierarchical way of working among us. This tension kept Vector somewhere in the middle, while transforming and becoming

1. Dan Acostioaei, Dragoş Alexandrescu, Matei Bejenaru, Felix Drăgan, Cezar Lăzărescu, Florin Grigoraş, Mihai Voicu and Bogdan Teodorescu, all artists. In 2005 five other members with various backgrounds joined: Alexandru Bounegru, Genţiana Baciu, Cătălin Gheorghe, Vlad Morariu, Livia Pancu and Iulia Tencariu.
2. See http://ro.tranzit.org/en.
3. See http://www.tranzit.org/.

were a permanent condition. More than ten years since its inception, Vector and its members found themselves at a crossroads needing to decide how to continue.

Iași is a city in eastern Romania. Our closest peers are in Bucharest, which is 406 km away, in Cluj, 390 km away, and Chisinău, in the Republic of Moldova, 180 km away. Before Vector was established, no contemporary art institution with connections to an international art network existed in the region. The motivations for initiating Vector included a certain sense of responsibility towards the local context.

For those running Vector it was essential to facilitate the production of art that connected with the international scene and with large-scale exhibitions, as a means to create and educate an audience. Throughout the years a big institutional infrastructure was simulated by organising a wide variety of projects, including an international biennial, the long term socio-cultural project cARTier, running a gallery space and a residency programme, as well as publishing magazines and books.(4) The complexities of these projects unavoidably led to a discussion on the potential of overproduction. All our projects provided means for self-education, both for the public as well as for ourselves. However, these situations also expressed Vector's ambitions to become an institution for contemporary art in dialogue with discussions happening elsewhere.

Our knowledge of contemporary art came from a rather limited network of artists and curators to begin with, based on our personal networks and contacts, and our projects were supported by a handful of funding structures and organisations that had specific demands on our activities. Today we still see elements that are remnants of the curators and art institutions that worked with Vector throughout its first years. The disadvantage of this was that we behaved in a mimetic manner, trying to follow and apply models that came from somewhere else. However, the most important role in projecting the ambitions of a big institution wanting to contextualise its activity and its interest in creating

4. Vector's history is intertwined with the history of the Periferic Festival and Biennial, the first biennial in Romania, which was initiated by Vector's co-founder Matei Beienaru (1997–2008). Vector was the organiser of cARTier project (2004–07), Vector Gallery (2004–07) and partner in the Backyard Residency (2006–07) and Accented Residency (2009–10) programmes, and published *Vector* magazine and *Vector – critical research in context*. Currently Vector's activities are invisible and more focused on positioning itself in its own history as well as in the surrounding society, apart from its participation in the ENPAP project (European Network for Public Art Producers) (2010–12).

a legacy was played by Vector members themselves. All our programmes reflected and simulated an institution, and formed the strategy we chose to articulate ourselves within the local and the international artistic contexts. I would, however, claim that what we did was rather embody the Almost Institution.

We wished to create a stable organisation that could transcend the individuals that had formed it, and the use of the term institution was somehow inflicted upon us. Our legal status as an association sat us closer to the self-organised format, rather than that of the institutional. We often described ourselves as 'a group of people', while our behaviour could periodically be characterised by strict rules and hierarchy.

When this discrepancy was occurring, we were actively discussing the institutionalisation of Vector. It was necessary to present the organisational structure as sustainable, which would benefit the dialogue with potential funding bodies, where use of the right terminology was instrumental in securing financial support. Within the organisation we thought that the Almost Institution could offer this image more strongly than that of the artist-run organisation. Although this image only remained a simulated projection, as we never allowed ourselves to become personally detached from Vector, and the knowledge we gradually developed over time stayed within our own group.

Another external pressure was constituted by the fact that when Vector was initiated there was no museum or other kind of national institution focused on contemporary art in Romania. Vector and other active organisations were therefore acting as substitutes, and were taking responsibility for critical discourse across the country. The National Museum of Contemporary Art was only inaugurated in 2004 in Bucharest. Soon after, the activities of this museum became almost irrelevant for part of the Romanian contemporary art scene, or part of the scene became irrelevant for the museum, which is why existing organisations across the country kept their roles and positions.

Because of the lack of strong institutions, and the need for production platforms for contemporary art, Vector had to present itself, adapt and act in many different ways, matching the type of projects we were running. At the time we could not see this as being flexible, since we were always changing. Thus, the only way we could characterise ourselves was through a promise: the promise of institutionalisation. We ended up using self-organisation as the only possible method to evolve and transform towards the institution, a stable model.

Vector members dreamt about this transformation for different reasons. The initial group consisted of eight artists who by 2006 had different motivations for still being involved. Nevertheless, their main drive was the possibility to produce their own work, exhibit, and get critical feedback from art professionals. Therefore their role in Vector transgressed from being organisers who occasionally would take part in exhibitions that they produced into being artists represented through Vector's activities. For the initial group Vector's institutionalisation was introduced out of the necessity as formulated by the new members, who slowly took over the organisers' role. By that time Vector was already over-producing. We had to deal with a huge amount of work,[5] which required at least ten people,[6] who were all gradually learning along the way. In retrospect it is clear that this made us focus solely on the realisation of projects and did not allow any room for reflection on the contents and the direction things were taking. We were merely trying to stay afloat.

By the end of the 2008 Periferic Biennial, the last biennial to date, Vector's members and close collaborators were exhausted and lacked the motivation to continue. Many of them had second jobs to earn a living, others went abroad to study, and the rest wanted to focus on their own artistic careers. Many of the relations between the individuals in the group were eroded and there was a lack of energy needed to work towards getting new members. In 2010 co-founder and director Matei Bejenaru decided to let go of Vector. He organised a conference with former collaborators (artists, curators and representatives of other institutions) to debate the future of Vector and later that year we published a small book on Vector's activities 1997–2010.

With the support of the former director I decided to use this moment to change the strategy of Vector. Instead of working in our own geographical context, where we had been active for ten years, we accepted every international invitation to collaborate abroad. This allowed us to focus strategies needed to present Vector elsewhere and formulate notions of the kind of work we had done to date. Vector's year

5. In 2005-2006 Vector was responsible for the Periferic 7 (three sections with four curators), the cARTier Project, the Vector Gallery with exhibitions every three weeks, the residency programmes, publications, the website as well as the visual identity for all the projects, layout and proofing for all the publications, application writing, budgeting, etc.

6. Dan Acostioaei, Dragoş Alexandrescu, Matei Bejenaru, Cătălin Gheorghe, Andrei Gavril (finance), Vlad Morariu, Cristian Nae (on a specific section of the biennial in 2006), Livia Pancu, Iulia Tencariu and Bogdan Teodorescu.

on the road became a turning point which constituted a moment for much needed contemplation and reflection, and came at the precise time when most of us realised the degree of disconnection we were facing between each other.[7] My attempt to run Vector in a very horizontal manner was due to fail because it could not be applied realistically within our group. What I had inherited was a great portfolio from an organisation that had been active until 2008, but that was exhausted. The dramatic differences in our expectations of what Vector was and should be had simply grown too big, and it seemed impossible at this point to engage with an audience, when we couldn't even find a common ground to work from among ourselves. We might have been able to go on simulating a while longer, but I'm not sure we would have been able to maintain respect for each other. Instead, by the end of 2011 artist Florin Bobu and I proposed to pause our programming and push all of us to focus on Vector as a group.[8]

As a consequence of ceasing the programme Vector became invisible to everyone outside the group.[9] The simple decision that rendered Vector invisible was not easy to make, since we had to step back from projects that we had already committed to.[10] The pressure from the outside had been growing, but in a way this also helped us reach this radical decision and to implement it immediately. However, the question remained how to communicate this decision to our audience and peers. Do you start being invisible by making a very visible public statement and transforming this into a new strategy of appearance?

For many, the fact that Vector was not doing what it had previously done, could mean that it was dead, or that it was falling prey to a slow death. If the process of becoming invisible is not declared publicly and

7. The phrase *'Vector's year on the road'* came about in a discussion with curator Jesse McKee. It included the following: participation in the Frame section of the Frieze Art Fair in London in October 2010; an exhibition project at Western Front in Vancouver in February 2011; participation in the Vienna Art Fair in May 2011; and participation in Preview Berlin Art Fair in September 2011 (the latest included a separate faction of Vector: studio for art practices and debates).
I must also mention that during this time a core group took over, formed by three previous active members, two founding members who had more or less stepped back in recent years, and two collaborators.

8. Florin Bobu is an artist based in Iași and the only (invisible) active Vector collaborator who specifically spent time and ideas on what the new Vector could be. At his wish, he is not a Vector member.

9. This decision was also influenced by a very productive meeting with ENPAP fellows, a closed and confidential one, during which we had to expose ourselves as an organisation and receive critical feedback.

10. Florin Bobu came up with this formulation in one of our intense dialogues. See also *Faculty of Invisibility Project* initiated by Inga Zimprich, department of Learning, tutor Nebojsa Milikic.

explained there is a danger for these interpretations to start circulating. Another danger seemed to be that it seemed we did not know which future we were heading towards. As with a biennial, the only time for invisibility is when preparing for the announcement of a new curator and preparing the concept of the next edition. Similarly for Vector the future had to look bright in order for this period of invisibility to be acceptable within its national and international networks. It is important to note that this text could be interpreted as the first sign of visibility for Vector since I was its director, but I would like to state that since I am writing in retrospect from a very personal perspective, these views might not be shared entirely by my colleagues.

Vector was now working very slowly on its mechanics and we were trying to fight the desire to produce and allow this state to gradually take its own course. The stakes were high, but the benefits were equally as promising: the former image of Vector was transforming and slowly disappearing, which could potentially allow for a situation in which we would feel less inclined to work with projects created by inertia and instead be inspired by the reality surrounding us.

Of course, the image of the institution that we had projected so easily earlier was still haunting us. The image was something we all believed in and something we held on to, as it was necessary for our sense of belonging to the professional art world. Throughout the years of Vector's existence, only during three of them we were in a somewhat stable situation, which allowed us to run a gallery programme.[11] What we knew was that the biennial, the publication of magazines, and running a gallery space are activities that need a stable platform with a proper infrastructure to operate in a sustainable manner. The symbolic investment of all the people involved in projects over the years was compensated for by a shared dream of stability, which would eventually allow complete freedom to work, which was a utopia based on false premises. Stability meant first of all a singular vision in order to have a high degree of flexibility in approaching funding bodies. For stability to happen we needed a clear institutional vision to be shared by all members. Given the different visions among Vector's membership it is hard to imagine a situation in which no one would feel the need to compromise.

11. The singular period when Vector came closest to the image of a stable format of an institution was between 2004 and 2007, when the cARTier project took place.

What I am not able to answer is the question what Vector will become when it remerges. Previously it had always been about surviving and letting the models and idiosyncrasies inherited from the past live on, and letting the multiple agendas of the different individuals forming Vector run in parallel to the overall ambitions. After ten years Vector has remained a curiosity, even for local art professional, often described as putting on 'unconventional' exhibitions.

The notion of a directorship and a horizontal structure do not go well together. As a result a last solution came to me: to really perform the role of the director, which was even harder within the given conditions. Dreaming of the previous more horizontal formats of Vector was not productive, but I hoped we would nevertheless be able to act together as a group. What I imagined for Vector was to be actively aware and engaged with the fast-changing Romanian society, encourage collaborations with local and regional institutions, thus creating a real dialogue, while always being aware of what simulation in these circumstances can bring. The further development of Vector is, however, not my call anymore.

From May 2012 a new management and artistic team have been put in place. The new group will find new ways of developing both the organisation and the flow of individual energies, and I hope they will use the past year of invisibility to re-consider what activities are needed, and from there regenerate Vector. The invisibility should be seen as a brutal, but necessary, link in the chain of events in Vector's life, as an activity just as important as any other. Without previously having tested invisibility as an exercise, it was a sensitive activity to engage in. Sometimes it seemed to help the flow of ideas and sometimes we got stuck, mainly because of our separate agendas. Eventually the self-induced invisibility led to my departure, but hopefully also to the ideological coagulation of the people that have decided to take over.

Internationally, we created ourselves as a periphery, but at the same time we also created a centre to refer to. However, we ignored the fact we allegedly also took on the role of a centre for other peripheries.(12) According to the Vector model that I have tried to describe above, I dare say that the lessons learnt are that the periphery has to act with caution and that invisibility can also be a form of existence!

12. This idea was very much discussed by Florin Bobu, whose work was partly realised in Tecuci, his native city. Tecuci is an old city at the intersection of historical commercial routes, which currently has 40,000 inhabitants and is halfway between Iaşi and Bucharest.

114 – 133

POST-RESEARCH NOTES: (RE)SEARCH FOR THE TRUE SELF-MANAGED ART

Jelena Vesić

The theme of self-organisation has acquired wide currency in contemporary international art. Critical practitioners, working in a network culture in the wake of the absorption of institutional critique, often talk about producing new culture through cooperation and sharing, through platforms and networks and through working outside 'isolated' and 'traditional' state-run institutions and their representative and repressive socio-political functions. Declarations of the value of self-organisation proliferate from an ever-increasing number of (so-called) 'independent' cultural actors, regardless of their actual material ties to institutions of culture and governance. Despite such self-assuring claims of independence, the old Marxist question remains to be addressed: Do these newly won cooperative freedoms truly liberate us within the field of labour, power within the field of labour and power distribution?

In the post-Yugoslavian context, the idea of an independent cultural scene brings with it numerous kinds of unease. Some are implied by the very name - independent - but also stem from, as I will show, ongoing discrepancies between nominal and actual positioning in the broad space of culture. Like anywhere else, cultural independence in post-Yugoslavian space, has a particular history. Cultural systems in the countries of former Yugoslavia, during the 1990s and later, were characterised by retrograde processes of the cultural renationalisation, on the one hand, and the introduction of market principles on the other. The atomisation of the modernist public sphere has been followed by the atomisation of labour in the institutions of culture as well as in ever-increasing numbers of free actors without permanent employment.

The tendencies that began in the '90s intensified after the war with the establishment of democratic governments which request that institutions enter into the market and become self-sustaining - that is, accept, whether they want to or not, the idea of self-sustainability. Actors in the field of contemporary culture and education are expected to be invested in reinvention - reinvention in the field of the cultural industries - attempting to find economic solutions through the system of project management (projectisation in an EU context). This is most often connected with processes of European integration and corporate foundation ventures for social responsibility.

Institutions that were previously wholly public in funding and mission are falling into a schism of 'double measures'. On the one hand, a persistently tight connection to the state produces pressure to perform in terms of national cultural programmes and their prerogatives. On the other hand, increasingly liberalised or flexible relations with the state necessarily produces another kind of entity - institutions (and individual agents) left to their own devices to find their own way on the market or on project fundraising.

The Marxist question, concerning the relationship between self-organisation and liberation, has been revisited in this context, with historical reflexivity, by two recent exhibition research projects which I address here: The Belgrade-based Prelom Kolektiv's *Two Times of One Wall: The Case of the Student Cultural Centre (SKC) - Belgrade in the 1970s* (first exhibited at Gallery SKUC Ljubljana, May 2008)[1] and *Removed from the Crowd: Dissociative Association - Associations outside the programmatic collectivities in the art of the 1960s and 1970s in the Socialist Republic of Croatia* by the Zagreb-based Institute for Duration, Location and Variables (DeLVe) (first exhibited in Museum of History of Yugoslavia, November 2009).[2] Both exhibitions focused on so-called 'non-conformist' art (given the art historical moniker New Artistic Practices)[3] and were comprised of different performative, conceptual, processual and de-materialising forms of artistic work. Both exhibitions explored critical artistic positioning in relation to the idea of collective, self-managed art in the context of socialist Yugoslavia. Both exhibitions also used this conceptual terrain for self-reflection, given that both organisations, Prelom and DeLVe, operate as self-organised collectives within a changed political landscape while forging ongoing links between art and life.

Prelom Kolektiv's curatorial research exhibition, *Two Times of One Wall...* explored the flux between self-organisation and the institution. Treating the history of the Student Cultural Centre of Belgrade as

1. Curators of the exhibition on behalf of Prelom Kolektiv were Dušan Grlja and the author in collaboration with Vladimir Jerić, Zorana Dojić and Radmila Joksimović. Information on this exhibition exists online in the form of an exhibition notebook, video interviews and audio materials edited by Prelom Kolektiv. See Prelom Kolektiv, 'SKC in ŠKUC: The Case of Students' Cultural Centre in the 1970s', http://www.prelomkolektiv.org/eng/PPYUart.htm

2. DeLVe is comprised of Ivana Bago and Antonia Majača. The exhibition and research materials appear also in the form of 'performative text'. See Ivana Bago and Antonia Majača (DeLVe), 'Dissociative Association, Dionysian Socialism, Non-Action and Delayed Audience. Between Action and Exodus in the Art of the 1960s and 1970s in the Socialist Republic of Croatia' in Ivana Bago and Antonia Majača in collaboration with Vesna Vuković (eds.), *Removed from the Crowd. Unexpected Encounters I.* BLOK and DeLVe. 2011. p. 250-307. http://www.academia.edu/1225411/Removed_from_the_Crowd._Unexpected_Encounters_I

3. The term 'New Artistic Practices' was introduced to the local context by art historian and art critic Ješa Denegri, who used it for the first time in his essay following the exhibition *New Artistic Practice 1966-1978*, staged in the Gallery of Contemporary Art in Zagreb in 1978. The term was borrowed from the critical practice of Catherine Millet, who visited SKC Belgrade in 1971.

an exemplary archive or case study, the exhibition consisted of images, texts, films, video testimonies and researchers' notes, organised into three chapters. The first chapter traced, through a kind of montage, different aspects of self-managed politics from political theory books to historical documents, proclamations and photographic records. The second addressed cultural policy in socialist Yugoslavia before and after 1968, as seen through the lens of institutional statements and actual practice. The third chapter of the exhibition followed specific artistic practices tackling the issues of self-management and artistic labour, such as *October 75, the International Strike of Artists* in 1979 and different acts of work and 'laziness' in the New Artistic Practices (performed by Mladen Stilinović, Raša Todosijević, Goran Trbuljak, Goran Đorđević, et al).

DeLVe's curatorial research exhibition, *Removed from the Crowd..* traced the history of artistic self-organisation – from the Gorgona group, established in the 1960s, through to the Group of Six Artists, active during 1970s, and from the fictional group/art project, Pensioner Tihomir Simčić, to artist-run spaces such as Podroom [Basement] – the Working Community of Artists – and PM Gallery, which operated in the late 1970s and early 1980s. The exhibition paid attention to artistic initiatives that took as their sites of action 'streets, nature, bathing places, university buildings, house entrances, balconies, cellars and windows that are not only extra-institutional locations but places of temporariness as well, which are also considered to be places of indefiniteness and, ultimately, as places with no programme'.(4)

It is worthwhile revisiting these two contemporary curatorial research projects to consider the way in which both took as a central concern art workers' own material performativity and relational comprehensions of connections between well-known and lesser-known circumstances of art production in a (post-)Yugoslavian context. Both exhibitions re-presented artistic work and thinking around artistic work by means of allusive montages of visual and textual material, associative diagrams and fragmented art-historical narratives. Making rich (re)use of prior artist groups' own particular decision-making and formats, each curatorial research project disclosed – with a different effective focus –

4. Ivana Bago and Antonia Majača, 'Removed from the Crowd: Dissociative Association – Associations outside the programmatic collectivities in the art of the 1960s and 1970s in the Socialist Republic of Croatia' in Zorana Dojić and Jelena Vesić (eds.), *Political Practices of (Post-)Yugoslav Art*. exhibition catalogue. Prelom Kolektiv. 2010. p. 100.

the numerous contradictions permeating the complex net of relationships between the institution, state, community and individual at particular historical moments, which informed the production of collectivity and artistic subjectivity.

Further, I want to argue that the critical materiality of the many alternative projects in socialist Yugoslavia of 1960s and 1970s – which the exhibitions by DeLVe and Prelom showed such interest in – was pointedly conceptual; that is, above and beyond such artistic practice's participation in the transformation of languages used to discuss art and in the redefinition of artistic acts amidst the emergence of Conceptual Art. In other words, what can be tracked in these projects is a critical reflexivity on paradoxical relationships and impasses negotiated in specific relation to the concepts informing 'art and labour' organisation. This conceptualism specifically manifested itself in each project's persistent (and intentionally naïve) commitment to ideas – the ideas behind Conceptual Art's iconoclastic critique of modernist representation and, in some cases, as I will detail later, representational political forms.

A Note On Self-Organisation

The common understanding of self-organisation points to a system without a central authority – a system that reveals itself through the calculated spontaneity of certain practices, ideally structured according to horizontal models of decision-making, power distribution and forms of participation. At the same time, self-organised practices are nowadays assumed to oppose traditional institutional models and state apparatuses; as such, they are generally understood to be alternative and progressive in relation to the notion of modernist cultural institutions populated by the (oppressive) mechanisms of bureaucracy and hierarchy.

Prelom Kolektiv and DeLVe Institute returned to the practices of self-organisation and self-management in 'really existing socialism' precisely in order to discuss their complexities, differences and (sometimes) similarities with what we experience as compelling forms of self-organisation and self-management in the neoliberal present. This return also meant revisiting and challenging the binaries that often emerge in 20th century art histories of Eastern Europe or geopolitical art histories of the countries of the socialist bloc, which have unfortunately been carried over into the broader sphere of art history to assume an almost universal character. One binary would encompass the concept of *authoritarian art* (variously allocated to socialist realism, Nazi kunst and fascist art, without any ideological differentiation), in opposition to the concept of *free art* (attributed to various avant-gardes and modernisms); another binary would assume juxtaposition of the concept of *official art* (art considered to develop in accordance with the dictates or at least support of the state), with the concept of *alternative art* (understood as standing in direct contrast with the state, 'hiding' in dark alternative spaces, artists' apartments or in nature, far from the eyes of the 'general public'). Given that such simplistic and clichéd distinctions between institutional cultural work and self-organised work persist in various interpretations, it is clear that these presumed oppositions warrant some questioning and situated reflexivity.

Research is a search, a quest, the recipient of which exists in the present moment. It is always about actualisation. In the present moment, contemporary art workers (almost anywhere) encounter self-organisation in terms of a two-fold trap that must be negotiated daily negotiated: a sense of anxiety and grief over the loss of the state and its social care, combined with the enjoyment of mobility and freedom in the sense of avoiding the paternalistic controls of permanent employment, the boredom of an everyday repetitiveness, institutional confinement and various impositions by the cultural bureaucracy.

The expanded terrain of research actualised by the two curatorial projects under discussion interrogated notions of artistic liberation-by-self-organisation and self-management. It also asked what it might mean to lose not only the maternal but also the paternal protection of the state through a (pseudo-)severing of the bonds between state and capitalism, ideology and economy, individual and collective, and the disappearance of the idea of society.

In (re-)tracing their *own* histories of self-organised collaborative practice from the socialist past, the underlying investment for these two post-socialist self-organised collectives was in a deeper understanding of the transformation of the meaning and potential of collective work. DeLVe foregrounded this by citing an early example of the same kind of questioning of 'collective work' relations by the Zagreb-based group, Gorgona, which consisted of nine artists and art historians operating along the lines of an anti-art agenda in Zagreb between 1959 and 1966:

> Collective Work is the complete opposite of the efforts we are constantly making as individuals: to affirm the person, who is confirmed and realized in their individual work. The individual testifies to his/her

destiny. S/he cannot testify to someone else's without being untruthful and artificial. BUT, do I desire Collective Work all the same? I do. Is a Collective Work possible? I suppose that it would require a common goal and equality of thought and will. Kindred feelings, and some at least minimal common enthusiasm. A 'constructive' Collective Work certainly also demands a common programme for the work.[5]

In the contemporary moment, it is difficult not to be affected by this interrogation of collectivised self-organisation at the very level of a questioning of desire. The comparative restaging of the desire for collectivity, achieved by DeLVe, foregrounded certain uncanny similarities, in tone and content, between the interests of alienated cultural workers working locally before and after the collapse of the Yugoslavian state.

Locating Self-Organisation

How should we approach the concept of the self-organised state or the idea of self-management as the state's principle, as encountered in socialist Yugoslavia?

According to the social science researcher, Marcelo Vieta, self-management can be described in terms of self-creation, self-control, self-provision and, ultimately, self-production.[6] At first glance, the very notion of the state would seem to mean something completely opposed to the terms of self-determination. Viewed from this angle, the state signifies a governed political entity or a social contract based on law and constitution - i.e., an organised political community living under a top-down structure of (representative) government. However, within the critical language of Marxism, we may find a way of unifying this opposition. Here, self-management is presented as a social process through which the state will wither away (given that socialism represents only a step towards communism, with the socialist state as a transient

5. This is an excerpt by Đuro Seder from 1963 from one of the 'homeworks' that the members of Zagreb art group Gorgona used to exchange within the collective. (See Bago and Majača, op cit. p. 260.) Seder formulated a 'critical-rational approach' to the idea of collective work in order to challenge it with an ensuing exposition of a 'Gorgonic approach', which 'mocked the preceding commonsensical and constructive premises, though in a way longing for them at the same time'.

6. See Marcelo Vieta, *Autogestión and the Worker-Recuperated Enterprises in Argentina: The Potential for Reconstituting Work and Recomposing Life.* http://yorku.academia.edu/MarceloVieta/Papers/549436/Autogestion_and_the_Worker-Recuperated_Enterprises_in_Argentina_The_Potential_for_Reconstituting_Work_and_Recomposing_Life

stage in abandoning the concept of state altogether).[7] It is precisely this 'withering of state' which seems to have obsessed the high-ranking politician and architect of self-managed Yugoslavian socialism, Edvard Kardelj. His view of the self-managed system was expressed in the pluralism of self-managed interests.[8] In Kardelj's view, rather than the political choices of organisation lying between single- or multi-party preferences, self-management was the promise of the choices and associations of socialism itself. Self-organisation allowed for a pluralism of interests that could be, in his words, 'incomparably closer to the individual and immeasurably more democratic than any form of political party pluralism which alienates society as a whole from the real man and citizen, even though it decides ostensibly on behalf of the citizen'.[9]

This vision of self-management called for the opening up of spaces for the autonomous development of different spheres of work and life under the umbrella of collective politics (which, understandably, were emphatically differentiated from the plurality of interests characteristic of capitalist individualism). Within socialist Yugoslavia, the principles of self-management emerged in the process of ideological differentiation from both Soviet and Western models of the state. This became a critique not only of Stalinist bureaucratic hegemony and the (totalitarian) state apparatus but also of so-called representative democracy. Over time, self-management became the dominant ideology, which - in theory and in practice - encompassed all the social spheres: economy, politics and culture.[10]

7. Self-management, first theorised by P.J. Proudhon under the term of *auto-gestion,* later became a primary component of some trade union organisations, in particular it was a theme within revolutionary syndicalism, introduced in late 19th century France.

8. Kardelj wrote: 'As far as Yugoslavia is concerned, the choice is not between multiparty pluralism or a one-party system, but rather between self-management, i.e. the democratic system of pluralism of self-management interests, or the multiparty system which negates self-management... The pluralism of interests is incomparably closer to the individual and immeasurably more democratic than any form of political party pluralism which alienates society as a whole from the real man and citizen, even though it decides ostensibly on behalf of the citizen.' Edvard Kardelj, *Self-Management and the Political System*. Socialist Thought and Practice. 1981.

9. Loc cit.

10. One of characteristics of socialist self-management was that the autonomous spheres of activity were proclaimed in the so-called Organisations of United Labour ('Organizacija udruženog rada', famously abbreviated with the acronym 'OUR') presenting the 'basic units' of the more complex mechanisms of a 'self-managed labour system'. Another characteristic is that the idea of property also received its own novel definition; it was neither the classical socialist concept of *state property,* nor the capitalist concept of *private property*, but the new concept of *social property*, by which Yugoslavia remained distinctive in its specific model of socialism.

In this context, workers' self-management or 'workers' control' signified a process of decision-making in which workers themselves negotiated the circumstances of production, instead of being dependent upon the set of rules defined by an owner or manager-supervisor. Ideas from this period generated traces, echoes and re-formulations in cultural production, which may be seen in the rhetoric of the New Artistic Practices and their various direct or implied treaties of self-association. Furthermore, the insistence of some of the protagonists of these practices on the self-control and self-regulation of artists' working conditions could almost be read - albeit with certain caveats - as a 'politically correct' response to Kardelj's proposition of applying the term 'worker' to all the people, 'no matter if they conduct physical or intellectual work, no matter if they are involved in material production of goods or other social activities'.(11)

In parallel with this appreciation of the connection between governance and culture, it is worth emphasising also that the term 'working people' was used as a kind of euphemism for 'citizenship' in former Yugoslavia. Thus, the ideology of self-management assumed that all citizens were workers and that all workers were citizens, and the very logic of equating the two designated Yugoslavia a state of self-managed workers - that is to say, a self-organised state. The tendency to politicise work, which is inscribed into the idea of self-management, has been discussed at various levels. In Kardelj's conception, work was considered to be not merely a measurable process of effectiveness and productivity in the service of state prestige or a given factory; it also implied knowledge of the circumstances of production and the (formal) possibility of continually influencing the development of the apparatus of production. In the context of managing the state, however, there was a pragmatic and strategic implementation of such principles. As might be expected, the postulates of self-management in state structures and institutions dissolved into bureaucratic standardisations and apologetic rhetoric, while the true practice of workers' control, its critical re-thinking and self-reflection, happened in less officiated 'elsewheres'.

As described above, one of the unexpected destinations for the problematisation of worker self-management was the sphere of artistic

11. Kardelj also called for the 'free and self-determined advance towards all forms of mutual relations of collaboration and association, adequate to their production, economical, social and other interests.' See Pravci razvoja političkog sistema socijalističkog samoupravljanja, p. 26-27.

and intellectual work. This problematisation did not happen through official cultural policy programmes of self-management, which were often taken either too vaguely or too formally into the actual practices of various art unions and core governmental institutions, resulting in similarly vague understandings of the 'relative autonomy of culture' and the 'modernist tendency' to become the mainstream current of art, known as 'socialist modernism'. These tendencies of art under socialism were criticised by the protagonists of New Artistic Practices because of the way in which they neutralised artistic language, reducing art's potential to assume a critical position within society. It was this ongoing internal criticism that the curatorial case studies scrutinised.

Self-Organisation-Institution-Self-Organisation

Prelom Kolektiv's *The Case of Student Cultural Centre (SKC) – Belgrade in the 1970s* (2009) traced the rich and divergent experience of an experimental institutional/self-organised practice that developed against the backdrop of the 1968 'march through the institutions' – i.e. developed in dialogue with international art activism and new institutionalism. The Student Cultural Centre (SKC) came into being as a result of the political activities of a group of young intellectuals and workers who had led the '68 protests and were also engaged in the Students' League. After the student protests, president Tito made the paradoxical, arguably assimilative, comment in his ambiguous claim: 'The students are right!' At the end of the 1960s, the former building of the state security agency, which was undergoing reconstruction, was given to the Belgrade University and Student Association. The space started being used by young critics, curators, filmmakers, social theorists and political activists who established the Student Cultural Centre (SKC) there.

Over time, SKC became well known for its annual international coming-together of artists, known as *April Meetings – Festival of Expanded Media*,[12] which established a reputation for being one of the rare 'territories' that enabled the exchange of ideas between artists and art critics from both sides of the Iron Curtain. During the 1970s, SKC hosted a large number of public discussions that dealt critically with the new politics of

12. Also translated as *April Encounters*. A non-traditional international art festival bringing together young artists and performers, beginning in 1972, on the occasion of 4 April, the Day of the Students of Belgrade, and the Day of the Student Cultural Centre.

emancipation – from feminist movements to questions of decolonisation and the non-aligned movement. Also in its organisation of 'alternative Octobers'[(13)] – critical, programmatic responses to the *art pour l'art* orientation of the October Salon, one of the biggest state manifestations – SKC broadened debate and created a place of confrontation with state institutions of art.

The experimental counter-exhibition, *October 75*, to which Prelom Kolektiv gave special consideration, gathered various cultural workers – critics, gallerists and curators – to produce a series of critical public statements on the concept of self-managed art. The output from *October 75* was circulated in the form of a mimeographed script, which presented the proclamations of all the participants. As the following excerpts from the texts show, they sought no less than a truly self-managed and autonomous art.

Dunja Blažević, curator of the SKC Gallery, head of visual arts programme, writes:

> Art should be changed! As long as we leave art alone and keep on transferring works of art from studios to depots and basements by means of social regulations and mechanisms, storing them, like stillborn children, for the benefit of our cultural offspring, or while we keep on creating, through the private market, our own variant of the *nouveau riche or kleinbürgers,* art will remain a social appendage, something serving no useful purpose, but something it is not decent or cultured to be without. [...] THE SELF-MANAGING SYSTEM OF FREE EXCHANGE AND ASSOCIATION OF LABOUR THROUGH SELF-MANAGING COMMUNITIES OF INTEREST REPRESENTS A NEW NON-OWNERSHIP RELATIONSHIP that examines and revises the existing models of artistic work and behavior.

Raša Todosijević, artist and member of the editorial board of SKC Gallery writes:

13. Alternative Octobers were characteristic for the first five years of SKC activity and cultural policy of head of visual art department, Dunja Blažević. Alternative Octobers were counter exhibitions that coincided with and have been in critical dialogue with the October Salon – the official state annual exhibition that carried a bourgeois prerogative of a salon and was of pure aesthetic orientation. Alternative Octobers were countering October Salon also through their different use and behaviour in the gallery space.

> A continual wish for a total autonomy of art is nothing else but its effort to attain a self-conscious and efficient functioning within the framework of its own language. [...] It is only when functioning as a critique and self-analysis of its own language that art is capable of raising the issue of the analysis and critique of social practice and demanding its change. [...] Art that celebrates victory stops fighting.

The aim of the research and (re)production of documents presented within Prelom Kolektiv's *The Case of SKC in the 1970s...* was to precisely locate, understand and emphasise the complex tension between these poles of state/institution and movement/self-organisation. The material effects of the state's and students' agreement to situate the student movement under the roof of a state building at the conclusion of the 1968 protests was examined by this exhibition for the first time. SKC was placed within what we could term a dialectic between self-realisation and the pacification of social critique. As the Prelom Kolektiv's exhibition research showed – in part through interviews with the original protagonists of SKC and contemporary art historians interested in the New Artistic Practices – this unusual housing of the student movement tended to be interpreted in two seemingly contrasting ways. On the one hand, Dunja Blažević, the first curator of the visual arts departments at SKC, considered the state-supported location to have been an authentic place of self-realisation, won out of struggle, embodying and ensuring different cultural expressions and the free circulation of critical visions by a new generation of conceptual artists from all parts of the world.(14) On the other hand, Miško Šuvaković – an aesthetic theorist who wrote on New Artistic Practices and was part of the group 143, which was active in SKC during the second half of 1970s – saw the location as a smart control mechanism, instigated by the state, in which SKC presented a sort of organised margin or peripheral social laboratory, where critical ideas and practices could be detected, isolated and thus put under control. As is often the case with competing interpretations of cultural processes, both are possible, or, rather, one might say that SKC was in a state of constant flux between these two poles, operating as both self-actualising agency and critical ghetto.

14. See the interviews with Dunja Blažević and Miško Šuvaković in Jelena Vesić and Dušan Grlja (eds.), *The Case of Student Cultural Centre in the 1970s*. exhibition catalogue. 2008. p. 81-90. http://www.prelomkolektiv.org/pdf/catalogue.pdf

As an expression of a multi-layered and laminated rebellion, the SKC space in Belgrade was heterogeneous just as any other self-organisation without political leadership is essentially hybrid. It was the combination of leftist critical options – from French Maoism to Yugoslavian humanistic Marxism, feminism, and anti-colonial struggles, dissidence and liberalism, mysticism and nationalism, with a touch of soft hippie and, later, glam-punk subculture. What unified all these different stances was their critique of official state structures, which ranged from the radical left to liberal turns and proto-nationalisms (the latter gradually prevailed to become 'official options' during the 1990s). In other words, in a less overt and more moderate, culturally specific, form, SKC expressed a spectrum of critical views on the state, accumulated in various protests during the 1960s and 1970s.

Prelom Kolektiv was especially interested in tracing an artistic-cultural-political thread tied to the fluctuating dynamics of a leftist critique of the socialist state within SKC-associated practices, both inside and outside its permeable institutional walls. As heralded by the famous slogans from 1968 – 'We Fight Against Socialism With Socialism' and 'Down With the Red Bourgeoisie' – the activities of SKC recapitulated, in different ways, the students' ongoing calls for abolishing rigid and hierarchical party politics and their demands for firmer rooting of socialist ideas in the field of everyday practice. These two slogans are exemplary of the kind of non-representational and movement-based institutional formations (which seems to incorporate the institution's own exceptions and rejections) that are possible to categorise in the terms of a 'performative institution'.

Prelom Kolektiv developed a particular thesis on, and took special interest in, the corporality and performativity of the institution of SKC. Prelom Kolektiv's exhibition research considered that SKC's 'cultural policy' could be best understood by observing the processual distribution of ideas from the student protests within the broader cultural field, and in the SKC's role over time in becoming a kind of alternative university for its protagonists. In the work of SKC, Prelom Kolektiv identified the (performative) claim that alternative institutions are primarily comprised of the people involved and only secondarily by formal structures. This notion of performativity is best exemplified by a photograph of Milan Jožić, which Prelom Kolektiv took as the institutional representation of SKC. This shows artists, critics, gallerists and friends – protagonists of

New Art Practices – leaning, side by side in a straight line, against the wall of SKC's Gallery.

The photograph shows people who *used to be there* (to paraphrase Roland Barthes),[15] used to be that institution, who made SKC precisely what it was through their permanent presence, withholding it from the institutional map of classical artistic venues of their time and in contrast with the ideology of the 'white cube,' with its restrictive and controlled conventions of observation and contemplation of artworks. The frontal positioning is not insignificant to the tactical composures of artist collaborators. The art critic, Ješa Denegri, has noted a particular investment, within New Artistic Practices, in the 'artist in the first person' describing processes of subjectivisation that make it possible to connect aspects of performativity and processuality in artistic work to the position of direct speech at the borders of art and life. This conceptual commitment to 'lived' and embodied ideas placed artists of the group in the position to be both 'true believers' and 'fierce critics' of the ideology of self-management.

The term 'performative institution' is used here in another, related sense to describe an institution in which not only the representatives of formal institutional structures (managers, programme editors, designers, archivists, etc.) but also numerous other individuals (who acted in the same space, through self-organised structures) take part in actualising programming decisions through new formations of editorial boards, councils and groups. This kind of performativity might be recognised as the sum of all the institution's departures from the classical national welfare-state institution (i.e. an art museum), which expresses its power in terms of guardianship over a disembodied art-historical canon or, indeed, as disembodied canon-building. To call an institution 'performative' and to observe its performativity in this manner is, therefore, to acknowledge the impossibility of placing the entirety of its practices on either side of the binary opposition between institution and self-organisation. This division is often used as a euphemism for another rigid opposition – that between 'official' and 'alternative' art – which as I have already mentioned, is frequently employed as the main epistemological tool within recent readings of the cultural histories of the countries of 'real socialism'.

15. Barthes' idea that photography does not represent memory, an imagination, a reconstitution (...), but reality in a past state: at once the past and the real. See Roland Barthes, *Camera Lucida*. Hill and Wang. 1981, p. 82.

In contrast to such art historical shorthand, research by Prelom Kolektiv revealed SKC as an example of an approach to collectivity that generates a different model of production, which may be expressed through the formula: *self-organisation-institution – self-organisation.*[16] This means that, when viewed durationally, the strength or volatility of the organisation's self-organising productions were built upon the foundations of a self-organised generation-in-protest. This created the conditions for establishing a new institution 'from above', which enabled further support from the state, but which, at the same time, paradoxically, fed the self-organised critique of state-based self-organisation. What I am labouring over here is not the historical series of events (again) but the *formula* of a dialectical re-production of criticality around self-organisation, which funnelled 1968's communitarian modus operandi towards a range of practices and projects of self-organization tarrying (and not) with its very own 'institutional roof'.[17] In this case then, performativity comprehends a movement beyond dualisms, which the SKC contained within itself: as an 'institution (but) of movement', as a 'self-organised institution', and as an 'institution (but) of critique', and so forth. Such performativity appears almost as a substance that could corrode the firmness of the institution's walls and internally dismantle the elitism, isolation and self-sufficiency of a classic institutional space with respect to everyday life and sociability 'from below'.

'Being With': Individual-Collective-State

If Prelom Kolektiv focused on vacillating conceptions of SKC in relation to collective work, then DeLVe considered an apparently different set of inclinations towards communitarian practices within a shared framework of ideas and practices. *Removed from the Crowd...*

16. See Jelena Vesić, 'SKC (Student Cultural Centre) as a site of performative (self-)production: October 75 – Institution, Self-organisation, First Person Speech, Collectivisation'. *Život Umjetnosti*. 2012.
17. This formula could be applied to the economical, cultural and political background of SKC, which presented one hybrid institutional model, close to the contemporary concept of 'open institutionalism.' See Teodor Celakoski, Miljenka Buljević, Tomislav Medak, Emina Višnić (eds.), *Open Institutions: Institutional Imagination and Cultural Public Sphere*. 2011. SKC was partly funded from the side of the state, partly forced to employ entrepreneurial activity (i.e., dependent on fundraising and a proactive attitude towards its own sustainability), and partly drew upon voluntary and self-organised work. These tendencies appear to be very close to contemporary defunding of public institutions within public budgets, and to the attempts of new self-organised and project-based institutions to 'force' the state to take part in their operations and sustainability.

emphasised the elusive strategy of fleeing, of being in a constant state of escape from any kind of normative social contract. As the exhibition-project argued, such 'escape' was always caught in a relational bind and could, therefore, only be the product of a two-way relationship (or, at least, a relationship 'towards'). This may be seen not only in the complex relationship between the individual and collective but also in the common mechanism in which, even if it remains 'hidden', the presence of the state marks a departure point from which this impulse to escape begins.

DeLVe's curatorial research introduced the concept of 'non-programmatic association' as a figure of resistance to functional, operative and measurable artistic work in the practices they re-curated. Non-programmatic association signifies the capacity, and implies the need, for self-regulation of one's own artistic production and distribution. The narrative of self-organised artistic initiatives and the history of artistic association elaborated by DeLVe particularly foregrounded notions of community and temporality and the connection between these in self-organised modes. This curatorial research attended to the paradoxical enjoyment that exists for artists in the connection between action, work and life, and in an art that inevitably betrays and overcomes its own functionality and use value. DeLVe created an associative cartography of historical facts that entered into dialogue with the contemporary context of cultural work. According to the curators, this cartographic sequencing of texts and images created a 'series of speculations derived from the enlargement of details, deliberate omissions, arbitrary connections, all in the aid of articulating a different viewpoint, a temporary and unstable truth through a different 'performance' of the writing of the history of contemporary art'.(18) DeLVe saw their curatorial method as providing 'fragmentary interventions' into existing art historical and museological narratives based on artistic excellence and individual oeuvres. Indeed, in this curatorial research, these interventions occurred precisely through the curators' shift away from exhibiting artworks, focusing instead on the productive activities of artists and artistic communities and the circumstances of their production. Instead of showing one particular work of, for example, Mladen Stilinović or Julije Knifer or Sanja Iveković or Braco Dimitrijević, they focused on the artists' participation in different conversations or gestures that were rarely presented as a singular artwork or as part of the oeuvre of a singular artist.

18. Bago and Majača, 2010. op cit. p. 101.

The operational principle of 'being with', which the curators of DeLVe took from Jean Luc Nancy's theory of community, was explored by considering two tactics that mark the opposite poles of this approach. One is the escape into what could be called 'surreal life', epitomised in the proverbial Gorgonic declaration: 'Sometimes Gorgona did nothing, it just lived'.[19] Another approach was that of practising 'direct speech' in the artist-run space, Podroom - the Working Community of Artists - which entailed continual reflection upon the ideas and conditions of work and the group's reasons for establishing mutual relationships in the form of community. This negotiation could also be seen as a process of searching for the social contract, a kind of internalisation of the ideological role of the state. Two excerpts from the debate held in Podroom and published in the group's magazine, *Prvi broj* [First Issue] (one of the central case studies in DeLVe's research), may be cited to illustrate two different tactics of this internalisation. Here, Stilinović fantasises about the possibility of total separation from the state and state institutions of art, while Goran Petercol's self-critical view manifests deep scepticism about the possibility of escape to some projected externality.[20]

Mladen Stilinović: I work in Podroom because I am responsible for what I do. When we act through the other galleries or newspapers it is them (not me) who think they are responsible for my work. That bothers me, and it can not be true. Besides, I like that my work is being presented completely, that is, exactly as I envisioned it, from the poster and catalogue to duration of the exhibition and how the works are stored. I really like that sentence by Aretino, the one that says 'to be alive means never going to the Court'. When I go to other institutions, I feel like going to the Court. When I go to Podroom, then I go to Podroom. [...]

Goran Petercol: However, there is another thing that seems to me very problematic, that we still act like a gallery for the artists we invite ... we give them space, and through exhibiting here, they support the idea of Podroom. But then, this happens: when they make an exhibition, we have to wait until someone remembers to ask them whether they would come back and make another exhibition in a year or two or not. This is a kind of

19. Josip Vaništa, cited in Bago and Majača, 2011, op cit., p. 268.
20. For a detailed discussion of Podroom in relation to these issues, see Ivana Bago, 'A Window and a Basement: Negotiating Hospitality at La Galerie Des Locataires and Podroom - the Working Community of Artists'. *ARTMargins* 1 (2:3). p. 116-46.

relationship typical of a gallery: what's offered is the space, and the honor, to exhibit, but cooperation isn't on offer. *We should treat them on an equal basis* ... I think what happened here is a certain *accumulation of power* based on the past; that is, on the fact, the merit, that two years, a year and a half ago, we founded Podroom... and in addition to that, we own the space, that is, it so happened that we got the space...[21]

Removed from the Crowd... isolated traces of a quest for solidarity - the forms of 'being with' - separating them out from primary and secondary materials. In this precise way, the project presented itself as 'a search for the history of searching',[22] for the history of sharing and constituting a common, thinking and practicing self-organisation. The curatorial enquiry became a quest towards achieving a new understanding of the relations between the individual and collective and of the meaning of collectivity in the different present moment, without resigning similar efforts to a resolutely past presentational moment, i.e. the 'archive'.

Self-Organisation and Its Discontents (From Art to State and Back)

Insights stemming from these curatorial research projects by the Prelom Kolektiv and DeLVe may be useful for thinking further through the politics of being self-organised. In regard to the practices encompassed by these two research projects, we can speak of an ideology that alternative workers in culture shared with the official political establishment as it was paradoxically embedded in, for example, the concept of 'Fighting Socialism With Socialism'. In a sense, we can speak of the artistic groups and the state ideologists making a mutual 'response' to the proposition of self-management. Further, we cannot lose sight of the different practices (and therefore politics) through which this 'response' was manifested and distributed across the spheres of the 'alternative' and 'official'.

Locally, but also globally, these questions from the past gain new relevance today, framed as they are by the disappearance of the public good and of the public institution of art which characterised the welfare state regime more broadly. The retreat of the social security system is happening in parallel with the expansion of individual entrepreneurship, which is currently unfolding at an ever-faster pace. In the region of

21. *Prvi Broj* [First Issue], cited in ibid. p. 132.
22. Bago and Majača, op cit. 2010. p. 100.

former Yugoslavia, the majority of cultural workers active today (both locally and internationally) are choosing, or are being compelled to adopt, self-organised forms of existence, acting through small collectives, troupes, groups and alternative education projects. They are forming an alternative cultural sector - as so-called 'independent' initiatives - characterised by flexible and precarious working conditions as well as mobile and adaptable forms of life.[23]

These free actors - whose freedom is, of course, very much conditional - still tend to ground their position of relative independence through identifications with the nation state and with the traditional, professionalised division of labour.[24] At the same time, they are restoring interest in the working process, re-thematising and shaping cultural working practices in a space that we experience as a more public, more democratic and more collectivist. This is happening in the region for the first time since the 1970s.

The transition from 'really existing socialism' (as the social grounds of operation for the art of the 1960s and 1970s disclosed within these projects) to liberal democracy and a free-market economy (i.e. 'really existing capitalism') can also be seen as the ultimate victory of self-organisation and oppressive self-care. This implies a transition from 'childish immaturity' to 'full maturity', in taking responsibility for one's own beliefs and actions, life and work. Achieving such full maturity today means becoming a truly entrepreneurial individual - simultaneously being one's own labour-force and employer, one's financial and PR manager, creating rather than finding jobs, 'self-organising' one's health security and pension plan. In short, it means acting as a kind of 'funky businessman' in contemporary 'karaoke capitalism'.[25]

In this context, the apparent political confinement of artistic projects by a new generation of self-organised cultural workers is a consequence of the (extreme) reformist backdrop against which they exist or perform. On the one hand, the tendency of cultural workers to

23. For example, the network of independent initiatives *Druga Scena* in Belgrade or *Clubture Network* for self-sustainability of independent initiatives in Croatia. http://www.clubture.org

24. For example, an artist performs his work as an initial potential value; a curator, historian or critic increases the value through the elaboration of contents, through exhibiting and presence in the space of evaluation; and, in the end, the work is purchased by the museum, while its price, or money, or compensation, in this case, is the sum of all the values of the collective work which participates in this process.

25. See Prelom Kolektiv, 'The Neoliberal Institution of Culture and the Critique of Culturalization'. *Transversal*. EIPCP. 2007. http://eipcp.net/transversal/0208/prelom/en

self-organise can be read as a process of the genuine creation of micro spaces or micro fields, of better and fairer communities. On the other hand, they are firmly tied to the system of project-based art and largely vulnerable to attacks of the regulatory powers of the art market.

The curatorial research projects by DeLVe Institute and Prelom Kolektiv demonstrate that the principles of self-organisation cannot be thought of in terms of politics *per se*, or merely as direct opposition to dominant institutionalisms. Quite the contrary - to paraphrase Godard's frequently cited 'making art politically rather than political art' - it is necessary to think of self-organisation politically. In this sense, then, we may also question our participation in the production of culture through self-organised initiatives, social networks and temporary collectives and through identifications as flexible individuals. Do we embody a new kind of transformative social critique that could, by analogy with our self-organised predecessors, be expressed by the slogan 'We Fight Against Capitalism with Capitalism'? Is this quest for a more just capitalism at the same time a move towards a naturalised turning of (self-)exploitation into passion, a move that fits perfectly with the idealised image of new globally networked happy workers?

134 - 152

MOVEMENTS THAT MATTER: THE PROJEKT MIGRATION (2003–06)

Marion von Osten

The film, *Passagen* (1996), by the Viennese filmmaker, Lisl Ponger, which was shown in the *Projekt Migration* exhibition that was held in Cologne in 2005,[1] links two otherwise unconnected narratives: a collage of private Super 8 footage representing a tourist gaze on exotic localities voiced over by reminiscences recounted by people who crossed borders, went into exile or took flight. The film samples offer momentary glimpses of various journeys - ports, ships, waves, the sea, landscapes as well as people and animals crossing the camera lens - images brought home for friends and family as proof of a journey undertaken. Meanwhile, the soundtrack is assembled from different interview recordings conducted by the artist. Despite being positioned asynchronously, the levels of image and voice in *Passagen* nevertheless produce links that seem to obey the laws of coincidence. The cities mentioned in different accounts - Casablanca, Shanghai, New York - give the observer the idea that there is, after all, a connection between the travel footage and the reminiscences of the narrators. This ambiguity comes about because the places named represent not only a vision of a cosmopolitan life or a desirable travel destination but also refer to places of exile in the twentieth century. This relation between different sites and forms of travel becomes obvious when a man with a Viennese accent relays that 'In Nauders, it may well have been possible'. This hints at the geographical correlation that exists between tourist locations and border crossings, since Nauders is located - triangulated - between Switzerland, Italy and Austria. During the period

1. *Projekt Migration* exhibition was on display from 1 October 2005 to 15 January 2006 at Kölnischer Kunstverein and other locations throughout Cologne's city centre. Exhibition participants were: Vito Acconci, Advanced Chemistry, Agency (Int./*1992), An Architektur, Aysun Bademsoy, Joseph Beuys, David Blandy, Madeleine Bernstorff/Elke aus dem Moore, Pavel Braïla, Brothers Keepers, Vlassis Caniaris, Gustav Deutsch, DOMiT, Lukas Duwenhögger, Ayşe Erkmen, Harun Farocki, Jeanne Faust/Jörn Zehe, Hans-Peter Feldmann, FFM Berlin, Doris Frohnapfel, Morgan O'Hara, Farida Heuck/Birgit zur Nieden, Candida Höfer, Cerin Hong, Kanak Attak,Gülsün Karamustafa, Selahattin Kaya, kein mensch ist illegal, Ernst Kirschner, Alfred Koch, Brigitte Kraemer, Kemal Kurt, Brigitta Kuster, Labor k3000, Thomas Locher, Mabouna Il Moise Merlin, Angela Melitopoulos, Jean Mohr, Christian Philipp Müller, Tazro Niscino, Non Stop No Stops, Marcel Odenbach, Anny & Sibel Öztürk, Henrik Olesen, Boris Ondreička, Erik-Jan Ouwerkerk, Adrian Paci, Krsto Papić, Dan Perjovschi, Susan Philipsz, Lisl Ponger, Dont Rhine/Ultra-red, Jeroen de Rijke/Willem de Rooij, Julika Rudelius, Saisonstadt, Anri Sala, Bülent Şangar, Christoph Schäfer, Alfred Schmidt, Edith Schmidt/David Wittenberg, Anne-Marie Schneider, Ene-Liis Semper, Ann-Sofi Sidén, Nika Špan, Stadt und Migration (Kniess, Frings, Hauser, Lagos Karlhoff), Wolfgang Staiger, Mladen Stilinović, Andrijana Stojković, Marily Stroux, Heinrich Stuckert, Erika Sulze-Kleimeier, Wolfgang Tillmans, TRANSIT MIGRATION, Rosemarie Trockel, Guenay Ulutuncok, Manfred Vollmer, Hans-Joachim Weber, Clemens von Wedemeyer, Jun Yang, Tobias Zielony, Zelimir Zilnik. The exhibition project Projekt Migration, was jointly curated by Aytac Eryilmaz, Martin Rapp, Kathrin Rhomberg, Regina Römhild and Marion von Osten.

of German Nazism, this alpine region was used by the politically persecuted as a passage into Switzerland, and it remains an important route for clandestine migration today. In Ponger's film, a multitude of people who fled the National Socialist regime, as well as people from other regions and historical contexts, recount their crossings by boat, road or foot from the Congo, South America and the Balkans. Reasons for the journeys are not revealed, but the stark difference between the memories represented acoustically and those conveyed via exotic wistful pictures exposes the fact that western tourist views dominate the occidental memory.(2)

According to the art historian, Christian Kravagna, amateur pictures – like the pictures in tourist advertising and other forms of travel reporting – 'feed the collective imagination of a public at home with material for contemplating otherness'.(3) Kravagna calls such travel images 'a special and at the same time paradigmatic category of those images that consolidate or undermine concepts of identity and difference'.(4) These visual mementos not only evoke the longing for distant horizons; they also betray the hierarchies and privileges of the tourist journey from North to South. *Passagen* alludes to an area of contingency within such representations. The popularity of tourist images points to the invisibility of numerous other images of travel – those not included in the prevailing view. Ponger's montage technique not only reveals a criticism of the privileged position of one type of mobility over another, but it also includes an imaginary in which tourists and migrants meet on their different routes within the structural layout of the film. The reference systems of journey/escape/migration are temporarily freed from their political and cultural adscription. The respective narratives point to their 'normative' character. Here, tourists and migrants become new agents of post-national origin, whose stories of home seem to have been lost along the way, in transit, during the passage.(5) But, in the visual memory, the migratory journey

2. Tom Holert and Mark Terkessidis, 'Was bedeutet Mobilität?' in *Projekt Migration*. DuMont Verlag. 2005.
3. Christian Kravagna, 'Traveling Identitie. Ethnizität und Geschlecht in postkolonialen Reisebildern' in Sigrid Schade and Marion Strunk (eds.), *Unterschiede. Unterschieden.Zwischen Gender und Kulturen*. Zürcher Hochschule der Künste/Institut Cultural Studies in the Arts. 2004. p. 8.
4. Ibid.
5. An example of the collaboration between research, film and sound productions developed within TRANSIT MIGRATION frameworks is the film *Hotel Almanya* (2004) by Ebru Karaca in cooperation with Sabine Hess and Serhat Karakayali, and the sound work Grenze (2005), made from interview material produced by researchers Regina Römhild and Michael Thies. Both projects also refer to the current connection of spatio-temporal overlaps between travelling as a tourist and journeys made as a migrant worker and their divided infrastructures and conditions.

exists neither as a transformation (a kind of passage) nor as a possibility of 'becoming someone else' (a state of being in-between) nor as a contact zone in the manner suggested by James Clifford.[6] We certainly do not regard the image of migration as a romantic longing for distant parts or adventure, as in the visual mementoes of tourism or the colonial journey south.

Migration - moving from one place to another with the aim of a short- or long-term stay - has been a social constant throughout the world since before industrialisation. The person moving from a small town or village to the city also migrates in this sense. Yet, this internal migration is not necessarily grasped in everyday life. Instead, the term migration is colloquially used to refer to a border being crossed by non-nationals. Despite increasing mobility around the globe, the concept of the nation state and citizenship still hierarchically divides populations into 'locals' and 'aliens'.[7] Today, the concept of migration is stigmatised; it designates a differentiation that the concept of mobility apparently does not - a differentiation that may once have been described with the concept of class. Being addressed - and discriminated against - as a migrant mostly affects labourers in the low-wage sector, who are not granted social rights.

'Our gaze decides *whether* and *how* we regard migration' was how the *Projekt Migration* curatorial team - comprised of Aytac Eryilmaz, Martin Rapp, Regina Römhild, Kathrin Rhomberg and myself - began the foreword to the exhibition's catalogue in 2005.[8] In this way, the constructed character of 'migration' - and its representation in the media, scientific and political discourse and greatly informed by artworks - deter-

6. James Clifford, *Routes: Travel and Translation in the Late Twentieth Century*. Harvard University Press. 1997; on 'becoming someone else,' see Gilles Deleuze and Felix Guattari, *A Thousand Plateaus: Capitalism and Schizophrenia*, trans. Brian Massumi. Continuum International Publishing Group. 2004.

7. Different forms of mobility and their control can be newly conceived in connection with each other. This is explored in Mark Terkessidis and Tom Holert's publication *Fliehkraft* - dedicated to migration and tourism - that was initiated as a sub-research project within the framework of *Projekt Migration.* Among other things, the authors propose to more precisely describe the interconnections between the practices of mobility and migration and their mutual dependency. Both tourist resorts and gated communities are maintained by migrants and inhabited by actors of mobility. But also migrant workers no longer come just from the global South, while tourists and global players are also not necessarily from the North, as the studies and works by Peter Spillmann, Michael Zinganel and Michael Hieslmaier have revealed, as project collaborators. See: Tom Holert and Mark Terkessidis, *Fliehkraft*: *Gesellschaft in Bewegung - Von Migranten und Touristen*. Kiepenheuer & Witsch. 2006; www.backstage-tourismus.net

8. Kölnischer Kunstverein et al. (eds.), *Projekt Migration.* DuMont Cologne. 2005.

mined the research process for the project. Between 2003 and 2006, the project generated a series of symposia, screenings and discussions as well as a final exhibition at three different post-war venues located in the city centre of Cologne. *Projekt Migration* was launched by the German Federal Cultural Foundation on the fiftieth anniversary of the former German Federal Republic's 'Agreement on the Recruitment and Placement of Workers' with Italy in 1955. Further contracts soon followed, with Greece and Spain (1960), Turkey (1961), Morocco (1963), Portugal (1964), Tunisia (1965) and Yugoslavia (1968). But, beyond this historical and national frame, the core team expanded the brief and dedicated the project to past and present forms and practices of migration that have challenged Germany as a country of immigration against its will.

The research process of *Projekt Migration* was guided, on the one hand, by the Documentation Center and Museum of Migration in Germany (DOMiD e.V), established in Cologne in 1990 by migrants from Turkey[(9)] who were collecting documents and oral histories of post-war migration from Italy, Greece, Spain, Turkey, Morocco and Tunisia (to the former Federal Republic of Germany - FRG - in the West) and from so-called contract workers from Angola, Cuba, Mozambique and Vietnam (to the former German Democratic Republic - GDR - in the East). The second project, TRANSIT MIGRATION, from 2002 to 2006, developed a common research method that was built on the collaborative efforts of academics, filmmakers, media activists and artists. For over two years, researchers and artists focused on the formation of new European border regimes, in relation to Germany, and on migration movements to and from the southeast of Europe. The project was headed by the Frankfurt Institute of Cultural Anthropology and European Ethnology at the Johann Wolfgang Goethe University in Frankfurt am Main and the Institute for Theory of Art and Design (ITH) in Zurich, including collaborations with German activists from KANAK ATTAK and other European No Border movements. Last but not least, Kathrin Rhomberg, director of the Kölnische Kunstverein at that time, and I researched artistic practices that dealt with concerns raised by the research institutions involved.[(10)] Thus, the project tried to make possible a trans-disciplinary collaboration between migrant self-organisations, activists, artists and researchers in

9. The TRANSIT MIGRATION project was led by Dr. Regina Rhömhild and Marion von Osten.

10. The TRANSIT MIGRATION project was led by Dr. Regina Rhömhild and Marion von Osten.

Germany and beyond. One of the aims of creating a dialogue between different societal actors was to develop new narratives that could step beyond the classical modes of representation found in socio-historical documentation, scientific discourse and individual artworks. This brought about an experimental curatorial approach that consciously combined different visual and textual artworks and artefacts - sources with different perspectives, generated through the researchers' insights or artistic productions. This was possible because not only contemporary art curators but also researchers and activists were involved in defining the selection process and structuring content for the exhibition.

The title, Projekt Migration, alluded to the content-related foundation of the joint endeavour, in which we took diverse 'projects of migration' as a basis for reflection, research, cultural activity and visualisation. With this approach, we hoped to overcome the 'national view' of migration discourse and instead develop a transnational perspective from the very different movements of migration - to cast a horizon of our contemporary globalised world from below. Rather than viewing the nation state as the only framework for developing the concept of migration, we focused on the fact that migration challenges the nation state and its attempts to control and regulate.

One of the major concerns of the *Projekt Migration* exhibition was to refuse obvious images of migration. Through a research process that took account of archives of films, photographs, documents and discourses on migration, it became clear that a task of the project would be to re-imagine other narratives. In the imaginative work that accompanied the production of the exhibition, we decided that it was not a matter of committing ourselves to the 'culture' of conveying as authentic an image as possible of the life of migrants or their 'communities' in Germany. The aim was that migration movements would no longer be seen as completely curbed or regulated but as autonomous, as Sandro Mezzadra has put it.[11] Thus, the exhibition concept related much more to the double meaning of the word representation: to re-present migration, both current and historical, and at the same time to present what has been told and what has not yet been told but needs to be thought about, in the future. The works and documents in the exhibition intended, therefore, not simply to depict a history but to reconstitute, from the

11. See: Étienne Balibar and Sandro Mezzadra, 'Borders, Citizenship, War, Class. A Dialogue with Étienne Balibar and Sandro Mezzadra'. *New Formations*. No. 58. Summer 2006. p. 10-30.

existing field, a story that has not yet been heard. By commissioning visual artists, filmmakers and sound artists to produce new works on the basis of newly established discourses, we sought to question and extend the fund of images of migration and to disrupt, aggravate or expose it. In this way, through different events and outcomes, *Projekt Migration* became an intervention into prevailing migration discourse that operated with diverse media, forms and formats. In this article, some of the insights generated and problem areas sketched out by researchers, filmmakers and artists will be reflected and discussed in relation to the exhibition-making process.

Arrivals

Since the 1950s, when large numbers of workers were recruited to the FRG from the Mediterranean region, images of their arrival have been collected in official film and photographic archives, publications and exhibitions. Among these, a prominent trope is the 'train station picture', in which males - usually dark-haired and moustachioed and carrying suitcases - are represented waiting at a station, looking out of train windows, being jostled or waving. As DOMiD researchers witnessed in the archives of the Westdeutscher Rundfunk (WDR) Television Station, when these images of migrant men were first shown on German television in the 1960s, they were accompanied by a voiceover by a German commentator, but the actors themselves remained silent throughout. While Germans were making pilgrimages to the sunny beaches of the Mediterranean, advertised in colourful brochures, the migrants' origins were depicted as empty, run-down, impoverished and obsolete, through neo-Realist film techniques and photographic reportage. The official image of 'guest labour' had the side effect of favourably contrasting the early economic renaissance of a war-ravaged Germany with the image of an even greater destitution.

This topos of the country of origin of migrants as a 'premodern hinterland' is found in the first films about migration to America - like Alice Guy Blanché's *The Making of an American Citizen* (1913) - which were shown in one of Projekt Migration's film programmes, organised in collaboration with Madeleine Bernstorff. In such films, pre-capitalist forms of production and the destitution of peasants is linked to images of the sexual oppression of women within traditional family structures. The canon of unskilled male worker/peasant and oppressed woman has stubbornly persisted and serves as a way of strengthening state control.[12] The redundancy of these attempts to represent the region from which the migrants came as pre-modern and poverty-stricken links these images of post-war migration to a further source of images constituted by colonialism. Representations of the non-West not only had the function of downgrading the rest of the world as underdeveloped, but it also helped to establish the idea of a universal, enlightened and superior middle-class Northern European subject, whose dominance, economic progression and rationality was set against the image of those who did not belong to this territory. In the words of Dipesh Chakrabarty, this motif 'has banished them for all time to the waiting room of history'.[13] The European colonial project registered this fund of images in the popular imagination, opening up a mutually reinforcing sphere of perception. In this binary structure, people took positions either side of a colonial border, creating an absolute difference between self and other, constructed through a whole series of further differentiations. In this way, the sphere of imagination created by colonial and post-colonial travel has also characterised the image of Northern Europe in non-European or Southern European countries. In this setting, the North has been presented through the 'promise' of a better life.[14]

Archives of pictures and ideas related to the colonial journey south and the migrant journey north are – as Kaja Silverman formulates in relation to a similar body of images concerning representations of the feminine – like a 'screen' from which we cannot simply walk away as they stay active in the visual memory. Instead of neglecting the 'screen', the task would be to insert contradictions and about-turns in order to rob the 'images' of the self-evidential.[15] The screen is very similar to language, insofar as it is shared by each of us. According to Silverman, our perception of a person or object follows specific descriptive parameters, the number of

12. The film programme was called 'Familien Bande'. It has to be noted that migration appears in current cinematic narrations – as in AyÐe Polat's *Auslandstournee* (2000) – against the background of juridical and everyday exclusions as a disturbance in the concept of the nation's small family unit. Moreover, the road movie is a category of new migration cinema, which has tried to describe the transnational character of migration.

13. Dipesh Chakrabarty, *Provincializing Europe: Postcolonial Thought and Historical Difference*. Princeton University Press. 2000.

14. See: Arjun Appadurai, *Modernity at Large: Cultural Dimensions of Globalization*. University of Minnesota Press. 1996; Fernando Coronil, 'Beyond Occidentalism. Toward Nonimperial Geohistorical Categories'. *Cultural Anthopology* 11. No. 1. 1996. p. 51-87; and Timothy Mitchell, 'The World as Exhibition,' *Comparative Studies in Society and History* 31. No. 2. 1989. p. 217-36.

15. Kaja Silverman, 'Dem Blickregime begegnen' in Christian Kravagna (ed.), *Privileg Blick. Kritik der visuellen Kultur*. ID Verlag. 1997.

which is relatively large but ultimately limited. For Silverman, the 'screen' confirms what and how we see - how the visible is processed: 'Those among them which impose themselves almost compulsorily I call the (pre-seen)'[16]. By using Michel Foucault's hypothesis on the pre-seen as a kind of positive unconsciousness of seeing, which determines not what is seen, but what can be seen, Silverman argues that not all methods of 'making visible' are capable of being understood or used at any one time. In any given period, certain things will be seen and others not. Thus, the screen of migration is not easily destroyed in a 'storm of images' or answered by a lack of images. As images circulate without even being materialised as presentations; they rain down upon us in texts or in statistics and in the acts of governing migration moulded by laws.

Images of labour migration, for example, conform to the neoclassical language of a market based on supply and demand - exactly as the recruitment bureaucrats devised it - in which those who have no work are compelled to go where the work is. Meanwhile, the North brings in exactly as many workers as it needs and sends them back when they are no longer required. Thus, the train station trope expresses a political condition and will. In both the FRG and GDR, post-war governments vehemently believed that, with the introduction of the rotation principle, the movements of migration could be precisely supervised, so that the Mediterranean, African and Asian workforces would not settle permanently. This conviction was compounded by the idea that temporary work permits, accommodation in workers' shacks and restricted political rights would deter migrants from staying in Germany. On the part of the Federal government, however, this was a total miscalculation as some recruited workers stayed longer than predicted - either in the interests of industrial companies or through their own will as they had formed cross-cultural relationships. Others left temporarily, returning for a second or third time and bringing their families with them; children were sent to school and later fought for their residency rights. Others went from Germany to other European countries or accepted special return premiums to go home; others were deported without any premium at all. But some workers also returned to their home countries after arrival because of the poor conditions of Germany's post-war factories and workers' barracks. It did not occur to the recruitment bureaucrats that, as a post-fascist state, Germany might not be the first choice for many labour migrants, and it

16. Ibid. p. 58.

was understood very late that the Southern European military dictatorships of the 1960s, '70s and '80s had a causal effect on movements to the North from Greece, Turkey and Spain.

The post-war image of labour migration was superimposed with the narrative traditions of a nationally centred modern industrial society as well as with factory work and its masculine connotations. The guest-worker regime thus condensed the diverse movements of migration into a one-dimensional framework which marks the capitalist logic of Fordism – in which becoming a factory worker through migration was entirely detached from the process of becoming a a political subject. Naming migrants as 'guest workers',[17] 'refugees', 'asylum seekers' or 'illegal immigrants' is linked to governmental practices that attempt to identify and control each of the discrepant movements within migration. But, as the researchers of DOMiD and TRANSIT MIGRATION commonly highlighted, even in the post-war 'guest worker' regime, with its strict state-regulated immigration processes, tactics and strategies existed for avoiding recruitment, passport, body and border checks. In the exhibition, we thus placed historical documentation of clandestine migration alongside that of legal migration and thus began to write a history that includes the illegal border-crossings of the post-war era.[18]

Through the research process, it became obvious that a full range of images and stories were missing, like those of migrants from rural to urban regions, from Southern cities and industrialised regions to the North or of those professionally and politically educated people for whom work in the mines or on a conveyor belt represented a demotion in their social status and provided a reason for further political engagement. Politicians and entrepreneurs came relatively late to the realisation that migrants are political actors – acutely so in the summer of 1973, when there was a wave of strikes by migrant workers in different places across the Federal Republic. Documentation of these instances was collected by the DOMiD researchers, beginning with the Karmann factory in Osnabrück, followed by the Hella firm in Lippstadt and Pierburg in Neuss, culminating in the best-known instance, the Cologne Ford factory strike.[19]

17. The term 'guest worker' emerged only in the late 1950s as a direct translation of the German *Gastarbeiter.*

18. Manuela Bojadzijev, 'Bürgerrechte und die Perspektive der Migration' and Serhat Karakayali and Vassilis Tsianos, 'Die Figuren der Migration,' in *Projekt Migration.*

19. A representative of the Ford management resigned with these words: 'We [have] stated over the numerous years that the foreigners often came to us with a too highly developed self-confidence.'

Moreover, in the collective (visual) memory of the guest worker, it was rarely brought to light that a large number of single women came to Germany, or that female migration had completely distinct, even emancipatory, motives.[20] For the exhibition, Edith Schmidt and David Wittenberg's film, *Pierburg: Their Fight Is Our Fight* (1974-75), about female strikers from the Pierburg Factory, was presented in an attempt to disrupt this one-dimensional frame. The strike at Pierburg is considered legendary, since it was accomplished primarily by and with female migrant workers and was successful in achieving its aim of permanently abolishing the low-wage category for workers. Stills from the film were also used as visuals for the invitation card and on the cover of the final publication. This was complemented by materials collected from migrant workers who were part of the Lotta Continua, a radical student and labour movement from Italy, active, for example, in the the famous Frankfurt Häuserkampf fight. Newspapers, photographs and documents in the exhibition demonstrated that migrants were involved as the main actors in a series of wildcat strikes, civil rights and tenant fights for better housing.

Transit

Since 1989, new forms of labour migration have emerged, such as shuttle migration, a driving force of which is the large wage differential between Eastern and Western Europe. The shuttlers or transit migrants - who do not settle in one place but are in a state of permanent, temporary sojourn - articulate new patterns of migration. Today, transit migrants are a central informal labour force in the building sector, the fragmentarily structured textile industry, agriculture, the nursing sector and domestic work. In this way, the consequences of a 'global market without borders' and the 'freedom of movement for the few' have given rise to new movements across national borders. Here, Europe's current border policies have a regulatory function regarding the European labour market and migration. The fact that demand for low-wage labourers is one of the conditions of a limitless economy is hardly addressed in migration discourses. This formed the subject of Gülsün Karamustafa's film,

20. See Monika Mattes, 'Zum Verhältnis von Migration und Geschlecht: Anwerbung und Beschäftigung von "Gastarbeiterinnen" in der Bundesrepublik 1960 bis 1973' in Jan Motte, Rainer Ohliger and Anne von Oswald (eds.), *50 Jahre Bundesrepublik, 50 Jahre Einwanderung* Campus Verlag. 1999.

Unawarded Performance (2005) - commissioned for the exhibition and shown next to photographs, films and documents from the guest-worker era - and Adrian Paci's video work, *Turn On* (2004). In Karamustafa's film, a university graduate from Moldova works as an elderly person's carer in Istanbul to support her unemployed husband and children. Forms of clandestine migration, and questions about their representation, were also addressed in the exhibition with works by artists such as Jeanne Faust and Jörn Zehe, Christoph Schäfer and Tobias Zielony.

Practices and conditions of migration create a transnational way of life because the movement of people across borders establishes new forms of the social beyond a settled existence. The experience of transnationalism within families that live and communicate in and beyond different global locations radically disrupts the idea of a citizen's right to be bound to a nation. This is equally the case in the shuttle migration of Eastern European baggage handlers, global migrants in transit through the European Union (EU), seasonal workers in the construction and catering industries, domestic and care services, diverse ethnic communities scattered throughout and between major metropolises, etc. In this respect, different patterns of movement and residency point to a post-national future in which neither place of birth nor so-called origin can be decisive in the constitution of the civil rights of citizens. If we take this not to be peripheral or marginal but to be the core of globalisation processes, then political preconceptions are immediately challenged. Against this backdrop, consideration of civil rights needs to be detached from its national form, as Saskia Sassen expressed at the symposium, *Transnational Europe*, in Cologne.[21] With this debate on new concepts of citizenship informed by global migration processes, the notion of freedom to travel as the privilege of an economic elite - which, in current globalisation processes, is largely confined to goods, data, money flows and wealthy citizens of Western states - is called into question.

In the TRANSIT MIGRATION project, researchers and artists examined the tightly meshed, confrontational interactions between migrants and the EU border regime. The border is no longer a line separating one territory from another; it has changed its shape, transforming border controls since 1989. Border police have increasing authority within the EU on streets, at stations and on trains, checking

21. Saskia Sassen, 'Immigrants and Citizens in the Global City' in *Projekt Migration*.

passers-by irrespective of suspicion.[22] Caught up in the transnational dynamics of migration, migrants might seek a better life across several different homelands, through periodic diasporic relocation, but they can only do so if they disregard, or subvert, the increasingly discriminatory techniques, tactics and strategies that are being deployed to police Europe's borders, even if this becomes a matter of life and death.[23] Meanwhile, the transnational movements of migration are undermining claims to control, and the modern state is under pressure to re-adapt its functions and technologies as a response to the movements of people.

The border regime has reacted by Europeanising migration policies and extending migration control mechanisms transnationally. In this context, TRANSIT MIGRATION also paid special attention to the ambivalent contributions of non-governmental organisations and humanitarian relief agencies, which are playing an increasingly important role in the design of EU and transatlantic migration policies. Moreover, individual European nation states are increasingly being incorporated into a larger system of supra-states – trading blocs which are also 'managing' migration and thus questioning the sovereignty of the nation state. During the course of this research, it became obvious that cooperation between the various supranational data agencies like the SIS, Frontex and EURODAC – which attempt to record and regulate the movements of people across the world – remains beyond contemporary discourses of migration. Against this backdrop, the Netproject *MigMap* – initiated by the media art collective, Labor k3000 – conveyed a picture of how and where knowledge production is currently taking place in the field of migration, and who is participating in it. Responding to data generated by the research team, *MigMap* investigated precisely how the new forms of supranational governance function. It looked, for example, at the authorities, persons and institutions taking part in this process and at how European standards in politics and civil society are implemented. Finally, this project analysed how responsibilities are allocated and

22. With their audio-visual installation, *Zertifikat Deutsch* (2004), the artist, Farida Heuck, and the sociologist, Birgit zur Nieden, analysed, in the context of TRANSIT MIGRATION, the *Zuwanderungsgesetz* (the 'law for the controlling and delimitation of the immigration and for the regulation of the stay and the integration of union citizens and foreigners') which has been in effect in Germany since January 2005. This law draws attention to, among other things, a new paradigm in immigration policy which requires that language and integration courses are conducted with standardised final examinations, to which the extension of the legal stay for immigrants is coupled.

23. See TRANSIT MIGRATION Forschungsgruppe (ed.), *Turbulente Ränder. Neue Perspektiven auf Migration an den Grenzen Europas* (transcript 2007).

legitimised, and explored the theories, data and discourses upon which current paradigms are based.[24] This made an important contribution to the wider question of how to make governance perceptible.

Accompanying the forms of migration that have emerged since 1989, it has been possible to constitute a new way of viewing migration, in which images of travel have largely arrived via the official media to become an autonomous genre. This migratory image is, however, a thoroughly negative one, as the countless sensational images of border crossings at the external boundaries of the EU make clear. In this new trope, it is again mainly lone men (from the global South) who are the main subjects, presented as victims or violators of the border. These representations of migration have determined contemporary discourse on the subject and the ways in which we perceive migration in general. Images of people stranded at the borders of the EU also produce a new image of Europe, which is no longer internally structured by migration but 'threatened' by it at its periphery. According to filmmaker, author and member of the TRANSIT MIGRATION research team, Brigitta Kuster, the 'EU external border' has become a hotspot for the 'image of migration' - established in countless Arte TV programmes or documentary festival films - in which the border magically attracts the documenting (and controlling) eye of cameras. In this evolving way of looking at border crossing, the fact that migrants develop strategies through which they actively respond to conditions at the borders is largely erased. But, most of these clandestine journeys will not take place without social networks - friends and relations - who have pre-structured the path and are already living abroad. The ways in which the practices of the border regime, the controls and the new security provisions are ambivalently intertwined with the practices and strategies of the clandestine was not a topic of the documentary features analysed by Kuster. By contrast to the image of labour migrants from the 1960s, the present-day image radically denies the fact that the border is a filter which regulates demand for migrants as low-wage workers instead of deterring and deporting all those who seek

24. http://www.transitmigration.org/migmap/

to traverse it.[25] Nevertheless, the figure of the 'illegalised immigrant' also implies new knowledge about migration, via third-nation arrangements, identifying the holes in the fence of border controls, the means of becoming invisible or 'someone else', for or against the categories of identity maintained by the state, as the sociologist, Dana Dimenescu, showed in her study presented at one of our symposia, or the artist, Jun Yang, in his video work, *LOOK* like them - *TALK* like them (2002–4), exhibited in the exhibition.

Želimir Žilnik's film, *Kenedi, Lost and Found,* produced within the framework of Projekt Migration, recounted the experience of Kenedi Hasani, the protagonist of three productions by Žilnik, who embodies and performs possible and impossible forms of travel. Hasani has undertaken a series of clandestine travels to EU countries in which his father, mother, brothers and sisters live. During one of his crossings of the Hungarian-Austrian border in 2003, he was captured by border police and spent a couple of months in a refugee camp. He managed to escape to Austria and then to Germany and Holland. The film crew caught up with him in Vienna in January 2005, at a screening of Kenedi Returns Home at the university, bringing his transnational existence into dialogue with the social and cultural scientific world that studies migration. Kenedi, Lost and Found recounts the experiences of Hasani's two-year refugee status and return to Serbia, where he decided to build a house in Novi Sad, because other members of the family were in the 'process of readmission' and arriving soon.[26]

In Žilnik's so-called docu-dramas, different settings for the reversal of existing societal roles are invented, as protagonists of a societal field

25. These changes in the present-day border regime were examined by the research group, TRANSIT MIGRATION, and documented in the publication, *Turbulente Ränder*, and in an experimental, collective process between research, theory, cultural production and media activism (Labor k3000 Zurich), in an interactive mapping. The resulting online project, MigMap, addressed the question of what ethno-sociological research, such as TRANSIT MIGRATION, is able to represent beyond pure text work. At the same time, MigMap also maps those who usually map and control migration, like the Federal Border Guard or the IOM, and was thus able to show to what extent knowledge production is a constitutive component of the new border and migration regime.

26. In the third film, after having built the house for his family, Kenedi finds himself searching for any kind of work to support himself, for as little as 10 EUR per day, a scarce amount to help him relieve his debt. Ultimately, Kenedi decides to look for money in sex business. Initially offering his services to older ladies and widows, he expands his 'business' to offer sex to wealthy men. When he finds out about new liberal European laws on gay marriages, Kenedi sees prospects in looking for a 'marriage material', to renew his search for a legal status in EU. The opportunity arises during EXIT Music Festival, when he meets Max, a man from Munich. 'But will their promising relationship bring the solution to Kenedi's problems?' asks the promo text in the end.

create the film plot in dialogue with the filmmaker. On the one hand, they co-direct the camera's eye because they stage their experiences as a story, and, on the other hand, they also act in front of the camera. The audience of Žilnik's films is, therefore, repeatedly confronted with the question: Is this documentary or is it a fiction? The object of study from the classical documentary genre is not observed but put into the role of the artist, the storyteller. And, like Hasani, the plot-maker, turns into a film star. Not only are the screen and its visual vocabulary used to show an alternate narrative but the cinema apparatus is also used to call existing power relations into question; the desire for self-invention, storytelling and role-playing is contrasted with reality. In parts of Žilnik's EU-border films, the 'actor' takes on the role of interviewer or reporter, creating chance 'reality effects' in a concrete environment like a border police station. The films create a situation, 'acting' in the present rather than re-enacting a past. What the films in the Kenedi series have in common is that they show an actor in a double sense - as a director/actor in a so-called docu-drama as well as a multiple actor in and of the EU border regime. Thus, the film is able to make visible the fact that refusal of refugee status, harsh border police or policing in general will not hinder Hasani in repeatedly trying to challenge Fortress Europe. Instead, he chooses very different strategies and identities to subvert or affirm existing laws as well as to create niches of survival and self-creation. Actors in Žilnik's films are subjects with prospects, desires and failures; they are involved in deviant practices. They do not fit national 'integration' norms even as they try to fulfil their dreams of a decent life with western standards.

This specific form of narration - which we were searching for in our research process - made it possible to see that border crossings also produce new social spheres, relationships and transnational ways of living, which ignore national state boundaries and their one-dimensional concepts of affiliation.

On Display

The dramaturgy of the *Projekt Migration* exhibition - in which various procedures and methods of representation corresponded and made mutually reinforcing comments - related diverse perspectives and thus attempted something clandestine, by linking different narrative and visual strategies beyond their disciplinary affiliations. Those making an exhibition are accorded a similar role to the photographer, artist or filmmaker, as they put the discrepant methods of documentary, artistic or private picture production into a new communicative relationship and, in a specific context, produce a particular understanding of, and relationship to, culture. As in Ponger's *Passagen*, a montage of different representational contexts indicates the productiveness of such a practice for exhibitions and collaborations between research, art and social history. To have only curated existing documentaries, artworks and private mementoes and exhibited them separately would not have established a new narrative. By collaging different source material from the research processes or by commissioning new works, the 'screen of migration' became recognisable. The complex association of the previously seen and the seemingly obvious asked us curators to take a step towards the image and text and become aware of the implications of different presentation techniques - to use, reverse, appropriate and abuse them for alternative narrations and offer new possibilities of presence and absence in pictures, poems and presentations.

This curatorial position differs from the representation of history in museums, which tries to recall the past with artefacts and documents and, at the same time, claims an objective view on history. By contrast, *Projekt Migration* set itself up as an interpretation of various histories, approaches and viewpoints. Since the labour and social movements of the 1960s, many attempts have been made to bring into play subjects and narratives that have been excluded from the canon of historical evidence by means of popular counter-narratives, documentation centres and archives; neighbourhood museums and other temporary or long-established forms of self-organisation and self-representation stand in opposition to the official presentation practices of museums. In Projekt Migration, even this work of identification with the marginalised or marginalisation, and the associated demand for it to be integrated into the hegemonic canon, was reflected upon critically. All the partners, artists and researchers involved either took part in investigative activities or commissioned artistic works. *Projekt Migration* was a locus of antagonism, self-empowerment and ceaseless struggle for representation and citizenship.

It was an aim of the curatorial team to develop accounts of migration, past and present, without highlighting a linear chronology. After three years of common work in *Projekt Migration* as a whole, we wanted to present the central changes made by migration within Europe, from the perspective of migration rather than from the perspective of the nation. Thus, for the production of the exhibition, we developed a narrative, containing all those figures of migration that can disappear at any moment and appear as new figures and thus disintegrate in terms of evidence. Against the realisation that, even if instigated by non-governmental organisations or human rights groups, all categorisations are underpinned by the policies of governmental regimes, we looked for a place that could make new socialities and subjectivities imaginable.[27] The result of this decision was a dramaturgy based around discontinuities. We created a place in which constant negotiation existed about whether, and to what extent, members of the educated class, migrants, teachers, artists and activists are represented. This presented the audience with a post-identitarian prospect of a transnational future.

In terms of research, the exhibition also became a method through which the screen of migration could no longer be considered distinct from other representations, and the ways of positioning oneself and others in the social field (as academics, artists or representatives of a migrant organisation). For this reason, we decided to make the methodical procedure of art, social history and research an additional subject of the exhibition and to develop questions and forms of display in dialogue with artists. This decision not only stirred the imaginative work of the research; it also opened up new personal conditions and collaborative relationships between academics, activists and cultural producers. On the one hand, this led to questions about what an ethno-sociological study like that of the research of the TRANSIT MIGRATION team might be capable of presenting as a purely textual work.[28] Art itself was also acknowledged as a mode of research, and trans-disciplinary work on an exhibition enabled new subject positions and associations to emerge. *Projekt Migration* can be read as a 'project exhibition' that creates a temporary field in which people from many diverse fields of knowledge can develop research with, and for, an exhibition, while explicitly alternating subject positions in this temporary and larger cultural and political context. The use of this format for communication aims to produce new publics through the imaginative and collective work of the exhibition's making. A 'project exhibition' unambiguously takes a stand by not

27. On the nomadic subject, see writings by Rosi Braidotti: *Nomadic Subjects: Embodiment and Sexual Difference in Contemporary Feminist Theory.* Columbia University Press. 1994; and Rosi Braidotti in conversation with Rutvica Andrijasevic, 'Europa lässt uns nicht träumen' in *Projekt Migration.*

28. See TRANSIT MIGRATION, http://www.transitmigration.org

illustrating a theme but instead developing its own theses, methods and formats, and thus establishing a discourse.

Furthermore, with the empirical work of all research partners, it was possible to develop thematic narratives for the conception of the exhibition beyond the ambit of time and to effect a change in perspective in which migration did not become an object of contemplation, as in folklore, but the subject of our post-war history. This was produced, on the one hand, by a number of measures of state and border control policies and, on the other hand, through migrants' campaigns for civil rights, and it has had a formative influence on everyday culture.

At each of the various exhibitions embodying the weary mood of post-war modernism, it became possible to examine the thematic associations between the venue and the exhibition. We would not have been able to identify and present the multiple relationships and transnational areas which migration produces from a purely national perspective. This also meant adopting the perspectives of all those who are involved in migration, from both majority and minority societies. It was thus possible to show a picture of migration as a common history and a shared present.

ACTION RESEARCH: GENERATIVE CURATORIAL PRACTICES

Kate Fowle

In 1997, fifteen curators from around the world met at the Rockefeller Conference Centre in Bellagio, Italy, to discuss the emerging phenomenon of 'international' exhibitions.[1] Chronicled by art critic, Michael Brenson, who attended to write a report for participants and funders, conversations centred on whether biennials, or projects of a similar scale, could address the pressing cultural concerns of the time as well as the practical and conceptual issues that arise in producing such shows.

Brenson's account began by pronouncing that the 'era of the curator' was upon us, going on to outline what he described as the 'challenges facing the curatorial profession to think deeply about multiple audiences and to allow individual curatorial perspectives to be invigorated by radically, even shockingly, different experiences of space and time, memory and history'. Recognising the expanding responsibilities of the curator in providing a framework for art in relation to broader world politics - namely the 'meanings and possibilities of art in a post-Cold War, post-colonial, fin-de-siècle moment' - he warned that such high stakes do not reward 'curatorial business as usual'.[2] The time had come to understand, and act upon, what it meant to work in diverse cultural and geographical contexts.

This summit occurred during a year in which five biennials - Cairo, Havana, Istanbul, Johannesburg, Venice - and a documenta took place, in a decade that witnessed an unprecedented rise in interest around curating. According to a recent study, thirty-two biennials were instigated during the 1990s, in comparison to the twenty-seven that were created altogether in the period between 1895 and 1989.[3] The 1990s was also

1. Participants in the Bellagio conference were: Margaret Archuleta, Curator of Twentieth-Century Art, the Heard Museum, Phoenix; René Block, Director, Museum Fridericianum, Kassel; Michael Brenson, New York; Germano Celant, Curator of Contemporary Art, Solomon R. Guggenheim Museum, New York; Kinshasha Holman Conwill, Director, Studio Museum in Harlem, New York; Vishaka N. Desai, Director of the Galleries, Asia Society, New York; Okwui Enwezor, Artistic Director, Second Johannesburg Biennial; N. Fulya Erdemci, Director, 13th International Istanbul Biennial; Lillian Godoy, Director, Centro Wifredo Lam, Havana; Madeleine Grynsztejn, curator of Twentieth-Century Art, Carnegie Museum, Pittsburgh; Paolo Herkenhoff, Chief Curator, Fundação Bienal de São Paulo; Virginia Pérez-Ratton, Director, Museo de Arte y Disñeo Contemporáneo, San Jose, Costa Rica; Apininan Poshyananda, Associate Director, Center of Academic Resources, Chulalongkorn University, Bangkok; Mari Carmen Ramirez, Curator of Latin American Art, Jack S. Blanton Museum of Art, Austin; Remi Sagna, Secrétaire Général, Daka Biennial; Caroline Turner, Deputy Director, Queensland Art Gallery, Brisbane.

2. Michael Brenson, 'The Curator's Moment'. *CAA Art Journal*. Vol. 57. No. 4. Winter 1998. p. 16-27.

3. Sabine B. Vogel, *Biennials - Art on a Global Scale*. Springer-Verlag/Wien. 2010. p. 118-119

a time during which curatorial masters programmes were established.[4] These degrees were premised on the notion that, just as an artist could be trained to develop a practice, so too could a burgeoning curator. Perhaps more importantly, the programmes instituted the model of curators taking time out to talk about and reflect upon their profession, for the sake of future generations' learning. Over a relatively short time, this self-reflexivity has given us a curatorial discourse through which we make sense of the circumstances we find ourselves working in today.

In spite of this, however, many of the uncertainties raised at the 1997 summit still seem as relevant as they were then. The questions as to whether art can speak for itself when presented out of its cultural context and whether we should be seeking intrinsic meaning in the form of an artwork, as opposed to amplifying the value of what it represents, are still up for judgment. As a curator, is it really possible to produce exhibitions beyond your own cultural knowledge? How do you find out what you don't know? Are there ways to continuously process and update research in order to generate fresh perspectives? In an art world that is increasingly intertwined with 'real life' politics, how do you navigate the contradictions this can create, presenting work in contexts that neither obfuscate nor distort meaning? What *does* it mean to work internationally?

This text asks: which of the experimental *curatorial* practices of the 1990s can be brought to bear in understanding how curators have developed ways of working that respond to changing cultural and political imperatives in an ever-expanding art world. It begins at the outset of the decade – with the proliferation of the biennial format and the emergence of a new discourse around curating and exhibitions – charting the tensions between theory and practice in establishing curatorial precedents.

The notion of research is interrogated throughout, in a bid to assess what constitutes a curatorial research, as opposed to any other kind. In particular, the process is explored as a lens through which to make sense of any instinct toward unfamiliar situations and concepts as well as the propositions artists offer us. Finally, by recognising the decade of the 1990s as one that witnessed radical shifts within the infrastructure of art, this chapter starts to evaluate the relevance of informal, peer-to-peer networks in the reappraisal of what so-called cultural 'exchange' can be. By exploring the curatorial imperatives of the people that pioneered

4. For example, the École du Magasin in Grenoble, France in 1987; the Royal College of Art in London, UK in 1992; the Center for Curatorial Studies at Bard College in Annandale-on-Hudson, US in 1994, etc.

experimental approaches to global connectivity, the reasons for building generative practices become more evident and, indeed, pressing.

In exhibition history, the story of the 1990s begins at the end of the previous decade. Four years in the making, *Magiciens de la Terre* was conceived and promoted as the first 'global' exhibition of contemporary art. Curated by Jean-Hubert Martin and installed at both the Centre George Pompidou and the Grande Halle La Villette in 1989, the show was initiated as an alternative to the traditional format of the Biennale de Paris, which it temporarily replaced. *Magiciens* presented work by a hundred artists - fifty from the United States and Western Europe juxtaposed with fifty from Eastern Europe, Asia, Africa, Central and South America, Australia and Oceania - who were each, according to an early press statement, 'committed to the avant-garde'.(5)

Martin produced *Magiciens* in response to what he regarded as the structural and ideological problems of large-scale shows that predominantly relied on cultural diplomacy for the selection of artists and works. The examples he referred to included the Biennale de Paris, which had been in operation since 1959, as well as the Triennale-India (since 1968), the Sydney Biennale (1973), the Havana and Cairo biennials (1984) and the Istanbul Biennial, which started in 1987, midway through the curator's preparations. In his first statement on *Magiciens* in 1986, Martin emphasised: 'This exhibition will bring together artists from all over the world, not just from developed, capitalist countries. [...] The artists in the exhibition will not be picked and shown as ambassadors of their countries to demonstrate their nation's cultural, economic, and political skills, but as individuals from all the world striving towards spiritual fulfilment'.(6)

In outlining his selection criteria, Martin described his curatorial research process as one of looking for artists whose practice was experimental within their own traditions; this involved a search for art that reflected on relations between different cultures, and for practitioners whose methods of working could be displaced from their original site to be adapted to the specific conditions and scale of the Parisian venues.(7)

5. '*Magiciens de la Terre*. The Death of Art - Long Live Art'. Press Release. Centre Georges Pompidou. 1986.
6. Ibid.
7. '*Magiciens de la Terre*. One Exhibition, Two Sites'. Press Release. Centre Georges Pompidou. 1989.

His emphasis was on conducting fieldwork, travelling extensively to meet with artists in their studios or place of practice, as well as providing research trips to a few Western artists to inform new work for the show. Martin also enlisted the support of three curatorial colleagues as advisors on the exhibition concept, as well as involving other specialists - ethnographers, anthropologists, historians and critics - in helping him to decide where to go and who to meet without relying on official diplomatic networks.(8) Adamantly upholding his own vision, Martin claimed: 'This project can only be realised wholly independently of all political machinery, national or international. It will be the first properly international exhibition by one organiser who can guarantee the intellectual unity of his selection.'

While this aim of avoiding bureaucratic channels created the potential for developing a transnational network of peers, Martin's insistence on maintaining a singular perspective, 'open and receptive towards other civilizations, but [...] made from a Western standpoint'(9) propelled the exhibition into the heart of postcolonial debate. The process also revealed the problematic behind the nascent form of international curating: how does one begin to research and engage with art that exists beyond one's own cultural references, to create a 'new internationalism', as opposed to using the premise that the more countries represented through the selection of artists, the more 'international' the show?(10)

Many critics concur that, to his credit, Martin at least demonstrated wide-ranging research practices, particularly in his emphasis on selecting artists from cultures in transition. Chilean-born, US-based Alfredo Jaar - who presented a series of photographic light boxes portraying the impact

8. '*Magiciens de la Terre*. The Death of Art - Long Live Art'. Press Release. Centre Georges Pompidou. 1986. A number of sources cite different curators and researchers as central to the project. The following list is one produced for the credits in the exhibition materials for the opening: Jan Debbaut; Mark Francis; Jean-Louis Maubant; Fei Da Wei; Cherif Khaznadar; Thierry De Duve; Pierre Gaudibert; Yves Michaud; Aline Luque; Andre Magnin; Thomas McEvilley; Homi Bhabha; Jacques Souliliou; Bernard Marcade.

9. Ibid.

10. Michael Brenson, 'Review/Art; Juxtaposing the New From All Over'. The *New York Times*. May 20 1989. http://www.nytimes.com/1989/05/20/arts/review-art-juxtaposing-the-new-from-all-over.html
Thomas McEvilley, 'APENDIX A The Global Issue' in *Art and Otherness. Crisis in Cultural Identity*. McPherson & Company. 1992. p. 153-158.
Rasheed Araeen, 'Our Bauhaus Others' Mudhouse' in Rasheed Araeen and Jean Fisher (eds.), *Third Text: Third World Perspectives on Contemporary Art and Culture*. Kala Press, part of the organisation Black Umbrella (Project MRB). 1989. p. 3-14.
Third Text: Third World Perspectives on Contemporary Art and Culture comprises all but one (Lucy Lippard's text from Les Cahiers) of the articles from the special issue of Les Cahiers du Musée National d'Art Moderne, No. 28, published at the occasion of the exhibition *Magiciens* de la Terre at the Centre Georges Pompidou in Paris.

of illegal toxic waste dumping in Koko, Nigeria – suggested that the show was the first to present his work alongside that of artists from countries that were the subject of his concerns: 'Since I began working, I've dealt with the issue of the widening gap between the so-called Third World and the industrialized world. In this show, perhaps for the first time, my work was seen in its proper context'.[11] Jaar also suggested that the show was pioneering because of the number of artists that were invited, often for the first time outside their own country, to produce work on site. The incongruity of the installation period did not go unnoticed, however: 'One morning, there was Esther Mahlangu from South Africa painting her house. In front of her Cyprien Tokkoudagba from Benin was finishing a sculpture. Next to both of them, a group of Australian Aboriginal artists were working on their sand painting, and five meters further in the back, Richard Long was making one of his large mud drawings. What a sight! They were so close together and so far apart at the same time'.[12]

Lawrence Weiner, one of the artists Martin travelled with in advance of the show to 'initiate dialogues' and 'question the relationship of our culture to other cultures in the world', also reported a distancing when he went to Papua New Guinea.[13] On describing this trip, he admitted: 'I don't know where along the way, probably on the airplane, I realized there was something a little bit greasy about the whole thing'. Weiner went on to explain that, while there was plenty of shared ground from which to engage with local artists, he was more interested in the fact that dialogue was not actually happening between the generations living and working there, even at the art school:

> They were excluding a lot of kids who were not making things for the European tourism; meaning copies of what had been previously done, which they were calling their heritage. It was *their* heritage, but why would a fourteen-year-old be doing that? They wanted to make other things. So we made a coin that was exactly like the 'Kina' in New Guinea (which has a hole in the middle) and inscribed 'Now Him It Art Belong You & Me' around it, which just means 'The Art of Today Belongs to Us'. People could

11. Alfredo Jaar, 'The Peripatetic Artist: 14 Statements'. *Art in America*. Vol. 77. No. 7. July 1989. p. 131. Interviews conducted by Lilly Wei, Elisabeth Baker.
12. Ibid.
13. Benjamin H.D. Buchloh, 'The Whole Earth Show: An Interview with Jean-Hubert Martin'. *Art in America*, Vol. 77. No. 5. May 1989. p. 155.

wear it around their neck. It's not very profound. It was a way of saying you could love your children without them having to resemble you.[14]

In contradiction to the accounts from participating artists, the exhibition title, 'Magicians of the Earth', suggests that the artists possessed some kind of pre-rational or spiritual connectivity to each other and their surroundings. In actuality, the artists' only shared experience appears to be that of the early contradictions of globalisation. Somewhere between these two paradigms - the connectivity suggested by the title and the distancing described by the artists - Martin's curatorial strategy revealed (as described by critic, Eleanor Heartney) 'an awareness of the theoretical debates currently raging within the disciplines of anthropology and ethnography', but little acknowledgement of 'the reality of power politics'.[15] What's more, the curator's desire to circumnavigate the national and international 'political machinery' for the sake of 'intellectual unity' did not ensure that the artists involved or the art presented was removed from the burden of national or cultural representation. In fact, through the emphasis on anthropology, it could be argued that many of the artists were framed *more* by their cultural representation than their individual merits.

Martin's claim - that the show was not a 'World Art catalogue' but a site for dialogue and exchange - further highlighted the complex question of what constitutes being 'open and receptive to other civilizations'. In one curatorial statement, he described exchange as 'borrowings' and 'the theft of influences',[16] while 'dialogue', in the context of this

14. Lawrence Weiner in conversation with Hans Ulrich Obrist at Manchester City Art Gallery, July 2013. As part of the public programme for do it. Unpublished transcribed quotation from a response to a question from the author, 'Can you tell me about your participation in Magiciens de la Terre?'

15. Eleanor Heartney, 'The Whole Earth Show. Part II'. *Art in America*. Vol. 77. No. 7. July 1989. p. 95-96. For further examples see also Benjamin H.D. Buchloh, op cit. p. 211.

Jean-Hubert Martin: Rather than showing that Abstraction is a universal language, or that the return to figuration is now happening everywhere in the world, I want to show the real difference and the specificity of the different cultures.

Benjamin Buchloh: But what are the real differences between the different cultures at this point? [...] Don't you think that by excluding these political and economical aspects and by focusing exclusively on the cultural relationships between Western centres and developing nations, you will inevitably generate a neo-colonialist reading?

J.-H.M.: That implies that the visitors of the exhibition would be unable to recognize the relationships between the centres and the Third World.

16. 'Magiciens de la Terre. The Death of Art - Long Live Art'. Press Release. Centre Georges Pompidou. 1989.

'Magiciens de la Terre. The First World-wide Exhibition of Contemporary Art'. Press Release. Centre Georges Pompidou. 1989.

show, can only really be construed as terminology for the formal juxtaposition of works within the exhibition design. The curator's travel notes indicate that the meetings he had with various artists and advisors during his research could constitute conversations,(17) but, as Weiner's account reveals, the exchange that occurred as the result of research travel was not necessarily in line with the conceptual intentions of the show or the messages it was supposed to convey.

In her article for a special issue of *Les Cahiers du Musée National d'Art Moderne*, published to coincide with the opening of the exhibition, the cultural theorist, Jean Fisher, indicated that such research was a new guise of imperialism: 'The West's traditionally anthropocentric search for lost utopias has never resulted in equal exchange with others [...] [and] the recent interest shown by our cultural institutions in creative work outside the paradigms of modernism raises the suspicion that, as so often in the past, the West is turning to other worlds to revitalize itself in the face of a spiritual and sociopolitical bankruptcy'.(18)

As radically polarised as Fisher's and Martin's perspectives were, there was perhaps a tacit agreement around the so-called 'bankruptcy' of the West. The common quest was one of resolution, particularly in relation to that which constitutes effective exchange. Martin emphasised his perspective on this when writing about the meta-objective behind Magiciens: 'The particular needs of this project require that a constant exchange takes place between theory and practice, and that both constantly correct each other in the course of the preparation of this exhibition. It is not that discourse on intercultural relationships has been absent from French thought; what is missing are the pragmatic forms of putting this discourse into practice'.(19)

The attempt to merge theory and practice through exhibition-making, and Martin's emphasis on primary research, perhaps explains why Magiciens still resonates today. Throughout the development of the show, Martin can be seen testing ideas by thinking aloud through various press statements, travel journals and media interviews. The processes of creating the exhibition became a form of 'action research' and, as such,

17. Extracts from Jean-Hubert Martin's diaries; correspondence; press releases; exhibition materials were all given to the author by Fei Dawei as scans from his personal archive, part of which can be found in the Asia Art Archive, Fei Dawei Archive: Collection Description VI. Magiciens de la Terre. http://www.aaa.org.hk/Collection/SpecialCollections/Details/22

18. Rasheed Araeen and Jean Fisher, op cit. p. 79.

19. Benjamin H.D. Buchloh, op cit. p. 157.

a vehicle through which the curator continuously built knowledge and experience; even if this was largely through contradiction and opposition, as a curatorial strategy, this approach had few precedents at the time.

Four years after *Magiciens de la Terre* and a continent away, the 1993 biennial exhibition at the Whitney Museum of American Art in New York was one of a number of exhibitions in that year's art world calendar which foregrounded what was becoming known as 'issue-based' or 'socially-engaged' practice. Curated by Elisabeth Sussman as part of a team, the 1993 biennial addressed the theoretical issues of multiculturalism and the Culture Wars by presenting artists whose practice engaged, to a greater or lesser degree, with migration, diaspora, displacement, gender and race in the United States.[20]

Interestingly, the curators' selection criteria addressed almost the same interests as those Martin had focused on for *Magiciens de la Terre*, but the motivation appears to be quite different. As outlined by Sussman in her catalogue essay, the co-curators each researched artists who were: committed as much to ideas as to aesthetics (compare with Martin: art that was radical in its own tradition), making work that portrayed identities and nationalisms in flux (Martin: art that reflected relations between different cultures) and creating projects that revealed the 'collectivity of cultures involved in a process of exchange and difference' rather than as homogenising entities (Martin: work that could be removed from its original site and respond to specific conditions).[21] One crucial difference was that artists were invited to participate in the biennial specifically *because* of their emphasis on political and cultural engagement rather than their 'spiritual' responses. Furthermore, the exhibition directly confronted the issue of political machinery and its influence on the development of culture, rather than attempting to remain independent of it, as Martin had done.

Looking back at the biennial a few years later, Sussman described it as one of the exhibitions 'that fixed the terms of the critical debate in the late 1980s and early 1990s' as well as being important in introducing a

20. As touched upon earlier in this essay, the subject of multiculturalism was widespread at the time, with other shows including *Aperto* in Venice (1993); *Poliphonies* in Budapest (1993); *Culture in Action* in Chicago (1993). The curator of the 1993 Whitney Biennial was Elisabeth Sussman, supported by co-curators Thelma Golden, John G. Hanhardt and Lisa Phillips. Not all selected artists for the 1993 Whitney Biennial could be considered 'identity-based' artists under the post-colonial rubric, for example Robert Gober, Mike Kelley, Cindy Sherman, Chris Burden.

21. Elisabeth Sussman et al., *1993 Biennial Exhibition*. Whitney Museum of American Art in association with Harry N. Abrams, Inc., Publishers. 1993. p. 14-15.

new generation of artists - including Lorna Simpson, Glenn Ligon, Daniel Martinez, Renée Green and Gary Simmons - who, she said, demanded a 'rebalancing of the critical discourse'.(22) At the time, however, this attention to criticality partly explained why the show was negatively received, especially because journalists perceived theory to predominate over practice, to which they responded by stressing the primacy of the object in relation to the discursive tensions of multiculturalism.(23) Roberta Smith epitomised this sentiment in her review for the *New York Times* in which she wrote that the 1993 biennial 'frequently substitutes didactic moralizing for genuine visual communication'.(24)

Aside from the media responses toward the rise of the message over the object, the topic was given academic weight when the biennial became the focus of the first published October roundtable, in which Benjamin Buchloh, Hal Foster, Silvia Kolbowski, Rosalind Krauss and Miwon Kwon explored how political, socio-economic and institutional change was transforming the frames through which art was being produced and understood. This discussion was centred on the premise that art made in the US at that time was prioritising theoretical concepts or political positions, and the importance of conveying a message was deflecting the artist's interests away from the signification of material and form. This, it was determined, was changing how meaning in art was conveyed and affecting the potential for multiple readings of the work. The panel went on to sugg-est that the politics of form was increasingly dismissed in the production of work about identity, which instead championed personal experience or political expressionism. This, in turn, encouraged curators to use artworks to represent their own personal takes on social and political issues. Far from producing a more open artwork

22. Elisabeth Sussman, 'Then and Now: Whitney Biennial 1993'. *CAA Art Journal*. Vol. 64. No. 1. Spring 2005. p. 75.
23. Examples of media coverage: Christopher Knight, '1993 Year in Review: ART: It's Called Art, Not Politics': With identity politics overriding the art world, it was a relief to see shows by artists like Vija Celmins and Adrian Saxe'. *Los Angeles Times*. 26 December 1993. http://articles.latimes.com/1993-12-26/entertainment/ca-5558_1_art-museum; Peter Plagens, 'Fade from White'. Newsweek Magazine. 14 March 1993. http://www.thedailybeast.com/newsweek/1993/03/14/fade-from-white.html; John Dorsey, 'While the Whitney Biennial Focuses on Messages, They Don't Always Get Through'. *The Baltimore Sun*. 29 March 1993. http://articles.baltimoresun.com/1993-03-29/features/1993088159_1_whitney-biennial-work-of-art-today-art; Roberta Smith, 'At The Whitney, A Biennial With A Social Conscience'. The *New York Times*. 5 March 1993. http://www.nytimes.com/1993/03/05/arts/at-the-whitney-a-biennial-with-a-social-conscience.html?pagewanted=all&src=pm; Hal Foster et al., 'The Politics of the Signifier: A Conversation on the Whitney Biennial'. *October*. Vol. 66. Autumn 1993. p. 3-27.
24. Roberta Smith, op cit.

or exhibition, it was agreed that the demise of form was leading to the privileging of viewers with access to certain definitions of culture rather than expanding potential audiences. In other words, while the intentions were different, the biennial curators created a distance between the artists and their publics just as Martin had also done in the process of trying to evidence connectivity between artists and spiritual ideas.[25]

In his essay for the catalogue, post-colonial theorist, Homi Bhabha, offered a contrasting perspective on this notion of producing openness (or not), with an observation about the reception of such work, which he saw as existing on a boundary that was constantly moving. Through this, he emphasised not *what* the audience will experience, but *how*:

> Representing cultures at the borderlines, as this Biennial attempts to do, is a demanding double act between artist and curator. [...] Installed within the very act of display, in the contradictory structure of spectatorship itself, there exists ambivalence about the representation of cultural difference that creates a productive tension between the borderline artist and the frontline curator. [...] The intention of the object consists neither in the producers' mental image of it, nor in the fulfilment of the curator's pedagogy. The intentionality of display lies in opening up an active space between object and label that propels the spectator in a 'shuttling process,' back and forth, hither and thither, between culturally informative causes and visually interesting objects.[26]

Where Martin was convinced that a cohesive exhibition could be produced through a singular curatorial vision, Bhabha's emphasis on the viewers' 'shuttling process' between 'causes' and 'objects' suggests that responsibility for a sense of cohesion rests with the audience. The evocation of borderline and frontline suggest the risks at stake in the relationship between curator and artist. The meaning of the work (and the exhibition) is a negotiation between the sum of its parts – the objects,

25. Hal Foster et al., op cit. p. 3-27.

26. Homi K. Bhabha, 'Beyond the Pale: Art in the Age of Multicultural Translation' in Elisabeth Sussman et al., op cit. p. 63-64. It is interesting to compare Bhabha's analogy of the 'curator on the frontline' with Mari Carmen Ramirez' 'curator as cultural broker' noting the 'transformation of the curator of contemporary art from the behind-the-scenes aesthetic arbiter to central player in the broader stage of global cultural politics' which she first described in 1994 at Bard College during a lecture for the curatorial programme and was subsequently published as Mari Carmen Ramirez, 'Brokering Identities: Art Curators and the Politics of Cultural Representation' in Reesa Greenberg, Bruce W. Ferguson and Sandy Nairne (eds.), *Thinking about Exhibitions*. Routledge. 1996. p. 15-27.

concepts, labels and spaces or tensions between works – in the context of a particular site. Furthermore, Bhabha suggests that, rather than with individual works, openness rests with the method of display, which is also the key mechanism through which representation can gain ambivalence, creating space for viewers' independent perceptions. As such, it could be said that, rather than exhibition-making constituting the completion of a thesis, the presentation of works creates the potential for testing ideas that would not otherwise be possible, thereby becoming a research tool itself. With this in mind, Sussman's belief that an exhibition could 'fix the terms of critical debate' gains credence, as does the decision by *October* to use the biennial as the frame of their first roundtable discussion.

The notion that curating and exhibition-making could be vehicles to further new socio-political readings was central to the development of a new style of art organisation in London around the same time. The Institute of International Visual Arts (InIVA) was set up as a production company with an emphasis on partnerships and collaboration and no exhibition space. Equally focused on ideas and making, its four spheres of activity were: exhibitions (many of which were produced to travel regionally in the UK), education and training, research and publications. Ground-breaking at the time, not only for its organisational structure but also for its mission – to support dialogue and practice that was not focused on the intellectual and cultural priorities of the West – InIVA was an outcome of the Black Arts Movement of the 1980s. It provided crucial access to the artists, theorists and philosophers who were starting to influence the art world, producing public events that gave access to the cross-disciplinary debates which were otherwise happening behind closed doors. In this respect, InIVA was among the first non-academic organisations anywhere in the world to champion research-orientated programming.

InIVA's inaugural event was a conference that took place at the Tate Gallery in 1994. Entitled *Global Visions: towards a new internationalism* in the visual arts, it was the first time artists, cultural theorists and curators – including Rasheed Aareen, Jean Fisher, Hal Foster, Geeta Kapur, Sarat Maharaj, Olu Oguibe, Elisabeth Sussman and Fred Wilson – came together to publicly discuss, and then publish, cultural perspectives on internationalism and multiculturalism.[27] The conference started from

27. Jean Fisher (ed.), *Global Visions: Towards a New Internationalism in the Visual Arts.* Kala Press in association with the Institute of International Visual Arts. 1994.

the principle that 'Postmodernity demands a different concept of internationalism', acknowledging both the practical and intellectual urgencies at stake, particularly the need to embrace pluralistic views prompted by multiculturalism. Speakers were invited to address the questions: How does the term 'international' fit into definitions of contemporary practice at the close of the millennium? Is there a desire for a new concept of the international? Which questions are posed for curatorial work, collecting and the construction of postmodern art history?[28]

A comprehensive overview of the event is beyond the scope of this essay, but it is relevant to briefly reflect on the contributions of curators Hou Hanru and Gerardo Mosquera, each of whom focused on the discrepancies between ideas of cultural marginalisation, on the one hand, and the decentralisation of culture on the other, drawing on their experiences of international curating from respective bases in China and Cuba.

Hou Hanru, who had just relocated from Beijing to Paris, stressed the difference between New Internationalism and previous internationalisms which imposed a Western utopic model on the world, suggesting that; '"New Internationalism" reflects the pluralisation of international political, economic and cultural relationships, as well as the contradictions and conflicts that have emerged'.[29] From this perspective, the binaries of Western modernism versus postmodernism, or even colonialism and post-colonialism, did not have the same resonance in China and could not, therefore, be the lens through which foreign curators and writers could understand Chinese contemporary art. The real problem with the notion of an international art world, at least from the perspective of places like China, was a lack of knowledge about the impetus for art practice, which was further exacerbated by the tendency to perpetuate clichés: 'The writers of most articles on Chinese contemporary art, instead of discussing the artists' creative efforts and the cultural-intellectual values of the work, concentrate their energy and interests on revealing how the 'unofficial' artists suffer from political pressure in the country, as if the significance of both artists and work can only be found in ideological struggles'.[30]

Hou went on to explain that this pervasive judgment from the outside was affecting internal production on many levels, not least

28. Gavin Jantjes, 'Preface' in Jean Fisher, op cit. p. 7-8.
29. Hou Hanru, 'Entropy; Chinese Artists, Western Art Institutions, A New Internationalism' in Jean Fisher, op cit. p. 79.
30. Ibid. p. 82.

because of the impact of the market on certain types of work which, in turn, undermined what he termed 'avant-garde research', which, he emphasised, was also central to the development of the Chinese art system. Furthermore, he suggested that the practices of many artists – such as Gu Dexin, Huang Yongping and Jang Jiechang – which were consistently concerned with the urgent problems of being International, were frequently considered nothing other than Western-influenced: 'The problem is that the authors understand multiculturalism as a kind of 'regionalism' or 'nationalism' while the artist understands it as internationalism, never refusing international exchanges and mutual influences'.[31] The slippage Hou described, between what the artist is communicating and what is perceived, raises serious questions about cultural translation, or the lack of it. There is no guarantee that meaning is communicated through the direct translation of language and little attempt to dig below the surface on the part of the critics and curators researching the work. Perhaps more importantly, Hou highlighted how so-called interest in art practice outside of one's own context amounts to little more than an affirmation of one's existing prejudices.

In his presentation, 'Some Problems in Transcultural Curating', Gerardo Mosquera opened by stating that 'There are many different centres and peripheries and relations among them', but that globalisation had created a false perception that everything was interconnected. In fact, the situation was one of 'axial globalization' between centres of power, interspersed with 'zones of silence'. His central concern was that, with the rise of the curator as author of international exhibitions, the chosen mode of research was increasingly that of explorer, which was both inevitable and problematic: 'It implies an acceptance of the curators' capacity to make transcultural judgments and, from here, the belief in the universality of art. To deny it would imply an anagnoresis: acknowledging that a selection is made from local criteria (from a particular institution, culture and aesthetic) leaving behind any globalizing discourse'.[32]

Mosquera spoke of working outside his own immediate knowledge during his research for the Havana Biennial,[33] through which he determined that 'one has to start by accepting an ample margin of contradiction' and the need to curate with 'both eyes and ears' as well as developing

31. Ibid. p. 81. The three artists cited were all selected to participate in *Magiciens de la Terre*.

32. Gerardo Mosquera, 'Some Problems in Transcultural Curating' in Jean Fisher, op cit. p. 136.

33. Ibid. p. 133-136.

small and diverse curatorial teams as opposed to using advisors. Mosquera's notion of team curating was only just gaining traction at the time of this conference, with the first large-scale collaboration happening in Venice in 1993, when 13 curators were invited to curate sections of the *Aperto*.[34] The same was true of biennials developing outside traditional art centres, which were also just starting to proliferate: for example Dak'art began in Senegal in 1992; the Asia-Pacific Triennial was instigated in Queensland in 1993; Bamako Encounters in Mali (1994); the Gwangju Biennale and the Johannesburg Biennale were initiated in 1995; and Shanghai, Mercosul and Manifesta biennials began in 1996, to name but a few. To conclude, he outlined that the truly international circulation of art ultimately had to mean more than the democratisation of current circuits, going on to anticipate the evolution of curatorial thinking and infrastructural development that would occur in the new millennium: 'The transformation has to include the internal mechanisms of circulation. This implies a change of formats, cultural extension, work within schools and communities, the use of press and mass media, and the development of many other ways emerging from local characteristics, interests and inventiveness. It must become a part of the responsibility of every curator of the Third World, as well as elsewhere, who aspires to a true plurality of the diffusion of art'.[35]

In a roundtable discussion, entitled 'Global Tendencies', published by *Artforum* in 2003, Hans Ulrich Obrist looked back on this phenomenon: 'The peripheral biennials, at least until the end of the decade, were not just 'another biennale again'; it was really a time when they were tools, helping a new generation of artists from different cultural backgrounds become internationally visible and also helping curators test ideas'. Later in the discussion, he described the impact of the decade on his own work: 'When I started to curate at the beginning of the '90s I very often had two or three years to research exhibitions. By the end of the '90s I often only had six or eight months'. He went on to explain how, when he and Hou Hanru started work on *Cities on the Move* in 1996, 'We couldn't just say, "We want three years for our research" because then the show would never have taken place. So there was a kind of given parameter. The question became: How, within this parameter, do we change the

34. Curators of *Aperto* include: Helena Kontova, Francesco Bonami, Jeffrey Deitch, Nicolas Bourriaud, Matthew Slotover, Berta Sichel, Kong Changan, Robert Nickas, Thomas Locher, Benjamin Weil, Mike Hubert, Antonio d'Avossa and Rosma Scuteri.
35. Gerardo Mosquera in Jean Fisher, op cit. p. 137-139.

rules of the game? And we thought it might be interesting to develop a show that wouldn't always stay the same, but to actually have research occur throughout the travel schedule'.[36]

Ten years on, in an interview with the author, Obrist reiterated that it was as a result of travelling to Bangkok to give a talk for the exhibition *do it* in 1996 that he understood the potential of this generative strategy. In particular, he responded to the artists and the energy of the art scene in a place he might otherwise not have visited:

> The penny really dropped about how important Asia was going to be for the twenty-first century and so I called up Hou Hanru, whom I had first met in the late-'80s through Yan Pei Ming and Huang Yong Ping, and said let's collaborate. I don't think I would have done *Cities on the Move* without this experience. It just became so apparent that it was really the urgent show to do. Then this led to research in Korea, Indonesia, Malaysia, and Singapore. All these places revealed themselves to be incredible art centres.[37]

Obrist's portrayal of the importance of a collegial network independent of institutional structures is indicative of a significant moment in the development of the profession. Between curators living and working in different geographies, there was burgeoning recognition that expertise could be shared and built upon. In turn, this collaborative practice enabled experimental research methods and the generation of more responsive curatorial forms; *Cities on the Move* is one such example.

A travelling exhibition like no other before it, *Cities on the Move* literally played out the contradictions between local traditions and rapidly expanding globalised societies being experienced in Asian mega-cities. Initially developed for Secession in Vienna, it was imagined as a complex, self-perpetuating system, spreading through the galleries, into the offices and out into the street. Intended to travel from the outset, the show was established with a roster of up to 100 artists and architects at any given

36. Tim Griffin et al., 'Global Tendencies: Globalism and the Large-Scale Exhibition'. Artforum. November 2003. p. 152-163. Roundtable participants include: Tim Griffin, introduction; James Meyer, moderator; Francesco Bonami, Catherine David, Okwui Enwezor, Hans-Ulrich Obrist, Martha Rosler and Yinka Shonibare.
37. Kate Fowle and Hans Ulrich Obrist, 'Progress Report' in Do It. Independent Curators International and DAP. 2013. p. 49.

time, changing and evolving over two years, across six venues in Europe, the US and Asia.[38]

In order to create a flexible, yet coherent, framework that would allow the project autonomy in the different spaces where it would be installed, the curators worked with architects, Rem Koolhaas and Ole Scheeren. They developed a system which re-used materials at each venue to create the future structure of the exhibition. This revealed construction methods and transformed existing architectural elements to shift the perceptions of the regular visitor while also enabling a low-cost process of accumulating materials to emulate environments that inspired the subject of the show. Spaces were carved into typologies of the city called 'the architecture compression centre', 'the pleasure district' and 'the political protest room', among others, with artists producing ad hoc interventions within this infrastructure. Providing opportunities for unmediated relationships between works while generating its own mutations, the exhibition embodied the chaos, claustrophobia and cacophony of the cities that artists were working in and the subjects with which they were dealing. Attention-seeking and headache-inducing, the exhibition was as performative as the work it presented.[39]

If it was Martin's desire for *Magiciens de la Terre* to be a site for dialogue and exchange, it could be said that Hou and Obrist wanted *Cities on the Move* to be a space of contamination and reinterpretation, exposing relationships rather than facilitating them. By constructing an imaginary in which artworks could coexist, the possibility of representing culture at borderlines, as Bhabha would have it, was redundant. In fact, this exhibition removed the border completely, becoming a frontline upon which the audience unwittingly stumbled. Nothing and no one was 'represented'. Everything just was in that moment in time. To then restage the project over and over again, responding to new sites and introducing new works, was to remove any possibility of the exhibition proving a curatorial thesis or producing a fixed meaning. Instead, exhibition-making was

38. Vienna Secession, Vienna; CAPC Musée d'Art Contemporain de Bordeaux, Bordeaux; MoMA PS1, New York; The Louisiana Museum of Modern Art, Copenhagen; The Hayward Gallery, London; Bangkok (as a city-intervention project) MoMA PS1, New York; The Louisiana Museum of Modern Art, Copenhagen; The Hayward Gallery, London; Bangkok (as a city-intervention project)

39. For descriptions of the project see: Andrew Gellatly, 'Cities on the Move'. *Frieze*. Issue 48. September-October 1999. http://www.frieze.com/issue/review/cities_on_the_move/; Douglas Fogle, 'Cities on the Move'. *Flash Art*, No. 199. 1998. http://www.flashartonline.com/interno.php?pagina=articolo_det&id_art=382&det=ok&title=CITIES-ON-THE-MOVE; Also see http://www.buro-os.com/?s=hans+ulrich+Obrist+

established as an evolutionary process, which, according to Obrist, is 'how the show learns and grows', reinforcing the notion that a show is somehow a living organism through which curators develop their practice.

Viewed retrospectively, 1997 – the year *Cities on the Move* began to travel – may be seen as a landmark for exhibitions, not least because of Catherine David's documenta X and Okwui Enwezor's Johannesburg Biennale. Both shows are now widely discussed for their expanded formats, their initiation of discursive frameworks and 'platforms' and, crucially, for confronting both the issue and subject of globalisation. As Michael Brenson proclaimed, in response to the Rockefeller summit of the same year, the age of the curator had indeed begun. As this essay has demonstrated, this was not only because of the increased number of shows and curatorial opportunities, or the so-called power this bestowed on curators, but also because of the growth of a profession into a practice, which created a field – or set of coordinates – of its own.

If the 1990s witnessed the rise of international exhibitions and the biennial boom – which opened the potential for dialogues between divergent practitioners around the world, as well as the establishment of contemporary curating as we understand it today – it could be said that the 2000s brought new institutional models to fruition, initially with curators taking the helm of older European and US spaces and transforming their functions and then with the emergence of institutions in new geographical locations. From the Colección Jumex in Mexico City and Inhotim near Bello Horizonte, the Mori Art Museum in Tokyo and the Ullens Center for Contemporary Art in Beijing to Garage Center for Contemporary Culture in Moscow and Tranzit in Vienna, Prague, Bucharest, Budapest and Bratislava; from Sán Art in Ho Chi Minh City to Salt in Istanbul, from the Centre for Contemporary Art in Lagos to the Raw Material Company in Dakar, these institutions are introducing new programming priorities, new audiences for contemporary art, new funding structures and yet further expansion of the curatorial role.

What these institutions have in common is that they have established more permanent platforms around the world from which to generate collaborative programming and accumulate research that goes beyond the mandates of the traditional contemporary art museum and biennial. But, as these new infrastructures, networks and curatorial strategies have emerged as decentralisation and instability have been accepted as operational norms, how far has the curator come in successfully navigating both the expanded contexts and ongoing questions of what working internationally really means?

By 2011, the art world appeared totally absorbed with, and implicated in, global politics. The initial flare was the march on Washington in late December 2010, following the Smithsonian's censorship of artist David Wojnarowicz's video in the National Portrait Gallery's *Hide/Seek* show. This artwork, produced in 1987 in response to the AIDS crisis, was removed after a handful of conservative radicals objected to a brief scene showing ants crawling on a crucifix. This ignited vivid recollections of the Culture Wars for those opposing the clampdown. Then, on a completely different scale, in the early months of 2011, the beginning of the Arab Spring made a huge impact as the Internet and social media fuelled worldwide calls for allegiance and participation in uprisings, bringing viral solidarity in the global art community. Attentions were momentarily diverted on 17 March, with the launch of the petition to boycott Guggenheim Abu Dhabi over migrant workers' rights in relation to the building of a museum on Saadiyat Island, when artist, Ai Weiwei, was detained in Beijing on 3 April for what officials alluded to as 'economic crimes.' This happened just days before curator, Jack Persekian, was sacked from his position as the director of the Sharjah Biennial, triggered by the more specifically political content of a work.

These protests and the prolific ensuing media commentary on the breakdown in international art relations were all eclipsed on 17 September when the Occupy Movement ignited around the world. Penetrating institutions of culture and commerce alike, while creating a fresh language of rebellion, Occupy created a feedback loop between art and activism that has, in equal parts, been taken advantage of and contested during the two years that have followed.

On the one hand, art and its infrastructures have become fully embedded in contemporary culture at large and increasingly located at the heart of global economics, while, on the other, it is evident that we are in a stage at which the production of biennials and the international circulation of projects and ideas has reached the limits of the official infrastructures that support them. Meanwhile, the new institutions are not yet fully established, and the ways in which they will create context-specific operational methods are still open to question. Time will tell what impact these new venues will have once they have proven sustainability, but it is already possible to ascertain that widespread connectivity with art – rather than a distancing from what it stands for – has started to expand audiences as the places and forms of its presentation continue to develop.

With the creation of a curatorial discourse and its widening dissemination beyond academia, curatorial knowledge has grown exponentially around the world; we don't find ourselves facing exactly the same practical and ideological dilemmas as Jean-Hubert Martin in 1986 when he made the first statements about Magiciens de la Terre, but the question of 'how' to practice remains as urgent, if for no other reason than that our options are so much broader. In a very short time, we have arrived at a point at which there are tensions between curatorial theory and practice, as well as cultural or political theory and curatorial practice. This is beginning to divide the field between those who think of curating as a means to an end and those who want to refine the practice for the sake of its form. As with any discipline, there is room for both. What is more important is the ways in which this plays out as the places in which contemporary curating occurs expand geographically, bringing new cultural and political imperatives into the equation.

Providing the tools with which an audience can ask questions and draw independent conclusions has become as important as providing curatorial frameworks for artistic practices. In an art world that is increasingly intertwined with real life politics, to curate *is* to navigate political machinery while revealing it, and the responsibility of the curator is to present work in ways that neither obfuscate nor distort meaning. Rather than just concerning ourselves with the balance between the representation and form of the artwork, we are now also responsible for thinking about the representation of emerging contexts as they continue to diversify.

We are fast arriving at a time when a new generation of curators will come of age. Starting to practice in the new millennium, this is a generation that has worked outside the traditional Western centres and museum structures as much as within them. These curators take for granted that wherever they work is also a centre. They have gained their experience through the new institutions and curatorial models that have emerged in the past two decades. They base their practices on responding to local situations, adapting what they learn from elsewhere to what matters where they are.

When this new generation take the reins, perhaps we can start to fathom what a truly international art world looks like and what new forms it can take. To paraphrase what Gerardo Mosquera said more than twenty years ago, it seems certain that one who aspires to a true plurality of the dissemination of art has to start by accepting an ample margin of contradiction.

173 - 185

HOME WORKS

Sidsel Nelund

Home Works: A Forum on Cultural Practices has been organised by Ashkal Alwan: The Lebanese Association for Plastic Arts in Beirut, Lebanon, since 2002, curated by Ashkal Alwan's founder and director, Christine Tohmé, every one to three years.[1] It takes place over one to two weeks as a series of artistic interventions, exhibitions, lectures, panels, publication launches and screenings. Participants are artists, intellectuals, performers and writers who present their reflections on themes of particular significance for the region.[2] For example, in 2008, after the 2006 bombings of Lebanon by Israel, the themes of disaster and catastrophe were chosen by the curators; in 2010, as the Abu Dhabi Tourism and Culture Authority began constructing a Guggenheim, Louvre and New York University outpost on Saadiyat Island, in a bid to influence the politics of cultural practices in the region, the theme of Saadiyat Island was selected.

Focusing on the themes of Home Works and their responsiveness to the region helps us to understand how this forum on cultural practices might be thought of as an act of curating research. Taking Home Works as a case study, I propose that 'curating research' does not mean exhibiting research, but rather setting up topics which are investigated through various media, sensibilities and practices. These investigations create a constellation which, in and of itself, can spark reflection and discussion. Curating research thereby operates on two levels; the first is in choosing and framing the topic, the second is in selecting and gathering different investigations, which (together and via the programming) enable and enhance reflexive dialogues among audiences and participants. 'Curating research' thus includes a verb, which differs from the noun and its descriptor found in 'research exhibition'. This suggests an emphasis on action; however, in the case of Home Works, the how seems to be as important as the what. It is to the how and what of curating research that I will turn in the following

1. Co-curators and assistant curators are Masha Refka (2005), Zeynep Oz (2010), Victoria Lupton (2013). For the 2013 edition, the exhibition programme was curated by Tarek Abou El Fetouh.

2. The themes have been dislocation (2002); the promise of globalisation (2003); presence (2005); disaster and catastrophe, recomposing desire and sex practices (2008); education, Saadiyat Island, sound and citizenry, the odd years, and militarism (2010); and the notion of trial (2013).

analysis of Home Works in relation to knowledge-producing formats, production conditions and audience intimacy.[3]

Producing Knowledge

Of Lebanese descent, Christine Tohmé started organising exhibitions in 1994, in Beirut's urban areas, which was novel at the time. Her intention, in bringing people together around the production and sharing of knowledge via the serial forum of Home Works, was to make people 'sit and talk' with one another. Rather than making an exhibition or a biennial, this implied creating sustained dialogue in a region in which she found things were not being rigorously discussed after the Lebanese civil war (1975–1990).[4] The ethical dimension of facing one another explains why Home Works was called a forum and not a festival or exhibition,[5] because forum emphasises a coming-together in public space and a focus on the people 'living here' – in Lebanon and the region.[6] It is perhaps because of this that no edition of Home Works is similar to another; it changes every time, according to the possibilities provided by the city and its people and institutions. One thing that is stable, though, is the core audience that follows the programme and, no less importantly, meets in public space for informal gatherings around eating, drinking and transportation. Moreover, the original Roman use of the term 'forum' denotes 'a public square or marketplace used for judicial and other business'.[7] Facing one another thus also connotes the juridical and alludes to a process of reconciliation, which Lebanon was deprived of after the civil war ended. The main distinction is that, in Home Works, the reconciliation process occurs not in a courtroom, via testimonies, but in a cultural setting in which different kinds of interdisciplinary, reflexive and affective expressions take place around given topics. The initial impetus,

3. It is necessary to mention that I am academically indebted to Ashkal Alwan and Home Works. After being an MA co-student with Christine Tohmé at the Department of Visual Cultures, Goldsmiths, University of London, in 2006–07, I went to Lebanon to research the visual archive of Ashkal Alwan for two months. I later came back to attend Home Works IV and V in 2008 and 2010. During the process of writing this article, I participated in Home Works 6 and visited Ashkal Alwan twice to carry out research about Home Works in relation to my PhD.
4. Interview conducted with Christine Tohmé on 6 February 2013.
5. A precedent is the Ayloul Festival for Arts in Beirut, organised annually by the writer, Elias Khoury, and the cultural broker Pascale Feghali, from 1997 till 2001.
6. Interview on 6 February 2013, op cit.
7. New Oxford American Dictionary.

to facilitate a reconciliation process through cultural practices, has led to further discursive and practical consolidation of the art scene in Lebanon.

Out of many possible moments in the history of Home Works, the focus of the following is on two events that produced knowledge in relation to the local scene. One event is a lecture by the French curator, Catherine David, from 2002, which created a discourse about the Lebanese art scene. Inviting David to take part in the first Home Works demonstrated a desire to solicit an analysis of Lebanese art practices, and her lecture serves as an example of the ways in which the Lebanese art scene is being framed, aesthetically and politically, through academic and curatorial research undertaken in relation to Home Works. The other event is a performance lecture by the Lebanese artist, Walid Raad, from 2005, which merged the political and affective in a research-based format. The performance lecture is a format that fits well with tendencies in the Lebanese art scene, which is known for being cerebral while attending to images in a careful way.[8]

The lecture given by Catherine David at the first edition of Home Works - entitled 'Learning from Beirut: Contemporary Aesthetic Practices in Lebanon: Stakes and Conditions for Experimental, Cultural and Aesthetic Practices in Lebanon and Elsewhere' - paved the way for a consideration of local cultural and political reality. David argued that, despite the civil war causing a vacuum in cultural production, Beirut was a 'privileged' art scene because, in the absence of institutions, practices had not been fully instrumentalised. For her, these conditions had given rise to a critical, 'experimental contemporary aesthetic practice'.[9] Taking inspiration from Jacques Rancière's politics of aesthetics,[10] David defined aesthetic practice as a 'contemporary project that can articulate the discursive and the visual, at times, in a complex manner'[11] and she framed both the

8. Kaelen Wilson-Goldie, 'Home Makeover'. Scene and Herd. *Artforum*.com. 2013. http://www.artforum.com/diary/id=41652. Rabih Mroué has moreover also worked carefully with the performance lecture format.
The practices of Joana Hadjithomas and Khalil Joreige, Lamia Joreige, Rabih Mroué, Walid Raad and Akram Zaatari all attend, in different ways, to 'the image' in relation to topics such as memory, politics, the archive and history. For an analysis of some of these practices in relation to 'the image', see T.J. Demos, 'Out of Beirut: Mobile Histories and the Politics of Fiction' in The Migrant Image: The Art and Politics of Documentary during Global Crisis. Duke University Press. 2013. p. 177-200.

9. Catherine David, 'Learning from Beirut: Contemporary Aesthetic Practices in Lebanon; Stakes and Conditions for Experimental, Cultural, and Aesthetic Practices in Lebanon and Elsewhere' in Christine Tohmé and Mona Abu Rayyan (eds.), Home Works: A Forum on Cultural Practices in the Region (Egypt, Iran, Iraq, Lebanon, Palestine and Syria). Ashkal Alwan. 2003. p. 32.

10. See Jacques Rancière, The Politics of Aesthetics. Continuum. 2006.

11. Catherine David, 2003, op cit. p. 36.

Lebanese art scene and the forum, providing a vocabulary with which to speak about the scene, noting that the void of institutions gave way to new kinds of art projects of a discursive and visual character.

Speaking not of artworks but of discursive and visual projects is pertinent to Home Works. Not all exhibitors have a visual arts education; some are philosophers, filmmakers and architects who use aesthetics as a means of commenting on political and social matters. This interdisciplinary appeal is different from more traditional exhibition models, in which, put simply, the limit between artists and non-artists is marked by artists participating in the exhibition and non-artists in seminars and publications around the exhibition. In Home Works, artists can be theorists and theorists can be artists as long as they contribute significantly to discussion of the chosen topic. Again, we see how the established features of the Lebanese art scene are reflected in the format of Home Works.

As Home Works has nurtured an identity, providing discourse about the Lebanese art scene, it has also encouraged the development of formats, one of which is the performance lecture. A prime example is Walid Raad's I Feel a Great Desire to Meet the Masses Once Again, which reflects on border crossings, interrogations and suspicions around artistic practice after 11 September 2001. The performance narrates Raad's exile from Lebanon to the United States in 1983, interwoven with descriptions of an interrogation he experienced while flying from Rochester to New York City, in which his artistic practice was suspected of terrorism.[12] Raad tells the story from the perspective of a character who is trustworthy in style, story and appearance, providing photographic documentation and demonstrating attention to detail. Through his fragmentary descriptions, though, the artist-narrator exposes the fragility of his memory, which prompts us to question whatever he tells us. Ultimately, the question is: Is artistic practice similar to terrorism? Treating artists as terrorists is an ethical issue, which, told in this way, is rendered surreal. However, the fiction embroils the audience in a train of thought that veers close to real events and the blur of memory and perception. In this way, the complex performance lecture conveys, on the one hand, that fiction is a way of understanding past realities and, on the other hand, that reality may seem unreal.

12. Raad's performance lecture also tells the story of the artist Steve Kurtz from Critical Art Ensemble, who was imprisoned for cultivating chemicals. The chemicals were intended for an exhibition, but the CIA interpreted them as weapons of terrorism. Steve Kurtz likewise participated in Home Works III.

The format of performance lecture fundamentally questions positivist and fact-based regimes of academic knowledge production.[13] Raad's variant shows that sharing a personal account – whether fictional or real – has an impact upon the broader political context, by providing a space for the affective.[14] The knowledge produced is of an experience-based character, coming together via narration, political content and images. Younger artists connected to the Lebanese art scene have taken up the affective space of the performance lecture. The latest edition of Home Works presented two such examples. Marwa Arsanios's 'Have You Ever Killed a Bear? Or Becoming Jamila' considered the role of the female fighter in resistance movements of the 1960s and 1970s, and Haig Aivazian's 'To Neither Confirm nor Deny That the Matter neither Reflected nor Absorbed Light' was about the geopolitical implications of the then Managing Director of the International Monetary Fund, Dominique Strauss-Kahn, being charged for sexual assault against a hotel maid in New York in 2011. These two examples show that the format of the performance lecture, keeps being developed as reflexions on pressing topics at the boundary between the personal and political.

David's lecture and Raad's performance lecture (and the ways in which it has been taken up by younger artists) demonstrate that Home Works allows for a sustained development of research-based formats (like the performance lecture) and for continuous discourse production not only in relation to the topics of each forum but also to the specificities of Lebanese art production. The forum, as a coming-together in public space, simultaneously allows for the affective (personal-public) and cognitive (traditional academic lectures) as the art scene's practices are developed and sustained.

13. Patricia Milder, 'Teaching as Art: The Contemporary Lecture-Performance'. PAJ: A Journal of Performance and Art 33 (1). The MIT Press. 2011. p. 13–27.
14. When using the term affective, I refer to the work of Kathleen Stewart on 'ordinary affects' as being at once publicly circulating and personally intimate and the work of Lauren Berlant on 'intimacy' as that which makes an impact on us and produces something. See Kathleen Stewart, Ordinary Affects. Duke University Press. 2007 and Lauren Berlant, 'Intimacy: A Special Issue'. Critical Inquiry 24 (2) (January 1). The University of Chicago Press. 1998. p. 281–288.

Providing Production Conditions

But how are the practices developed and sustained? The first edition of Home Works counted four types of activity - lectures, performances, exhibitions and films - whereas the 2010 version counted ten, including categories such as publications, workshops, panels, artists' talks, music and research projects. The activities have possibly increased as a result of participating practitioners naming their own activity. The format of Home Works has thus expanded according to the projects it has included instead of adjusting projects to existing categories. Allowing the forum to shape itself in such a way is another aspect of the responsive curatorial strategy. But there are also controlled elements in its realisation - for instance, the non-commissioned performances, lectures and artworks brought from outside of Lebanon - which work like pillars in the programme and serve as inspiration within the local milieu.

Funding for Home Works has largely come from Europe (Prince Claus Fund and different national council funding), the Middle East (Fondation Saradar, the Arab Fund for Arts and Culture and others) and the US (Ford Foundation), which was a necessity as there is little public funding in Lebanon for events like Home Works. This funding has allowed the forum to expand not only in its activities but also in scope and size. The first edition of Home Works was regional in outlook, but, with the second, its perspective changed to 'concentrate on kindred artistic and intellectual concerns that are operative all over the world'.[15] Whereas the twenty-five participants of the first Home Works were largely native to the region, the two last editions each had a hundred participants from various parts of the world, including Pad.ma from Mumbai (2010), Judi Werthein from Buenos Aires/New York (2010) and Cao Fei from Beijing (2013).

Despite the change from being regionally focused to being internationally connected, there is a local grounding in the recurrence of Lebanese artists in the programme. For example, the actor, director and visual artist, Rabih Mroué, has presented work in all six Home Works. The visual artist, curator and co-founder of the Arab Image Foundation, Akram Zaatari, actor and visual artist, Lina Saneh, philosopher and artist, Jalal Toufic and filmmakers, Joana Hadjithomas and Khalil Joreige, have participated

15. Christine Tohmé, 'Introduction' in Christine Tohmé (ed), Home Works: A Forum on Cultural Practices. Ashkal Alwan. 2005. p. 11.

in five Home Works.[16] Many of their projects have been commissioned, with the forum operating as a generator of artistic production. This is significant as there are few local funding sources for artists, which means that Home Works has economically sustained local production over the years. In addition to this, foreign artists, like the Otolith Group, have participated at various times and created commissioned artworks for Home Works. That both local and foreign cultural practitioners participate in *reflecting* on themes of urgency creates a sustained professional and public dialogue and a possibility for creating affinity bonds over the years.

In a critique of Home Works, however, the Rotterdam and Middle East-based curator and critic, Nat Müller, raises the problem that the focus on the international arena has kept the local Lebanese public away.[17] She compares this shift to the importation of Western museum models to the colonies in the late nineteenth century, thereby positing Home Works as part of a self-colonising strategy that is no better than traditional museums' way of organising national history and knowledge.[18] Müller's point is highly relevant as Home Works must be aware of how it challenges and attends to its topics as well as which frameworks it creates for the sharing and production of knowledge.

The amount of foreigners attending the forum increased until 2010 before stagnating in 2013. It might be due to growing political instability in that period or to curators responding to the critique of catering to foreign audiences. But the balance between the local and aforementioned kindred spirits all over the world is important to maintain, because it contains the possibility of learning from other perspectives and, thereby, qualifying cultural intellectual thought and practice. What is significant, though, is that those Lebanese cultural practitioners who have had the chance to participate in, and attend, Home Works have gained in terms of

16. Other recurring artists and theorists are Abbas Baydoun (2002, 2005 and 2010), Ghassan Salhab (2002, 2003 and 2008), the Otolith Group (2005, 2008 and 2010), Marwan Rechmaoui (2003, 2008 and 2010), Tony Chakar (2005, 2008, 2010 and 2013), Ayreen Anastas (2005, 2008 and 2010), Walid Raad (2005, 2010 and 2013), Stephen Wright (2003 and 2008), Emily Jacir (2003 and 2008), Rasha Salti (2002 and 2003), Lamia Joreige (2003 and 2008), Elia Suleiman (2002 and 2003), T.J. Demos (2008 and 2010), Hassan Khan (2002 and 2008), Wael Shawky (2008, 2010 and 2013), Roy Samaha (2003, 2008 and 2013), Maher Abi Samra (2005 and 2008) and Wissam Sadeh (2005 and 2008).

17. Catherine David has expressed a similar critique, insinuating that Home Works had lost its potential to create truly interesting discussions due to its internationalisation. Unpublished conversation, entitled 'Encuentro con Catherine David', held at Centro Gabriela Mistral in Santiago de Chile, 2010.

18. Nat Müller, '006.01 Interview with Ashkan Sepahvand by Nat Müller'. 006.01 See http://www.artterritories.net/?page_id=1716.

production conditions, inspiration, affinities, sustained and professional dialogue and an open environment for developing formats.

Animating Intimacy

All Home Works events are free to attend and often start in the afternoon, which allows international guests to have meetings during the day and for locals to join in after work. Being a forum, and not only an exhibition, creates a social environment in which people take part in social and intellectual activities before, during and after timetabled events. Historically, Beirut has not had an obvious location - a museum or art institution - that could host the whole event (this changed, to a certain extent, with the opening of Beirut Art Center in 2009 and Ashkal Alwan's own space in 2010), which has meant that activities took place (and still do) in theatres, cinemas, galleries and other locations throughout the city. While Home Works increasingly provides shuttle buses between venues, this dispersal of events throughout a city with no public transport prompts audience members to organise themselves, bargaining with one of the many 'service'[19] chauffeurs or getting a lift with other attendees. The importance of sharing transport - the non-discursive taking place in and around timetabled events - is difficult to theorise but crucial to Home Works. For want of a better word, I describe this as intimacy, as it spans the seriousness and playfulness of close and shared experiences of significance between private and public.[20] Focusing, however, on timetabled events, the following tentatively suggests how the politics of affective intimacy is brought about in two instances: a face-to-face encounter and a collective experience.

It is afternoon, a Saturday in May 2013, in the Metropolis Empire Sofil cinema in Ashrafieh, on the Eastern side of the city centre. The artist, Kader Attia, presents a 'reparative' art project, which consists of repaired everyday objects from Rwanda and Algeria. The objects embody Attia's idea that 'repair is a ground for a new aesthetics' - not a return to something, but a reworking of something.[21] He relates the reworking and repairing of objects to the history of Algeria and Rwanda and their attempts to politically and legally come to terms with - or repair - past civil

19. Shared taxis with a price fixed according to distance.
20. Once again, I am evoking Lauren Berlant's concept of intimacy (see note 14).
21. Unpublished lecture by Kader Attia, entitled 'Rwanda, Algeria - from tradition to modernity of forgiveness', held at Home Works 6 in Beirut, 2013.

wars and genocide. In a question and answer session organised around the presentation of the project, an Algerian woman raises her hand. She does not agree with the term 'civil war' in relation to Algeria: rather, she argues, in her environment people talk about the 'black decade'. Attia responds that starting to call it 'civil war', or at least talking about what to call it, is part of the reparative practice. The woman keeps questioning him, and both mention their affective involvement and lost relatives. Even though the situation remains unresolved, something seemed to happen.

The following Wednesday, a live broadcasting event is taking place in a run-down showroom in Mar Mikhael, the newly trendy Armenian neighbourhood further to the east. The London-based artist, Lawrence Abu Hamdan, is orchestrating a radio project on the poetics and politics of language, Our Lines Are Now Open, in collaboration with London based curator, Nora Razian, and Beirut-based research project, 98weeks (founded in 2007 by the cousins Marwa Arsanios, an artist, and Mirene Arsanios, a writer). 98weeks consists of research projects running for 98 weeks and, like Home Works, their approach is topic driven, but with a reflexive, material and playful approach.(22) The first selected topic was Beirut's urban space; then it was Arab cultural and art historical magazines from the 1930s to today and now it is feminism. Based in Mar Mikhael, their project space is inclusive; workshops are open to the public for a relatively small fee and attract not just artists. The space serves as a base for the current research project, a small-scale publishing house and a venue for talks, events and screenings by artists and theorists passing through Beirut. A popular part of the programme is cabaret nights, in which the floor is open to anyone who wants to perform. Many artists from this generation also participate in, and attend, Home Works, but it is telling that 98weeks insists on a less institutional framework and is considered more a part of the artistic practice of the founders. For Home Works 6, 98weeks rented a closed showroom across the street to house their temporary radio project.

A microphone stands on an oval table in the centre of the room, and people approach it one by one to read aloud from banned or smuggled literature. One is reading The Da Vinci Code; another a 'trashy spy novel' about the 2005 assassination of the then president, Rafic Hariri. Both

22. I am also academically indebted to 98weeks, which I have followed since its inception in 2007 and collaborated with since 2010. For Home Works 6, they invited me to participate in the radio project Our Lines Are Now Open on the poetics and politics of speech and feminism.

are banned in Lebanon; The Da Vinci Code in other countries worldwide. Other books are in Persian, French, English and Spanish. Some are read via Skype; some lie on the table for further inspection. The collective act is playful and performative. Voices mingle – some invited, some responding to an open call – plausibly tempted by the importance of articulating the absurdity of illegality via a public radio frequency that probably remains beyond the interest of local surveillance. From time to time, liquid drips from the leaking ceiling. People move in and out, drink beer, listen and chat, heated by the sun.

The topic of Home Works 6, in which these two moments took place, was 'trial', which especially related to the breakdown and reformation of political regimes throughout the twentieth century (in, for example, Algeria, Indonesia, Kosovo, Mozambique, Romania and Rwanda). Given the initiating impulse of Home Works in creating dialogue and facing one another, the notion of trial has been tangible throughout the six forums. As the Attia Q&A showed, arguments are put forward but Home Works rarely provides a judgment, and Tohmé and her team of curators stay in the background, listening and concentrating on the organisational aspect of the programming. Instead, the forum allows for a collective reflexion, featuring different voices with which each attendee or participant is left to grapple. Collectivity exists around an engagement with topics, as in the reading of Abu Hamdan, in which bodies partook in an intimate act of talking, sharing and blending. This collectivity becomes comparable to an organism in which research, knowledge and positions are shared and reshaped vis-à-vis affective situations. The programme fulfils, and sometimes exhausts, the audience, yet the commitment lasts days, weeks or years.

Opening Up

Considering the project of Home Works as a whole, the different layers of the how in relation to the what are now easier to separate. The urgency of topics is the main drive of organisers and participants, who, on the one side, want to create encounters and, on the other side, want to partake of these encounters. The curatorial practice of responsiveness allows for discourse production, the development of formats and voices in sustained artistic production. The more controllable part of curatorial practice is the non-commissioned projects and performances that work as pillars in the programme and provide inspiration for the scene. This mix of responsiveness and control, in a carefully planned programme with theoretical and practical affinities developed between participants and audiences over years, allows for a sharing of intimate events on the verge of the personal and the public. Curating research in this context arises from urgency and the movement between curatorial response and control, the public and personal, affect and discourse.

We have heard about 98weeks in Beirut, which represents a younger generation than Christine Tohmé and the regular participants of Home Works. Home Works has not only been influential in the regional context of the Middle East. In London, the work of Tohmé has inspired another ongoing research project – The Edgware Road Project, part of the Centre for Possible Studies hosted by the Serpentine Gallery, since 2009. In this, a series of artists is invited to work with the area around Edgware Road in London, home to a concentration of Arabic immigrants since the late 19th century. Christine Tohmé has been a consulting curator on the project, and the approach of the Centre for Possible Studies is highly inspired by both Ashkal Alwan and Townhouse Gallery in Cairo, both of which have 'the encounter' as one of their primary formats. As the statement of the Edgware Road Project reads, 'In each of these projects, the opening up of political dynamics in the local is contextualised by a series of global comings and goings, producing active cartographies, subversive diplomacies and imaginative modes of exchange'.[23] Having such an approach to Ashkal Alwan and seeing Home Works in that light is productive as it does not think in terms of insiders and outsiders but rather in terms of epistemic partners and research collaborators.

As mentioned, one of the challenges of conducting research in contemporary art is how to provide the space around which alternatively produced knowledge can be engendered. The ways in which Home Works will continue to pursue the task of curating research are not easy to predict. Many parameters have changed since Ashkal Alwan opened a new and spacious Home Workspace (named after Home Works), which now also hosts an art study programme, Home Workspace Program, a café and a research hub with a library and multipurpose auditorium for talks and events. Ashkal Alwan is expanding and the spatial context and intellectual production environment of Home Works is therefore changing. The fact that the curating of the exhibition part of Home Works 6 was

23. Centre for Possible Studies, 'About'. http://centreforpossiblestudies.wordpress.com/about

delegated to the Egyptian curator, Tarek Abou El Fetouh, and that the Turkish curator, Zeynep Oz, and the 98weeks research project participated with sizeable research projects suggests a desire to organise differently and include the voices and strategies of research of a younger generation in the regional art scene. However, a responsive curatorial style means that future ways of curating research will take shape alongside political, practical and intellectual developments that are yet to happen.

186 – 194

EVOLVING ARCHIVE: ASIA ART ARCHIVE

Hyunjoo Byeon

Between the *language (langue)* that defines the system of constructing possible sentences, and the *corpus* that passively collects the words that are spoken, the *archive* defines a particular level: that of a practice that causes a multiplicity of statements to emerge as so many regular events, as so many things to be dealt with and manipulated. It does not have the weight of tradition; and it does not constitute the library of all libraries, outside time and place; nor is it the welcoming oblivion that opens up to all new speech the operational field of its freedom; between tradition and oblivion, it reveals the rules of a practice that enables statements both to survive and to undergo regular modification. It is *the general system of the formation and transformation of statements.*(1)

Michel Foucault, 1969.

Research is an essential component within curatorial production. This has become increasingly apparent in recent years, as curatorial methods have been intensively discussed. In an effort to define the constitution and legitimacy of curating, a discursive field has been constructed, and various definitions of the curatorial have been formulated. These are seen to be different; however, there seems to be a mutual understanding that the curatorial encompasses not only the production of exhibitions but also the practice of generating knowledge and enquiry. In developing this new knowledge, research functions as a fundamental modality. Thus, when exploring expanded notions of the curatorial, it is significant to discuss the specific role of research. With this in mind, I aim to investigate Asia Art Archive (AAA) as a model of research practice, in a bid to illustrate how the archive incorporates research into the curatorial process through a series of attempts to examine the recent history of contemporary art practices. This will pave the way for an examination of how AAA has evolved into an organisation that performs the notion of the curatorial within a mode of research practice.

Founded in Hong Kong in 2000 by Claire Hsu, Johnson Chang and Ronald Arculli, Asia Art Archive - as its name indicates - has been documenting Asian contemporary art practices by collecting, archiving and conserving research materials. Claire Hsu initiated AAA in response to the need for an archive of contemporary art in Asia.(2) While studying History of Art at the University of London's School of Oriental and African

1. Michel Foucault, 'The Historical a priori and the Archive'. *The Archaeology of Knowledge*. Random House. 2010 [1969]. p. 130. Italics in original.
2. Cathy Yan, 'Conserving Asia Art'. *The Wall Street Journal*. 14 December 2010.

Studies, Hsu experienced difficulty in accessing information on contemporary art in Asia. After graduation, she began to work at the Hanart TZ Gallery in Hong Kong, and again realised the urgent need to make an information resource about Asian art, when working on the exhibition, *China's New Art, Post-1989* (which took place at various venues in Hong Kong, the US, Australia and Canada in 1993). Co-curated by Johnson Chang and Li Xianting, the exhibition outlined China's experimental art scene during the late 1980s and the early 1990s and required massive amounts of information. In response, Hsu decided to establish AAA, registering it as a non-profit organisation with the support of Chang, owner of Hanart TZ Gallery, who became one of AAA's board directors.

AAA is located on the 11th floor of a building on Hollywood Road in Hong Kong, where many commercial galleries and antique shops are situated. It may be hard to imagine that an archive of contemporary art is located in this region - known to be a popular tourist destination - yet more than 2,000 people per year visit the archive. Among them are students, teachers, artists, curators and collectors, and one third of the total visitors come from abroad to access materials that can only be found in AAA. In this way, the archive functions as a research platform for art practitioners, which was its stated intention. Hsu has said that 'AAA's collection is a valuable resource for curators planning their next exhibitions, professors designing courses of study, and students conducting research. It is an independent source of information for collectors and auction houses. And it is a source of inspiration for artists and theorists'.(3)

Starting out as a single bookshelf, AAA focused on collecting documents from Hong Kong, Taiwan and Mainland China in the first few years of its existence. Since then, it has grown to become one of the most comprehensive Asian art archives, containing approximately 45,000 records. The regions AAA covers have expanded to other Asian countries such as South Korea, Japan, Singapore, Thailand, India, the Philippines and Pakistan. In 2010, China and Hong Kong were represented by the largest quantities of materials (44 percent), followed by Japan (11 percent), Taiwan (10 percent) and India (6 percent).(4) The imbalance between countries is determined by the size, production rate and accessibility of information in each country, rather than a lack of

3. Roy Voragen, 'The Asia Art Archive in Hong Kong'. *IIAS Newsletter.* Spring 2012. p. 44-45.
4. Daisley Kramer (ed.), *Asia Art Archive: Ten Years.* Asia Art Archive. 2011. p. 36-45.

perceived importance or interest. The archive's collection is categorised into monographs, exhibition catalogues, reference materials, periodicals, invitation cards, leaflets, AV files, etc. While more than 40 percent of its collection is made up of traditional reference materials, AAA is steadily attempting to include non-traditional materials, categorised as 'grey literature' and 'primary source material'. The first of these categories refers to publications that are available in limited quantities with no ISBN or ISSN, often not for sale. The second of these categories refers to sketches, correspondence, photographs and other unique material from artists, critics, galleries or collectives. Moreover, the contemporaneity that AAA illustrates is measured by the date range of the collection's publications. More than 75 percent of the books were published over the past ten years and 95 percent of the collection was published within the past 20 years. This represents AAA's philosophy in its research praxis, which aims to reflect various artistic practices.

Although the organisation began from one person's initiative, it has evolved into a collective effort. AAA is funded through multiple sources, including government agencies, foundations, corporations and individuals. More than 85 percent of the collection has been donated by various contributors and its annual fundraiser – a banquet and auction of donated artworks – is also an important means of fundraising. This signifies that AAA has been expanded through community effort.

In collecting materials, the archive's research team also plays an important role in the regions of Asia. Since 2002, AAA has been establishing research posts in various cities, including Taipei, Beijing, Bangkok, Seoul, Tokyo, Singapore, Manila, New Delhi, Mumbai and Lahore. Researchers in these regions gather rare materials, conduct interviews and collect information on exhibitions and art events. However, they not only collect information; they also help to organise and preserve materials. For example, when Typhoon Ketsana hit the Philippines in 2009, many repositories for art-related materials were submerged. Fortunately, an AAA researcher, Ringo Bunoan, helped to document and digitise materials, especially those of Roberto Chabet, a prominent figure in the country's art scene; about 8,000 of Chabet's items were rescued, because Bunoan had already digitised them. Furthermore, some of the researchers working in areas where materials are relatively diffuse have been dedicated to collecting documents such as books, photographs, paintings, posters and newspapers. For instance, Sabih Ahmad has described how, while in India for 14 months, he often worked from 10am to 9pm, gathering more than 10,000 items from Geeta Kapur and Vivan Sundaram, who are important art practitioners in the Indian art scene.[5] The collection encompasses documents relating to events, including exhibition catalogues, newspaper clippings and artists' slides in India's art community over the last 50 years as well as documentation of artwork and writings by Kapur and Sundaram. These efforts resulted in the project called *Another Life: The Digitised Personal Archive of Geeta Kapur and Vivan Sundaram*, which is presented on AAA's website.

As proven in the case of the Philippines, digitising documents is an essential part of preserving materials. This also fulfils AAA's new core mission for the next ten years, which is to create a collection that belongs to the public. In the publication *Asia Art Archive: Ten Years*, which was published to celebrate AAA's tenth anniversary, Hsu states that the accessibility of the archive is fundamental to its new vision; the organisation's main objective for the next decade is to open the archive to the public. By building up areas of specialisation, increasing digital access to the information in its collection and fostering individual connections and interventions, AAA will strive to use the foundation it has created to support openness in the next phase of the archive.[6] With this in mind, in 2009, the organisation began to digitise documents and activate its website as a portal to the archive, extending the collection beyond its physical location. In June 2012, AAA launched the 'Collection Online', comprised of more than 300,000 digital items, including scanned images, artists' personal documents, audio and video documentation of performance art and diverse art events. The digital archive is growing continuously, and is accessible without charge from anywhere in the world.

One project that shows the archive's substantial online collection is *Materials of the Future: Documenting Contemporary Chinese Art from 1980 to 1990*. This project was initiated in acknowledgement of the increased interest in collecting and organising Chinese contemporary art that accompanied the country's dramatic economic and cultural shifts. During the Mao Zedong regime, artists were under the control of the state, and the value of their work was measured by its reinforcement of the Communist Party leadership. In the 1980s, under the pragmatic economic programme of Deng Xiaoping, the objectives of the leadership

5. Joyce Lau, 'Keeping Track of Art All over Asia'. *The New York Times*. 2 July 2012.
6. Daisley Kramer (ed.), *Asia Art Archive: Ten Years*. Asia Art Archive. 2011. p. 3.

changed. While there remained a resistance to bourgeois liberalism, which was considered part of a Western influence, artists were encouraged to 'modernise' and challenge the Cultural Revolution. During this transitional period, a number of books were published, ranging from accounts of traditional Chinese antiquity to translations of Western texts. Hou Hanru argues that books published during the 1980s have had a lasting impact on Chinese society as well as on the art world, because, in addition to supplying technical information, these books 'underpinned social values'.[7] Needless to say, this intellectual and social backdrop means that the art produced during that time is significant. In a bid to capture the historical narrative of this period, AAA collected art publications and obscure critical writings from artists and curators including Mao Xuhui, Wu Shanzhuan, Zhang Xiaogang, Fei Dawei, Lu Peng and Zheng Shengtian, as well as books, periodicals, newspapers, exhibition brochures, invitations, video recordings, correspondence and other relevant documents. In addition, the archive conducted over 75 in-depth interviews with artists, curators and critics who were prominent in the 1980s. The interviewees talked about their practices, inspirations and influences. All the documents that were collected in this way through AAA's expansive research present the era from various perspectives, and are available on its website.[8] Furthermore, the online archive is occasionally linked to the physical world, in a bid to collect more extensive opinions from different experts. When launching the project *Materials of the Future* in 2006, AAA collaborated with the Museum of Modern Art (MoMA) in New York to organise *Contemporary Chinese Art: Primary Documents*, which included panel discussions that were documented in a MoMA publication of the same name, edited by Professor Wu Hung, followed by serial events held in Hong Kong, Beijing and Shanghai.

The 'Collection Online' projects not only function as a web portal but also embody the organisation's curatorial practice by selecting subjects to research and rearticulating the past in the context of the present. By curating its archive, AAA determines its legitimacy by deciding what to archive and disseminate. In the introduction to *Materials of the Future*, Jane DeBevoise, one of the board directors, says, 'we hope that the traces of the past that we have preserved will inform the perspectives from which new narratives will be assembled

7. Jane DeBevoise, 'Interview with Hou Hanru (DVD)'. *From Jean-Paul Sartre to Teresa Teng: Cantonese Contemporary Art in the 1980s*. Asia Art Archive. 2009.
8. www.china1980s.org

and tested'.[9] She adds that, 'like Bart deBaere, we also believe that the archive is about potentiality and the "stream of possible narratives; from storage and access to stories, to connections and palaver" that give rise to the contingencies embedded in our cultural history'.[10] In stating the objectives of its project, AAA demonstrates how the expanded role of research encompasses curatorial practice, as well as how research practice performs an expanded notion of the curatorial.

Other archives reflect their curatorial practices by curating collections, and many archives and libraries organise art events. Nonetheless, AAA may be distinguished as an 'evolving archive'. It not only follows conventional models but also traverses the traditional boundaries of an institution. This has emerged through AAA's public programmes making it a proactive archive. Among its activities, AAA's exhibitions are remarkable for challenging dominant narratives related to artistic practices and reinterpreting the past by focusing on the archive. *Uncatalogued: The Case of Oil Street Artist Village* – a two-part exhibition which took place at the Hong Kong International Art Fair and AAA's library in 2012 – is a prime example. The exhibition was derived from a box, containing portfolios, petitions, news clippings and photographs relating to Oil Street, which was donated by a member of Hong Kong's artist community in 2006. From the late 1990s until early 2000, Oil Street operated as a cultural village, attracting a number of artists, designers, actors and filmmakers with the lure of affordable rent and the opportunity to conduct unconstrained experiments. However, the government began to evict tenants due to the residents' lack of permits or insurance. This gave rise to a 'Save Oil Street Campaign', which included a mass protest and press conference. Ellen Pau, founder of a non-profit art collective called 'Videotage', recalls that 'the campaign was the first gathering of many artists drawing a lot of attention'.[11] Regardless of these endeavours, the movement failed, and the last tenant was forced out in 2000. *Uncatalogued* nostalgically recalled this movement through two timelines. One of the timelines, from 1998 to 2000, focused on the rise and fall of the artists' village, reflecting on subjective memories by asking the artists to draw the site as they remembered it; the other explored the history of the site from 1908 to the present day. In so doing, the exhibition addressed the complexity

9. In *Introduction by Jane DeBevoise* on www.china1980s.org
10. Ibid.
11. Payal Uttam, 'A Forgotten Enclave Comes Into View'. *The Wall Street Journal*. 17 May 2012.

and ambiguity of a research process that began with a single box, and demonstrated how research and archives can be transformed by creating a new narrative with different perspectives.

The Oxford English Dictionary defines the word 'archive' as a collection of historical documents or records providing information about a place, institution or group of people. Departing from this, AAA continues to reconfigure conventional understanding of an archive through the expansive scope of its activities. In this regard, it attempts to stimulate artistic production by hosting residencies. The archive's residency programme invites art practitioners, such as artists and curators, to spend time in AAA, and provides opportunities for them to reinterpret materials in its collection and evaluate its position as a vibrant archive. In March 2011, Seoul-based art group, Young-hae Chang Heavy Industries (YHCHI), was invited for a residency. Comprised of Marc Voge from the US and Young-hae Chang from South Korea, YHCHI pioneered use of the Internet as an artistic platform in the 1990s. Their works are characterised by text-based animations referring to film and poetry, synchronised with an upbeat musical score. YHCHI's residency was significant as it took place while the organisation was opening up its 'collection online'. Integrating the archive with visual material relating to the idea of an archive, YHCHI produced two works - *HOLLYWOOD* and *IT'S A PLEASURE TO BE HERE: WE HAVE NOTHING TO SAY: COLLECTORS CIRCLE TALK AT WILLIAM LIM'S STUDIO* - and presented them on AAA's website. More generally, the residency programme reveals a way in which an archive becomes an art arena for exchange and communication.

AAA's mission to open the archive to the public is also manifested in its discursive programme - including artists' talks, symposia and workshops - providing a platform for the sharing of various discourses regarding contemporary artistic practices in the region. This non-exhibition-based approach creates discussions around specific art events as well as the phenomena of culture and politics in relation to artistic production, reflecting the recent growth of discourse-orientated artistic practices. Among the symposia that have been hosted by AAA, *The Subject of Archives* was closely associated with its project, *Another Life: The Digitised Personal Archive of Geeta Kapur and Vivan Sundaram*. As stated above, this project brought into the public realm a broad range of materials, collected by Kapur and Sundaram since the 1950s, by digitising and presenting them on AAA's website. Expanding discussion beyond the website, *The Subject of Archives* was held at the auditorium of the School of Arts and Aesthetics, Jawaharlal Nehru University, New Delhi, in 2011. It dealt with growing interest in the subject of archives, the custodianship of memory and that which can be contextualised when personal documents are opened to the public.

AAA's 'learning and participation' programme functions as a principal channel for communicating with the public, encouraging a better understanding of art. Growing out of the need of art practitioners, AAA keeps attempting to reach a wider audience, and its programme reflects the organisation's investigation of new pedagogical modes through the format of the archive. Various learning programmes are provided to students, teachers and other members of the community. For example, representatives from AAA regularly visit university and high school classrooms to introduce the organisation and its task as well as arranging group tours to the library so that the archive can serve as an alternative learning environment.

Over a decade ago, AAA was launched with the passion of a handful of founders who sought to construct an archive of Asian contemporary art. Despite its modest start, AAA has become a collective effort by a group of people who share a need for it. AAA's team and researchers maintain the archive and expand it beyond its physical limitation and increase accessibility to art. Furthermore, the organisation develops and constantly redefines the archive, activating Foucault's notion, from *The Archaeology of Knowledge*, that 'the never completed, never wholly achieved uncovering of the archive forms the general horizon to which the descriptions of discursive formations, the analysis of positivities, the mapping of the enunciative field belong'.(12) Through its collective efforts, AAA will continue to open up a discursive field in which different statements can coexist, form and transform; and it could suggest a model of research practice that functions within curatorial production in the forthcoming decades.

12. Michel Foucault, op cit. p. 131.

IN THE TIME OF TRYING: IF I CAN'T DANCE, I DON'T WANT TO BE PART OF YOUR REVOLUTION

Vivian Ziherl

Exhibitions go up and come down like refrains in a song. It is in this way that their protagonists - artists, curators, critics, technicians, etc. - dance to rhythms set by the circulation of art and ideas through economies of cultural capital. When we speak of rhythm, time is at issue - in this case, time organised into a framing and punctuating metric that serves as an infrastructure for curatorial acts. The temporal basis of art institutions is seldom articulated; it is a latent pre-supposition, an unhailed infrastructure conditioning the roles and relations of production and display.

Emerging from the interstice between contemporary art and theatre, the Dutch performance and feminist-focused institution, If I Can't Dance, I Don't Want To Be Part Of Your Revolution, has evolved as a singular and contingent formation over the past decade. Lacking a permanent display space, its curators have explored a series of temporal displacements and re-figurations in pursuing the fundamental question of how to work together on commissioning performance-based projects. Through deferral, distension and repetition, the organisation has foregrounded a temporal architecture, investing in a speculative method that is always already one of enquiry.

Affixed to the wall of the If I Can't Dance office is an ink-jet printed A4 page that cautions against reading the organisation as a case study. The page bears a schematic diagram of a tall, narrow bench, fitted with wheels, annotated with the title; 'Rolling (Curatorial) Platform: patent pending'. The hook of this gag - the surtitle 'patent pending' - gestures towards the ongoing deferral of If I Can't Dance's formalisation into an institutional prototype. This highlights the need to tread carefully in order to avoid assigning to an assemblage of strategic choices the mantle of a model, to aver from fixing token to type.

(1)

If I Can't Dance was initially established not as an organisation but as an experiment - a year-long exploration of margin-thinking and doing, undertaken in the interstice between disciplines and relative peripheries. The process commenced in late 2004, when three curators each independently took up positions overseeing the visual art programme of regional theatre festivals in the Netherlands. They were Frédérique Bergholtz, Tanja Elstgeest and Annie Fletcher in Utrecht, Leiden and 's-Hertogenbosch respectively. Discovering their parallel situations, the three arranged to pool their resources and collectively explore the potentials specific to presenting art in the context of theatre.

The founding of If I Can't Dance results, then, from a fortuitous coincidence in motivation among its founders. All three recall a frustration with curatorial strategies, combined with a deep enthusiasm for intensively working with artists to develop new work. In their first publication, the curators outlined their move away from a 'paradigm of exhibition-making that relies mainly (though not always) on ideas of curatorial originality and of the completed finalised project on display'.[1] This willingness to experiment has since become folded into the institution's novel praxis. Almost a decade later, If I Can't Dance remains unconventional enough to occasion a blurb on its structure each time it is introduced anew. In short, it is a contemporary art institution with an episodic programme focused on new work and research commissions. It is physically located within an office in Amsterdam while creating and moving through lateral networks across Europe and inter-regionally.

The programme of If I Can't Dance is structured by thematic 'editions'. Four such editions have been completed to date, with the thematic of each merging into the next in a trajectory of enquiry that is marked by overflow, speculation and return. The first edition, *Theatricality*, opened an exploration of performativity and performance art histories which led into *Feminism, Its Legacies and Potentials*. The third edition, *Masquerade*, took up Joan Rivière's *Womanliness as a Masquerade*, a text that had been foundational to the second edition. At the time of writing, the fourth edition, *Affect*, is set to lead directly into the fifth, *Appropriation and Dedication*, which will involve a reconsideration of artistic strategies of appropriation of the 1970s and '80s through the retroactive lens of affect, in a bid to analyse artistic agency.

If I Can't Dance's disinterest in the curatorial mastery and authorial mode - often assumed in the group show - has, from the outset, been accompanied by a re-focusing upon deep investment in the singularity of artistic practice. A sense of excess and overflow arises in conversation with artists involved in the early editions. 'It was palpably distinct at the time,' Gerard Byrne says of the invitation he received in 2005. 'It was clear that it was premised on an ongoing engagement with practice,

1. Frédérique Bergholtz, Tanja Eltgeest and Annie Fletcher, *If I Can't Dance, I Don't Want To Be Part Of Your Revolution*, If I Can't Dance, I Don't Want To Be Part Of Your Revolution. 2006. p. 10.

rather than hinging on the delivery of the work [...] In a way, it's important to say that it wasn't that strategic. It was more generous'.[2]

(2)

The structural shift of If I Can't Dance would at first appear to be spatial – a move away from city centres and beyond the art institution as an architectural fact. Time, however, has been the crucial stratum of the organisation's formation. Transitioning between disciplinary spaces, the curators of If I Can't Dance introduced a series of temporal interventions into the structure of their shared programme, thereby wedging open intervals for indefinite permutations of artistic practice. This was achieved by dispersing a programme of six commissions across the three festivals for which they were collectively responsible, thus segmenting each commission into three chapters of an ongoing and indefinite process. This disaggregation opened up the possibility for returns – for projects to be tested, repeated and modified – tempering the curatorial charge of 'care' with an ethic of rescindability.

Immersed in a theatre setting, the curators and artists experimented with tropes of stage production, such as the rehearsal, the try-out and the read-through, each of which posits a temporality of tentative, continuous or contingent time. These temporal shiftings and stutterings take the time of display beyond itself. They replace that which is final – both with that which is not yet done and that which will be done again. From the outset, If I Can't Dance re-named its rhythm, citing Hanne Darboven's methodology of 'contemplation interrupted by action'.[3]

Initially, this approach was confined to the theatre festival. Subsequently, the methodology was transposed back onto the art museum. A case in point is *From Dusk Till Dawn*, a project held between the closing and opening hours of the Van Abbemuseum, Eindhoven, in 2010. Part exhibition, symposium, performance programme, screening, radio broadcast and publication launch, the project weighted together the many arms of If I Can't Dance's activity into a condensed programme as the culmination of *Edition III: Masquerades*. The project guide depicts the event as a spiralling timescale encircling the floor plan of the museum,

2. In conversation with the author, 2012.
3. Frédérique Bergholtz, Tanja Eltgeest and Annie Fletcher, *If I Can't Dance, I Don't Want To Be Part Of Your Revolution*, If I Can't Dance, I Don't Want To Be Part Of Your Revolution. 2006. p. 9.

echoing an inverse of the corkscrew halls of the Solomon R. Guggenheim Museum, which stands as an art-architectural monument. With *From Dusk Till Dawn*, the museum floor was literally contained in time and permeated through different kinds of use – a performance re-enactment by artist Keren Cytter, for example, or a breakfast lecture by Peggy Phelan.

Through its operations of distension and repetition, If I Can't Dance exceeded the fixed presentation of display as a curatorial given. Herein, the orthodox rhythm of the exhibition is meted out as that of a dash/stop – a period of development, punctuated and concluded by a period of stasis. This conclusive fixity concerns not only a spatial arrangement of forms but also the arrangement of time itself. It is the stopped clock of the realised project – what Boris Groys has discussed as the 'infinite secular' time of the museum.[4] This pure time is the horizon towards which narrations of modernity were propelled as an improving force of history. Its legacy may be recognised in the permanent museum collection, partially disaggregated by the temporary exhibition and yet haunting the convention of the static display.

(3)

With its elliptical trajectory of returns, the investments of If I Can't Dance become cumulative deposits in an unfinished conversation. The texture of the organisation itself is woven across thematic overlaps, throughout phased commissions involving recurring conversation partners. Over its course the institution has developed a 'specific gravity', a certain autonomous density in its configurations of ideas, practice and presentation. In working among platforms of presentation, If I Can't Dance has developed an internal weighting through which its movement acts to temporarily recalibrate institutional rates of exchange.

The introduction of a circulatory pathway is form-giving, inserted as an envelope that regulates the passage of a parcel of aesthetic ideas. Circulations and their productive processes are an influential and often unremarked force in contemporary art. As critic and anthropologist, Elizabeth Povinelli, notes: 'Routes *figure* space – they create worlds – and are figured by figurated space, by the worlds through which they move'.[5] Different tiers of art circulation are productive of different genres of work,

4. Boris Groys, 'Comrades of Time'. *e-flux journal*. #11. 2009.
5. Elizabeth A. Povinelli, 'Routes/Worlds'. *e-flux journal*. #27. 2011.

each object in turn supporting and rendering differing ideas of art and its role, and each propelled by differing forms of capital. As an institution without walls, it is in this condition of reciprocal enmeshment that If I Can't Dance has grown to braid among hierarchical platforms of institutional legitimation. By the time of If I Can't Dance's fourth edition in 2011–12, for instance, it was viable for its programme to span platforms including major museums, fringe theatre venues, an international film festival and the basement of a partially-built office tower.[6]

This desynchronic movement produces dissonance as well as opening pockets of potentiality, however; where some areas of excess are privileged, other areas of deficit are incurred. The recognisability of If I Can't Dance has traditionally been an area of lack and of struggle. As authorship is habitually read towards architecture and away from a multi-vocal position, the curators have periodically found their projects attributed to host institutions.

A symptomatic explanatory anxiety is discernible amongst the proliferation of printed matter that materially accounts for the first five years of If I Can't Dance's activity. Across the pages of slim pamphlets, the institution's activities are strenuously ordered through a taxonomy of boldly headlined 'Acts' and 'Episodes' with attendant 'Prologues' and 'Epilogues'. Such effortful self-explication can be traced to a foundational dissonance between the institution and the ordering conventions of the world it ultimately inhabits - the aggregation of tacitly agreed preferences and methodologies known in plain terms as 'the art world'. This arduous inscription is indicative of a demand to confess - the burden of self-rendering into narratability that is the classic marker of difference in the liberal theatre of appearance that itself may be understood, via Hannah Arendt, as the condition of the political itself.

(4)

Inhabiting a zone beside and between conventional art institutions, If I Can't Dance shifted into a position in which the usual epistemological certainties of curating unravelled. From here, a process of enquiry

6. A re-staging of Guy de Cointet's 'Five Sisters' toured widely across Europe and the United States including Frascati Theatre - Amsterdam, STUK - Leuven, MUSAC - Leon, Museo Reina Sofia - Madrid, LACMA - Los Angeles and MOMA - New York. Wendelien van Oldenborgh's 'Bete & Deise' premiered at the Rotterdam Interntional Film Festival. Jeremiah Day's 'Of All Possible Things' was first presented in the raw basement of the Miles Building in Amsterdam's Zuidas business district.

naturally arose, necessitated by an exploratory imperative contained within the pragmatics of commissioning and presenting work within a heterodox scenario. The practical question 'How do we do this?' rebounds back to the premise 'Why are we doing this, with what resources and for whom?' This meets its eventual response: 'Let's try it this way', for the process is experimental and there will be a possibility to try it again. This is not a model of hypothesis-testing; the deferral of finality here differs from the repeatability of the positivist trial. It does not begin with a goal of producing an eventual sameness. Its logic is not to reduce or extract, but rather to assume an 'experimental disposition'.

The experimental disposition, a condition of enquiry rather than a research methodology, is discerned in the writing of Nietzsche by philosopher Avital Ronell. Departing from *The Gay Science*, Ronell identifies the 'test drive' as a prevailing rubric of neoliberal cultural life. She points to the unrelenting impulse to put everything to the test – sports equipment, citizen status, blood, security, love, etc. Against the defensive rhetoric of the trial, of 'try me', Ronnell contrasts the experimental imaginary of Nietzsche's 'versuchen wir's', of 'let's try'. She notes the transformation of the test into a gift, 'let's give it a try', citing *The Gay Science*; 'I favour any skepsis to which I may reply, "Let us try [versuchen] it!" But I no longer wish to hear anything of all those things and questions that do not permit any experiment [...] For there courage has lost its rights'.(7)

Rescindability, the possibility for repeal, is part of the courage assumed by If I Can't Dance with its institutional temperament of an experimental disposition. Through its praxis of try-outs and episodic projects, If I Can't Dance has eschewed the positivist hygiene of separation and exposed itself to become at once experimenter and experimentee. Integral to its investigation of the conditions of performance and the practices of artists, the matter of research is the form of the institution itself. It is an investigation of mutability, recognisability and meaningfulness encountered amidst the time of trying.

7. Avital Ronell, 'The Experimental Disposition: Nietzsche's Discovery of America (Or, Why the Present Administration Sees Everything in Terms of a Test)' in Diane Davis (ed)., *The UberReader: Selected Works of Avital Ronell*. University of Illinois Press. 2008. p. 297. Italics in original.

DRAFTS, ACTS AND LAPSES: EASTSIDE PROJECTS

Chris Fite-Wassilak

MANY THINGS PLACED HERE + THERE TO FORM A PLACE CAPABLE OF SHELTERING MANY OTHER THINGS PUT HERE + THERE [1]

Like many of these transformative ventures, merely to attempt a complete picture of Eastside is hard work. As a project with a mission, it clearly outlines its mandate for a conceptual, co-operative and process-led approach to exhibition production. *This is the Gallery* mirrors the core principle of Eastside, whose founders aim for a transformative potentiality inherent to the processes of exhibition production and formation. The first show began with a reconstructed empty space and evolved over a nine-week period into multiple exhibition forms and moments of public display, all of which are photographed by commissioned artist Stuart Whipps and shown on the gallery's website.[2]

Before it first opened, there were already photographs. It was conceived from the start as an artwork, Whipps shooting from set points. Consistent documentation of the experiment with which, from this far point, we can construct a time lapse of the evolution of the space. The resulting images display a shifting palimpsest of objects and constructions, some things which are visible for just a moment, others which vanish after a time. The exhibitions flow like clusters of sand dunes, one half leading into the next, as it morphs from a repurposed empty cabinet factory to an ongoing cultural institution. What the procession of images makes clearest is that

1. Phrases in Helvetica Neue Condensed Black are works by Lawrence Weiner considered for placement in Eastside Projects. One, *As Long As It Lasts*, was agreed upon with the artist, and placed, in red, down one side of one of the concrete supporting columns within the gallery as part of the inaugural show, *This is the Gallery and the Gallery is Many Things*, in September 2008. The work remained as one of the gallery's 'Long Term Works',* subsequently providing the title for the exhibition by Simon and Tom Bloor in Eastside in February 2009. As part of *Abstract Cabinet Show* in September 2009, The Hut Project presented *Moderne Vehme*, a work of 'magic' which would make one of the gallery's permanent works disappear. *As Long As It Lasts* was painted over with white paint in successive layers, until, by the closing of the show that November, it was no longer visible.

*These have included Heather and Ivan Morrison's *Pleasure Island* (2007), which acted as the gallery's meeting room, kitchen and director's office from 2008 to 2013, and Jennifer Tee's *Local Myths* (2010), a marble totem which remained in the gallery from her solo show in 2010 until Mike Nelson's exhibition, *M6*, in 2013 (at which point the front desk and light of the gallery, collectively named *Functional Configuration* (2008) by Support Structure, were also removed and replaced with a 10 cm high 12 x 14m concrete plinth, which hosted Nelson's exhibition and the subsequent Puppet Show); the piece was then moved to a semi-permanent outdoor site at a plaza in Millennium Points, as an entry marker to Birmingham's Eastside area.

2. Paul O'Neill, review of 'This is the Gallery and the Gallery is Many Things,' *Art Monthly*, 324, March 2009, p. 27.

the physical space, the transformation of the gallery, is both the context and the subject. Eastside Projects (EP) is a metonymy of space – the gallery's programme is the gallery itself.

MANY THINGS PILED UPON MANY OTHER THINGS

Comparisons to activities ostensibly outside the realm of exhibition making accumulate around the conception of the project. A member of the founding collective organising the space, artist and architect Céline Condorelli, asks:

> Why is it that libraries never host book production? A lot of writers go there to research and write texts, but no books are published in libraries, just as probably no consumables are made in shopping malls, and nothing that gets sold in supermarkets actually gets made in supermarkets. [...] If we use this to think about what we are trying to do with Eastside Projects, we want it as a place that hosts artists, art production, and its distribution. This is like writers being invited to the library to make books that are printed there and then put on the shelves.(3)

The Freee collective pose another: 'Let's build an artworld in the image of the hairdresser. The hairdresser attacks the way things are. The hairdresser ploughs through facts with the not-yet. The hairdresser scours reality with alternatives. The hairdresser makes systematic mercenary war on what in fact is. This is why even the most perfectionist hairdresser is ultimately on the side of wildness'.(4) FormContent conceives of Eastside Projects as a host:

> As a statement, Eastside Projects takes a very particular conceptual structure that can be conceived of as a practice of hosting.

3. Céline Condorelli, 'Functional Configurations,' *Manifesta Journal 10* (The Curator As Producer), 2010, p. 93.
4. Freee, 'The Whistle-blower's Pocket Guide to Dissent in the Public Sphere Incorporating Let's Build and Fuck Globalisation', 2010, quoted in *Eastside Projects User's Manual Draft # Five*, Eastside Projects, 2012, under 'Hairdressing,' page 17. From October 2010, Freee held a series of workshops and discussion groups in the gallery during exhibition hours as part of a year-long set of events on the subject of 'whistleblowing'. A billboard-sized poster, of an assembled group of people with the words 'Whistleblowing' imposed on top of them, appeared on the back wall of the gallery's main space during *Narrative Show*.

[...] The host welcomes relatives, friends and acquaintances, stray dogs, passers-by, back packers, and so on. [...] The host likes interruptions, interferences, twists and shifts, background noises. The host collects and produces, but never discards. Occasionally the host enjoys swapping positions with the guests, making the role interchangeable, shifting subjectivities. The host doesn't host, but absorbs.[5]

Condorelli's analogy is posed within an article structured as a 'play within eight acts', with the list of characters including Walther Benjamin and El Lissitzky. *Narrative Show*, which ran from May to September 2011, was presented in five 'acts', three of which were events and performances, while the remaining two took place as an exhibition within the gallery space, including a shifting set of participants.[6] If we go with the theatrical analogy for a moment, perhaps it might be appropriate to posit the exhibition as a script: a melodramatic genre script, the salient traits, tropes and stereotypes of which are known. The generative curatorship of the Eastside Projects space, then, could be cast as a director, or, perhaps more appropriately, as multiple directors, who interpret, re-interpret, transform and spin the script differently every time.

WITH RELATION TO THE VARIOUS MANNERS OF USE:
1. PREPARATION FOR
AND
2. PRESENTATION OF
3. POSITIONED OVER
4. HIDDEN FROM VIEW
5. RENOVATED
ETC.
ALTERED TO SUIT

5. Performance delivered at Public Evaluation Event, October 2011, quoted in *Eastside Projects User's Manual Draft # Five*, p. 17-18. FormContent curated the third scene of their shifting exhibition, *It's Moving From I to It*, in Eastside's Second Gallery in May 2012.

6. Rooms constructed for the Carey Young exhibition in November 2010 had been altered to house the subsequent Dan Graham show. Two of the grey, carpeted rooms remained as screening rooms in *Narrative Show*; in preparation for the subsequent William Pope L. exhibition that September, one was replaced by a raised wooden platform, covered in dirt, which appeared smack in the middle of the gallery in July, as a set for Pope L.'s film to be produced.

The [*Narrative Show*] exhibition is an experiential manifesto of an exhibition space attempting to continue pushing at its own boundaries. With different works being set off at various points and the inclusion of many works that exist only in performance, any view - or review - is necessarily fractured and incomplete. So like any manifesto, it might exist more in its self-proclamation than anything else. But the curators seem well aware that they have set themselves the impossible task of attempting to articulate processes, not products; the narration of the unfinished, the never finishing. Within the narrative of an artist-run institution, this is no doubt an interesting and entertaining exercise for the curators themselves. But this same plot, seen from the point of view of the person coming into the space, treads a fine line between bewildering indifference and challenging engagement, falling dizzily just on the side of the latter.[7]

Eastside Projects is a not-for-profit company limited by guarantee, conceived and initiated with self-titled 'artist-curator', Gavin Wade, as its director. Long-term collaborators of Wade's were invited to form the board of directors legally liable for the entity, including Condorelli, artists, Ruth Claxton Simon and Tom Bloor, and designer, James Langdon. A supporting Council of Management was also formed, consisting of shifting members including artists, curators, collectors, academic researchers, and gallery assistants.

'Organising: Eastside Projects seeks to continuously question its status as an organisation and respond to the pressures of becoming an institution. Our ambition is to incorporate the methodologies of art-making at all scales and functions of the organisation'.[8]

Since its inception, the gallery has staged on average of five exhibitions per year in its main space. Single-artist shows are punctuated by large-scale group shows bearing seemingly functional, straightforward titles such as: *Sculpture Show, Book Show, Puppet Show.* Each exhibition is curated by one or several of the directors, with occasional guest curators being invited to stage projects within the Second Gallery space.

7. Chris Fite-Wassilak, review of 'Narrative Show,' *Art Monthly*, 349, September 2011, p. 32.
8. Eastside Projects *Manual Draft # 5*, pp 26-7.

**WITH A RELATION TO THE VARIOUS MANNERS OF RESONANCE:
HAVING BEEN MOVED TO A POINT OF DISCORDANCE (WITH OR WITHOUT PURPOSE)
HAVING BEEN VIBRATED TO A POINT OF DESTRUCTION (WITHIN OR WITHOUT PURPOSE)
HAVING BEEN PLACED AS A MEANS TOWARDS RESONANCE (DESPITE EFFECTIVENESS)
HAVING BEEN PLACED AS A MEANS AGAINST RESONANCE (WITHIN THE CONTEXT OF EFFECTIVENESS)**

Every year since its inception, Eastside has published a User's Manual.(9) The first, from 2008, is a ten-page document which opens with a statement of materials used in the construction of the space and contains the footnote, 'We have joined together to execute functional constructions and to alter or refurbish existing structures as a means of surviving in a capitalist economy'.(10) There are diagrams of the space and the objects that will provide an office, a desk, an artist's studio. It concludes with a list of 49 names, of 'every individual who has worked with Eastside Projects since it was founded'.(11) The second draft opens instead with an introduction, a self-conscious proclamation: 'Spaces do not often come with instruction manuals. [...] As would be necessary for operating a machine or learning a subject a manual may be necessary for the full use of Eastside Projects'.(12) Overlaid on the standard black text is a layer of red print; on the second page, the words 'well as to multiple forms of involvement from artists' are crossed over, in red,

9. Visit http://eastsideprojects.org/eastside-projects-manual/ for downloadable PDFs of each draft.

10. Eastside Projects Manual Draft #1, Eastside Projects, 2008, p. 1. This statement, and the format and wording of this page, are quoted from the invitations used for Peter Nadin and Christopher D'Arcangelo's gallery, officially called the Peter Nadin Gallery, also known as 'The work shown in this space is a response to the existing conditions and/or work previously shown within the space', which operated in New York for nine months in 1978–9. In 2009, Nadin was interviewed by Condorelli and quoted in her 'Functional Configurations' article; Peter Fend and Lawrence Weiner both took part in the Nadin Gallery's cumulative programme, and were consequently invited to be part of *This Is the Gallery*.

11. Ibid., p. 19.

12. Eastside Projects Manual Draft #2, Eastside Projects, 2009, p. 1.

by 'THE ARTIST-RUN SPACE IS NOT A STOP GAP'.[13] Photographs are now included, the empty space in its initial preparations. The list of individuals grows, by the third draft, to 166 names. The fourth draft, for 2011, changes in its format from a brochure to an encyclopaedia or glossary of verbs, idiosyncratically defined and cross-referenced, modifying, introducing, circulating. The shift in tone, compared to the first three drafts, is from explanatory to densely didactic, the verbs feeling like the outcome of a corporate brainstorming event. The images are played-down, minimised in favour of an outpouring of words. The fifth draft modifies the fourth, inhabiting the margins in overlaid blue text, addendums, insights and corrections culled from the Public Evaluation Event. The list of names swells to 483. Problems become articulated, clarifications made. The manual becomes a web of references that is also self-critical, self-contradictory. Common to all five of these versions of the manual is the clear setting-out of historical exhibitions that provided reference points in the ongoing formation of the gallery's programme: the conscious curatorial and architectural accentuation of El Lissitzky's Abstract Cabinet (1926/1930), the cumulative layering of the Peter Nadin Gallery, and the collaborative, evolving formation of Bart de Baere's 1994 *This is the Show and the Show is Many Things.*[14]

The sixth and most recent version of the manual changes tact, shifting from a freely available PDF to a thirty-two page publication on sale for five pounds, re-posing the gallery's narrative as a children's parable. The exhibition references and list of names are gone, framing itself instead as 'A New Motto for Birmingham.'[15] The picture-led story introduces three archetypal protagonists drawn from Birmingham's city emblem: The Hammer, The Engineer, and The Artist, who all take part in building 'the city', here an idiosyncratic sculpture of wood, bolts and bric-a-brac. The finale sees the three characters devising what they envision as a new approach: 'The new motto for the city is 'Layered!;

13. Ibid., page 2. The front page features, in red, a credit: Support Structure, *Phase 9: In Support of a Public*, thereby claiming Eastside Projects as a work of Support Structure, itself a collaboration between Gavin Wade and Céline Condorelli which began in 2003. Functional objects within Eastside, such as the reception desk from 2008–2013, were appropriated as artworks by Support Structure. See http://supportstructure.org/. This credit is absent from later drafts of the EP User's Manual.

14. These references are thoroughly laid out in the User's Manuals, on Eastside's website and in publications such as *Upcycle This Text* (Stroom Den Haag, 2011). See also Lina Bo Bardi's interior design for Museuo d'Arte de Sao Paulo (1968), the Tralfamadorians of Kurt Vonnegut's *Slaughterhouse 5* (1969), or Dr. Manhattan of Alan Moore and Dave Gibbons' *Watchmen* (1987).

15. The Artist and The Engineer: Eastside User's Manual, Eastside Project, 2013, p. 30.

Welcome to our new layered city!'[16] Draft six presents Eastside Projects' aims as synonymous with the urban environment and city planning policy, proclaiming itself 'a model of a layered environment...creating a legible environment that is able to express complex narratives.'[17] The dense tangle embodied by the previous drafts is swept away for a simplified anecdote attempting to literally portray that layering, with overtones of aspirations to political ambitions. 'Users' of draft six are directed back to draft five to find documentation of EP's process up to that point.[18]

**ONE BEHIND THE OTHER
ONE ON TOP OF THE OTHER
ONE IN FRONT OF THE OTHER
UNDER ANY CIRCUMSTANCE**

People seem to need to create a difference between what is considered artwork and what is not, as if the gallery context itself was not work and could be ignored. It is difficult to explain until people come to Eastside Projects; the space just makes sense when you are part of it. Perhaps this is because it is so far from a white cube, and all the layers of the making of the space are apparent and overlaid, making it too complex to read from a distance.[19]

'The most interesting element of the exhibition was the install, something completely closed to the public'.[20]

'We do not make art for the public. We are the public that makes art'.[21]

16. Ibid., p. 28-29.
17. Ibid., p.31.
18. loc. cit.
19. Condorelli, op. cit. p. 91.
20. An Endless Supply (Henry Blackett and Robin Kirkham, both former EP employees), from a reading at Public Evaluation Event, October 2011, which detailed criticisms overheard while working at the gallery, either uttered by staff, visitors, people they met, or heard second hand, quoted in *Eastside Projects Manual Draft # 5*. Eastside Projects. 2012. p. 6.
21. From 'About', on the Eastside Projects' website, http://www.eastsideprojects.org/about/

PLACED OVER A SPACE WITH A PROBABILITY OF SHIFT (I.E. A LINTEL)

Eastside Projects is a public exhibition space which, like most contemporary art spaces, puts on successive expositions of artworks, organised by artist or theme. Underlying the structuring of that succession, however, is a re-prioritising of some of the values of exhibition making. It is a refutation of several blindsides, most apparently the accepted norm that one exhibition follows the next, each one self-contained and never acknowledging its precedents or successors (whereby no evidence of a production or installation is to remain, and, if it does, it is to be ignored). Emphasised instead are trace, modularity, accountability and duration. The re-use and re-configuration of structures and basic materials, the installation of one exhibition beginning in the middle of the one before, or the regular re-appearance of artists throughout the gallery programme, are attempts to both allow and articulate long-term processes of creation.

To call the space 'experimental' would necessitate the testing of a hypothesis. The closest we might come would be the modification of a question posed in the 2008 press release for the space's inauguration: 'Can we imagine a context for exhibitions and exhibition making that produces rather than embodies or represents the exhibition itself?'(22) Replace 'imagine' with 'create,' 'realise' or 'enact.' The priorities of the Eastside programme are perhaps closer to an attempt to create an ecology that makes curator and gallery synonymous in a long-term, gradually shifting, consistently unsettled and evolving environment, which the artist and the 'user' enter into and ambiguously engage.(23) Though, with this analogy, it would seem that the artist has more of a direct engagement in altering the environment; the 'user' must, as is were, acclimatise.

22. 'Launch of Eastside Projects', press release, Eastside Projects, 2008.

23. In relation to EP's attempt to engender a long term, open-ended curatorial process, we could use the fashionable ecology-turned-business term, 'sustainability', or, perhaps more appropriately, its 18th century precedent, 'competency:' 'a degree of well-being that was both desirable and morally legitimate' (See Daniel Vickers, 'Competency and Competition' in the *William and Mary Quarterly*, 47 (1), 1990, p. 3.), the 'well-being' here referring to a contextual realism combined with a playful provocativeness.

ONE OBJECT DEPENDENT UPON ANOTHER OBJECT TO FUNCTION APART

In 1986, Austrian architect, Adolf Krischanitz, designed a modular wall system for The Vienna Secession - sections of white wall on steel poles that could be mounted in floor brackets and rearranged as needed. In 2008, Eastside Projects installed scaffolding on both its outside front façade and the front and rear of its main gallery space as modifiable 'display devices'. For *Narrative Show* in 2011, six of Krischanitz's original wall panels were temporarily borrowed from the Secession, at some points holding several posters from Glasgow's Poster Club; at some, simply dividing the space; at others, leaning unused against the other structures in the space. For the closing event, Act 5 of the *Narrative Show*, Wade read out a list of every exhibition in which the walls had ever been used. A replica of the system, *Mobile Wall System with 41 permanent pole positions on a square and triangular grid (After Adolf Krischanitz)* (2011), was made as an artwork by Wade. Sophie Von Hellerman, one of the members of hobbypopMUSEUM, which exhibited at EP in 2010, co-curated *Painting Show* with Wade in November 2011, painting over his panels as scenes, backdrops and disruptions of the more than 30 artists in the exhibition.

Painting Show had no clear theme except for painting itself, and, even then, the term was shown to be slippery. In encompassing such a vast range of approaches and displaying them in a risky and unconventional manner, the exhibition communicated both the intellectual concerns and visceral power of the medium, with some clearly argued ideas about modes of display. To borrow from the title of the first show in this series, the issue of what constitutes painting today was answered thus: 'This is painting and painting is many things'.[24]

24. Chris Sharratt, 'Painting Show', *Frieze*,146, April 2012, available at http://www.frieze.com/issue/review/painting-show/

AS LONG AS IT LASTS

Eastside Projects is a deliberate multiplicity that layers production, dissemination and consumption in attempts to locate as-yet undefined means of engagement. Insofar as the project continues, we can only attempt to recognise what *types* of multiplicity it is. It is a conscious self-mythologising that requires incessant documentation and discussion and the constant clarification and re-qualifying of statements. It is a porous system, but not an open one; although an invitational platform for artists and an artist-run space, there is a discernably authorial tone that is predominantly curatorial. Its density promotes a quasi-hermetic involvement,(25) rewarding sustained attention and repeated exposure, frustrating the casual observer.

MATTER SO SHAKEN TO ITS CORE TO LEAD TO A CHANGE IN INHERENT FORM
TO THE EXTENT OF BRINGING ABOUT A CHANGE IN THE DESTINY OF THE MATERIAL

'Eastside Projects listens but it does not learn'.(26)

'¶ We must learn from our experiences. ¶ Make sure we really do'.(27)

PRIMARY – SECONDARY – TERTIARY

25. Two examples of engagement: On the one hand, as part of *This is the Gallery*, Kelly Large asked that, when the space was opened to the public each day, the fire alarm be activated. It would only be turned off once someone from outside came in to complain, or see what was the matter. On the other hand, the gallery's Extra Special People programme is a paid member's system with an active events and discussion programme which, in turn, feeds back into the running of the gallery.
26. An Endless Supply, Public Evaluation Event, quoted in *Eastside Projects Manual Draft # 5*. Eastside Projects. 2012. p. 9.
27. Extract of 'selected tweets from @eprjcts'. Public Evaluation Event. Quoted in *Ibid*. p. 40.

213 - 229

OUR OWN BUBBLES OF IGNORANCE: THE AESTHETIC OF RESEARCH OF SOME BIENNALES

Carson Chan & Joanna Warsza

JOANNA WARSZA There are around 400 biennial exhibitions around the world, and one could, theoretically, go from one opening to another every second day. And most of these biennales engage with a great deal of research done by all the critical people involved – artists, curators, project managers, coordinators and, of course, interns. But what do we mean when we talk about artistic research? Should we know exactly what we are doing when we research, or rather should we be losing control over the process? Is artistic research expected to bring the unexpected, or rather to affirm a couple of pre-determined agendas? When does it fail? And how?

CARSON CHAN I guess we were both involved in curating around one percent of those 400 biennials, and we once said that we would sit down and share biennale stories and horrors. In May 2012, Nadim Samman and myself closed the 4th Marrakech Biennale; the 7th Berlin Biennale, which you curated as associate curator to Artur Żmijewski, ended in July of the same year. I went on to curate the Biennial of the Americas, which took place in Denver in 2013, and you become the curator of the Georgian Pavilion at the 55th Venice Biennale. Let's take Marrakech and Berlin as the starting points of a discussion of research, as both exhibitions dealt quite concretely with politics. The Marrakech Biennale took place amidst the so-called Arab Spring, while the potential for politics in, and through, art was the main theme of your exhibition. At the same time, the respective research attitudes we took were almost the opposite of each other. You curated the project by responding to world news – its conflicts, injustices and oppressions and the artists' place within them. We tried to create an exhibition that would highlight the cultural life of Marrakech, rather than the more newsworthy question of its political instability; at the time, world headlines viewed North Africa through a purely political lens. In the Berlin Biennale, you wanted to see what kind of real-world ramifications art projects had, whereas I wanted to see what sort of latent political ideas would arise from works that wouldn't normally be called political art.

JW: Researching the 7th Berlin Biennale was a very particular endeavour. We were preparing the project throughout the very heated and exciting year of 2011, and it felt like being a journalist in pursuit of something that could be called 'citizen art' in the midst of much international turmoil. We just followed the news. Our question was quite simple: how can we do things with art, or rather: what kind of agency does art has in the civic process; can it performatively intervene beyond representation? Following those questions, we went to Hungary, which is dominated by the right-wing party, Fidesz; to Iceland, where a group of artists came into power in the aftermath of the financial crisis; to Russia, which was being rocked by anti-Putin protests; to the various factions of Occupy Wall Street; to Tunisia in the wake of the first free elections; and to post-revolutionary Egypt at the beginning of democratic change. This form of curatorial research didn't involve deadlines, hunting for interesting portfolios or studio visits. Instead, we tried to reflect on civic agency – or art activism, if you will – looking at the ways in which artists and non-artists participate in social processes or economic transformations. We examined how art disperses within society, how it exploits its potential for political action, civic disobedience and the aesthetics of protest. And I have to say the whole process of working on the Berlin Biennale, as it was set out by Żmijewski, was more about researching than curating. Research was ongoing, curatorship was limited, as he rather refused to act as curator and to practice curating in a normative sense.

CC: Was this meant to be research into the politics of art or expanding the definition of political art?

JW: The intention wasn't to present political art, per se, but to look for art that acts politically. I believe that art is not political just because somebody says so. Representing a phenomenon doesn't make it political. As Hito Steryl wrote, 'simply look at what it does – not what it shows'. Our task was to identify the performative capabilities of art, and I understand the performative as something which produces both possible results and a critical evaluation at the same time. One such attempt was the decision to contract the Voina group as associate curators of the Berlin Biennale. Voina is a sister collective of Pussy Riot, engaged in civil disobedience and anti-Putin advocacy through art, echoing the avant-garde claims of fusing art and life. Obviously, they weren't acting as curators at all. They did not come to Berlin even once for curatorial meetings, nor did they give any advice and the KunstWerke team never met them.

CC: So why did you do this? I can understand hiring them for political reasons, but for the biennial audience this gesture makes little difference, no?

JW: The curatorial alliance between the Berlin Biennale and Voina was meant to create a situation in which the institutional tools of the big exhibition – access to press coverage, legal representation and funding – could serve Voina's cause. With this contract, they backed up part of their strategy – being legitimised as artists and their 'guerrilla' actions deemed art. Witnessing the trial of Pussy Riot later in summer 2012, I wondered what would have happened if the biennale had signed the contract with Pussy Riot. Would the link with a big European exhibition have mattered during their Moscow *schauprozess* – the public trial in which their action was constantly questioned as 'so-called art'? Would legitimisation in the art world have helped? After all, is it only a judge who has the legitimacy to decide whether something is art or not and whether it can benefit from the constitutionally guaranteed freedom of art in Russia. In other words, the 7th Berlin Biennale's contract with the Voina group as spectral associate curators was a proposal to expend the institutional possibilities of biennales and question the growing power of its curators.

CC: The Pussy Riot scenario you just outlined is intriguing, but it's also hypothetical – and dangerously so as it seems to over-assign the power of contemporary fine arts within non-art realms. When Ai Weiwei was interned by the Chinese government – ostensibly for tax fraud, but in reality to silence his ongoing criticism of human rights violations and the cronyism of officials in China – there was a loud and sustained outcry from the international art world. Directors of prominent museums, famous artists and curators, all signed petitions and protested in front of Chinese embassies around the world. These protests struck me as extremely well-meaning, but also extremely naïve. Few in the art world who protested knew much about Chinese polity or regulations. It is more than naïve to think that protests outside of China could be effective in any way in changing political matters in China. It's a double bind: to not do something is to be part of the problem, but to act inefficiently is a waste of time and energy. More research, as it were, should have been directed at how actual change can come about.

JW: The art world generally overestimates its own capacities in this regard. As an artist or curator, it's perhaps a little too pretentious to think you can make a change on your own. Nevertheless, I do believe that art can work as a symbolic shortcut and have a major influence, but only if you manage to engage and inspire other agents and sectors of society. One of the recent recurring questions is how art and activism could empower each other – how could one create a situation in which an artist doesn't feel commodified but can symbolically back up those who act in a sustainable manner on the ground? To take an example from New York City. I talked to Tom Finkelpearl, the former director of the Queens Museum, when he was starting a long-term socially engaged project with Tania Bruguera in Corona, Queens. He didn't have any illusions about the fact that the artist would leave one day, so, in order to maintain the value of her work, he employed community organisers and conflict mediators from the start, who would work side by side with the artist. It's not only artists 'using' or 'misusing' communities – communities can also gain a big advantage from working with artists and their unorthodox research methods.

CC: Perhaps we should both define what we mean when we say art. For me, art is a thoughtful reflection on the world; it's a type of reflection that allows us to see the world differently. For art to be this mirror, it needs distance from the objects it reflects. This *seeing differently* could definitely come out of a naïve process, but the important thing is the comparison of differences. We need this difference, this imaginary world, against which to measure our lived reality. This is the non-linear logic of art, its essence. In this regard, curating is completely dissimilar. The role of the curator is, I believe, to negotiate between the exhibition's various interests – the institution, the various publics, the artists and their artwork. Mediating between all of the exhibition's stakeholders requires, to varying degrees, a linear work flow; budgets need to be met, visitors need to be attracted and the work needs to be shown in a communicative and aesthetic way.

JW: I also see art as a vehicle for re-contextualisation of the status quo and curating as a sort of refined mediation, and I especially felt it in my recent role as a curator of the Georgian Pavilion in Venice – in which you are entitled to mediate art as the representation of a country, in this case a young, post-Soviet state. As you know, countries like the United States, UK or even Poland enjoy the pleasure of spacious pavilions in the Giardini, others can afford space in the Arsenale, while the remaining ones have to rent a space in some palazzo that fewer people will visit. The politics of visibility is very uneven. And Georgia belongs to the last category. Together with the artist, Gio Sumbadze, we came to the idea that maybe we should just build a pavilion – since Georgia doesn't have one – as a simple addition to the existing medieval architecture, inspired by the extensions of Soviet blocs in the post-USSR era. We first thought to construct it on the roof of the Pavilone Centrale, the main exhibition venue. We believed that would be a meaningful intrusion, a parachuting pavilion emerging from Euro-Asiatic invisibility. I wrote an email with this proposal to Massimiliano Gioni, the curator of the 2013 Biennale. To my surprise, he answered quite quickly, saying that he liked the concept, and we started a conversation. Unfortunately, a few weeks later, we found out that, in order to avoid diplomatic tensions, an international agreement that no new pavilions will be built in the Giardini has been in place since Korea built the last one in 1996. Instead, the Biennale production team offered us the roof of a funny, undefined building at the end of Arsenale, facing the water and bordering the gardens, where we eventually built a pavilion-artwork called Kamikaze Loggia, together with a team of 12 artists. The project took a critical look at the ways in which economic and geopolitical contexts seem to reflect the transnational alliances and nature of the pavilions within the order of the Venice Biennale. I have to say I really enjoyed the process of negotiating over the importance, cultural significance, and necessity of the kamikaze loggia being represented at Venice. The talks and mediation with the Georgian Ministry – as well as with the Biennale director, curatorial team, the artists, of course, and finally the local architects, engineers and builders – gave me a funny sense of empowerment, also because I was mediating not for my own country. So yes, I agree that facilitation and mediation are crucial to curating. The Georgian Pavilion was quite the opposite of the 7th Berlin

Biennale in this regard. Żmijewski's method as an artist is often to create conflicts and tensions; as an artist-curator he didn't see a place for much mediation either.

CC: Did you find viable ways of delivering conflict to an audience in Berlin?

JW: What I learned from the Berlin Biennale experience is that the political moment is created not through a sole conflict, but through its sublimation or negotiation. Politics also entails an ability for creating relations and communicating your stance through art. What I also learnt from Artur is that one should not be afraid of conflict, since art can also be an agent of confrontation, and rightly so if we don't want to turn it into merely a pleasant experience which only reinforces symbolic and market values. Sometimes art should be against its audience rather than for it, reaching beyond what Renzo Martens calls 'beauty and kindness'. Żmijewski had the courage to go against the audience – a strategy we have known since the Futurists' evenings – but the refusal of mediation later appeared as a missing link.

CC: Every curator I know has a different method, but, if we could agree on a working definition of curating, curators could work in their own way to fulfil the curatorial imperative. I find looking at the site very important. The site informs how one curates; the site is where the research comes from. For the Biennial of the Americas, which I curated in Denver (2013), the site was the exhibition. The exhibition was, basically, downtown Denver itself, and all the various narratives that already exist. I saw my role as being the one who articulates these narratives.

JW: I used a very similar approach while working on the Biennale de Beleville in Paris in 2010. I looked upon the extremely heterogeneous district of Beleville as a potential readymade for the model of a biennale with national pavilions. And so the famous Chinese restaurant, Le President, obviously became the Chinese pavilion, Oskar Niemeyer's headquarters of the French communist party became the Brazilian one and a local supermarket the US pavilion. I invited the artists to intervene within those contextualised spaces. In other words, I used the infrastructure of the city to reflect upon biennialisation at large, the dichotomy between art and its urban, social and economic effects. In general, my ongoing curatorial method is to start projects with an existing trouble, an unresolved issue – perhaps a trauma – and, very often, to look at the concrete heterogeneous site, or an image that an artwork creates. Later, I commission artists who are interested in similar issues. I also like to add to art non-art, activism, science or everyday actions. The resulting art projects are not shipped and exhibited in a white cube but negotiated and staged. For example, for the Georgian Pavilion, the starting images were the so-called kamikaze loggias. Kamikaze loggias are informal structures that have been characteristic of Tbilisi since the 1990s. The leading questions were how the Soviet past has been appropriated and domesticated, via these performative architectural forms, and how parasitical and informal architecture generates an emancipatory potential in a country called, by some, 'Italy gone Marxist'. The final issue was the translation of the site. We aimed at a meaningful recreation of a kamikaze loggia in the Venetian context. In this way, a pavilion became an extension of the Venice Biennale's spatial logic. As you said in one of your recent essays, 'Space, Not Art, is the Curator's Primary Material'.

CC: I am advocating that curators understand the exhibition space as the tool with which to express ideas. In other words, the artist communicates through art and the curator communicates through the exhibition. The sequence of works, the lighting, the sight lines, the temperature, the sound level – these are all things that the curator can control to express ideas that relate the pieces in the show. As I mentioned, the city of Denver was the exhibition space for the Biennial of the Americas (2013). Instead of making an exhibition in a museum, as with the previous edition, we commissioned all the work to be exhibited in public space. Architects were asked to create building-sized interventions that responded to the urban condition of their respective sites, while artists, poets and writers were given billboards on which to exhibit their work throughout the city. To see all 71 exhibits would take visitors through more than a dozen neighbourhoods stretched over 25 square kilometres. It was an exhibition that was impossible to document with an installation shot, and you did't need to know you were at an exhibition to engage with the work. Instead of the white walls of a museum or gallery, the sights and sounds of the city provided context.

JW: And smells and tastes. You said that you also advocated licence for public beer drinking in order to enjoy the show.

CC: Right, all our senses inform our experience of exhibitions, and few curators research other fields – like psychology and video game design – fields that could inform this question. As curators, this is what we should be concerned with. Site and context were definitely informative in curating the Marrakech Biennale; in fact, I took many lessons from Marrakech to Denver. We curated the Marrakech Biennale in a very different way to the shows I made in Europe. One reason is that, by and large, Moroccans, as well as inhabitants of Denver, have very little access to contemporary art. There is no contemporary art museum in Morocco, and the galleries that exist there are geared towards retail and the elite. There is no tradition of large-scale art exhibitions like the biennials of Europe. There are, of course, notable but isolated instances of public art, but nothing has been established to the point at which it could be understood as part of Moroccan culture. The question we were faced with was what to show in Marrakech and how. How do we communicate something that is so foreign? What are the techniques to make it seem less so? Marrakshis have such a rich, living culture that absorbing artistic ideas was not a problem; there is so much curiosity and desire to engage with new things like contemporary art.

JW: How, then, did you mediate the situation?

CC: We tried to communicate the idea that art was simply another way of seeing the world. Many of today's contemporary art practices in Europe and the Americas rely on philosophical, conceptual and theoretical frameworks that require a lot of advance knowledge in order to understand them. So-called art for art's sake requires knowledge of Western art history – something I often cannot assume for Western audiences, let alone those in Morocco. We met many university students, from Cadi Ayyad University as well as some from École Supérieure des Arts Visuels (ESAV) film school, and saw them as our target audience – culturally curious, open to new ideas, worldly, online and willing to engage. We often measured the potential success of work by non-Moroccan artists in a Moroccan setting through our discussions with these students. How do we get these guys excited? How do we grab someone's attention for more than 30 seconds? I think you need at least this amount of time to get someone to start thinking and questioning, and I think this is where our curatorial strategies overlap. The performativity of an idea and the first-hand, physical experience of art is what determined the works we showed. Large-scale installations – things that one could walk into, videos, sounds – basically, we wanted to communicate through experience, rather than through text.

JW: This is what I call the economy of experience – the lived experience of an idea. What you cite as 'making one's way to an artwork'.

CC: I think that it's also important to preserve a space of discourse for art-for-artists – art that requires a lot of reading or advance knowledge, or art that's based on a lot of research – there's an audience for these practices as well. But biennials, generally being open to very many publics, are probably not where this work truly belongs.

JW: The appearance of biennales since the '80s was supposed to be a critical response to the hermetism of the art institutions. But what is not so well known is that the contemporary biennale boom is based on models such as the Havana Biennale in the 1980s – pluralistic, free from national rhetoric, critical, engaging, stressing the importance of the public realm – rather than on the old-fashioned Venice Biennale – which, for many years, was based on the international expo model of the 'best of'. But how concretely does a biennale arrive at a city such as Marrakech; how much is art a matter of class?

CC: The question of the exhibition's reception and how it might be divided along various social lines was a huge concern. Class was one issue, but so was language. Moroccans speak Moroccan Arabic or Darija – a creole of colloquial Arabic, Tamazight, French and Spanish – but Classical Arabic is used for official broadcasts on radio and television as well as in the newspapers. We tried to provide as much access to the art as possible. The exhibition was free to all Moroccans; we had a video art exhibition in the Djma al Fnaa square (the city's main square) and several works were shown in public places like the Cyber Park and the Koutoubia Mosque. We wanted to create situations in which people would stumble upon the work. This is a condition that you were also very conscious to create for the Berlin Biennale audience, right? With some of the works you showed, people didn't know they were looking at art when they saw it. This is an amazing way to exhibit art – you bypass the conditioning we all have when looking at art in galleries and museums.

JW: The Voina group says that art can only happen if you are unsure whether something is art or not. Art happens in a moment that puts you in a state of disturbance and hesitation.

CC: But we are the people who frame art – curators. We frame it into accessible contexts for the public to absorb, and, in the process, we institutionalise it. The fact that the Berlin Biennale institutionalised Voina as political artists might already jeopardise their role as an avant-garde. One reason why it's important not to think about art in terms of what it can do is because we can never guarantee its effects, in the sense that we can never predict how people will react to any particular work. In one of our venues in Marrakesh, the Théâtre Royal – a half-finished opera house commissioned by King Hassan II – we installed a huge, ten-metre-long wooden, inhabitable installation by Alex Schweder and Khadija Carroll, called *The Rise and Fall* (2012). The artists built a fourteen-metre-long stage that invited the audience to walk high above the orchestra pit. As individuals moved along, the floor rose and fell and you never felt totally safe. The artists wanted to reflect the political context quite physically in this work; like the political situation, the ground beneath your feet felt unstable. A month after the exhibition opened, I returned to Marrakech and interviewed many of our interns. I asked everyone, which was their favourite piece and one of them said that he liked The Rise and Fall best. I suspected the reason was because the piece was so big, because you can walk on it and it moves and that he's never experienced anything like it before. Instead, he said he liked it best because it was a collaboration between a man and a woman. I would never have anticipated this response. It's difficult to think of art as operative because artists can't predict how their audience will react. Curators who have to manage many works definitely can't predict how people will see the work.

JW: I nevertheless believe that art can sometimes anticipate or carve out a shortcut, achieving that would take sociology or diplomacy years to accomplish.

CC: I agree, though I also think we shouldn't overplay art's importance in society. Even here in Berlin, where art and other cultural events seem completely pervasive, in the end it only affects a small portion of the city's population. Curator, Ute Meta Bauer, told me that her mother would rather go home and watch television after work than go to an exhibition. This is perfectly fine. Not everyone needs to enjoy art - not everyone wants to. Is addressing social problems through art, then, really that effective or efficient? How many big media cases are there like Pussy Riot or Ai Weiwei per art project that no one ever hears about? We almost set ourselves up for failure when we try to address social problems through art or exhibitions. There is a movement in design right now called 'social design'. Designers, who are trained in schools to design products like chairs and cups, are forming design groups and think tanks to design workflows and problem-solving strategies. Particularly in Finland, where this field is quite active, groups like Sitra are working with the parliament - advising on many different aspects of governance. Bringing research expertise from one discipline to another is always great, and often very generative, but it is also important to address each discipline's limitations. Each discipline could be very active and effective within its field of influence. Working outside one's field does not guarantee results. If affecting legislation is the goal, is an exhibition the best way to go about doing this, or is some kind of political lobbying? Perhaps one in a million attempts by art to challenge legislation are successful, and I think we all gravitate towards those success stories; we can be realistic without being cynical. You said earlier that art could be used to fast-track political processes that would take diplomacy much longer, and it seems to me that Jonas Staal's *New World Summit* – a congress of associations listed terrorist – was exactly that. Terrorist groups – whether justifiably called so or not – were brought to Berlin for the congress in the name of art. This time, it was a meeting of different political or activist factions, but it's not hard to see what other kind of activity could be carried out in the almost infallible name of art.

JW: It is only through the constitutional freedom of art that this summit was able to happen; otherwise, it would have been forbidden to discuss those issues in the public realm. It is crucial to address the terms and conditions of the situation in which one works. This is the card that Jonas Staal played, as an artist active in politics. The aim of the project was not to praise terrorism, but rather to reveal and engage in the discussion on the so-called 'war on terror', which allows non-democratic mechanisms to operate within our democracies. *New World Summit* brought together lawyers, so-called terrorists and peace negotiators to debate case studies of how the EU, UN and US compile their lists of terrorists according to completely non-transparent and subjective methods. The whole project – and its prior negotiations to convince our donors to allow the congress to happen – were a fascinating way of staging democracy.

CC: It's definitely intriguing, but you see why it's also a dangerous position, no? For example, a neo-Nazi group could use the exact same strategy to enact their events. 'It's not discrimination, it's just art'.

JW: If you engage in the political field in art, you have to take such options into account and go into the situation prepared. But, changing the topic, did you ever feel as if you were part of a larger agenda that the biennial was supposed to fulfil? Large-scale exhibition are made for all sorts of reasons – to smooth over conflicts, to market cities.

CC: You answer first.

JW: Well, we were pretty much free to do as we wished, but, since the Berlin Biennale is state funded, whenever a sensitive political issue appeared in projects – like *Deutschland Schaft es ab*, by Martin Zet, around the best-selling book of Thilo Sarazzin and its racist content; the Key of Return, engaging the Palestinian diaspora in Berlin; the idea of supporting the Occupy Movement; or *New World Summit* by Jonas Staal – these projects had to be institutionally defended, as if they reached out beyond the field of art and representation. Looking back, I think that there must have been an agenda behind choosing Artur Żmijewski as curator in peaceful and politically correct Berlin. It was like a storm that traversed the city at its own request. Later, everybody was all of a sudden surprised that he didn't do a proper exhibition. Some people felt misused by the fact that he didn't fulfil the curatorial model. For me, the whole experience was clearly a difficult, fascinating and exhausting experiment. Obviously it was hard, to work as a curator next to an artist who refuses to be a curator. You are put into a situation in which your curatorial capacities cannot be exercised, and you have to find your place within it, and often mediate situations you disagree with. So, it was a crash course on many levels. Looking back, I believe that we do need this kind of experiment to prevent art from becoming a well-managed bureaucratic machine. The most valuable experience was, in fact, the common research on 'art that acts', which was later published in the reader, *Forget Fear.*

CC: An agenda that we felt compelled to address in Marrakech was the social and political unrest in North Africa. We asked ourselves: what could our exhibition add to the discussion around this political situation? Perhaps not much in the grand scheme of things, but, as I mentioned earlier, as professional curators, we have to understand the limitations of our profession. We decided that, as the world's media was reporting on the turmoil and injustices of the region, we would make an exhibition that would bring attention to the region's rich cultural life. In fact, going through with making an international art exhibition in North Africa during the Arab Spring was already a response.

The Biennial of the Americas was started by the city of Denver, and the organisers definitely had an agenda to market the city as a place of culture. It was enlightening to see that such an agenda often expressed itself simply as branding, which didn't actually include the arts. The institutional structures in Denver gave me good reason to work directly with the public by showing all the pieces in public space. We commissioned architects to design temporary structures that responded to the urban conditions of their respective locations, and about fifty artists, writers and poets to make new works for billboards around the city.

JW: It is interesting to hear that you were pushed into a less object-orientated biennale. Simon Sheikh has theorised that the rise of the importance of research in contemporary art, and its prevalence as the theme of artworks themselves, is directly related to the disappearance of the object as artwork. Part of what he's claiming is that, instead of producing just a final product, artists are presenting the process in the form of documentation, interviews and artists' books as the work itself.

CC: Yes, I have noticed this too, and I have always suspected that one reason for this trend is for artists to distance themselves from the commodification of art.

JW: What would constitute the aesthetic appearance of research?

CC: The aesthetics of research, or the aesthetics of academia, is what I call the phenomenon of taking on the superficial qualities of academic work, like publishing or speaking, without actually engaging in academic processes like archival work, sustained study or obtaining degrees. In this mode, it's enough to produce the books, for example; there is no need to care for their contents. The flipside of this problem is the issue of the education industry. Though less prevalent in Europe, it's a big question in the United States, particularly considering that the cost of tuition leaves many young artists unable to repay their loans. How many artists should we really train? Or doctors of Fine Arts? Some programmes seem very much designed to extract tuition fees from students. Of course, education is a business, and in America it's a good business. In Europe, students generally don't pay for education, but it brings many new individuals to the art industry every year. What this amount of activity brings us is hard to say. There is so much artwork being made, so many books, blogs and articles written, but there seems to be very little reflection. Books are being written and bought, but they are not being read and digested. Research, and the long-term embedding of culture that comes with it, is missing. A lot of ideas are being repeated, book after book, lecture after lecture. It's as if everyone is living in their own bubble of ignorance. This is the aesthetic of research.

JW: But our bubbles of research ignorance have also brought alternatives to the dry and goal-orientated educational model of many universities. Such long-term initiatives as The Public School, which you have been involved with in Berlin, makes learning into a lateral process in which members share knowledge and skills. Art also seeks new, exciting ways of learning, in what was coined, some years ago, as the 'educational turn'.

CC: I'm glad there's an optimist in this conversation! You're right to mention The Public School as an alternative model in this discussion about research and art. They've had many opportunities to commercialise themselves. They've been offered money from museums to take them in under their institution, and they've refused every time and never been co-opted. Speaking of being co-opted, to what degree is *exhibiting* someone the same as *co-opting* them? Under the auspices of the Berlin Biennale, members of the Occupy and Indignados movements used the ground floor of KunstWerke as their own space, but one can't escape the fact that what is inside an art museum is, in fact, being exhibited, and thus institutionalised. Having the Occupy folks in the museum really brought out the reality of how a group that is actively questioning and protesting state organisation is, in fact, funded by the state.

JW: Yes, it's complex, ambiguous and problematic. What I can say is that in 2011, there was nothing more interesting than the Occupy movement. The idea was to experiment with using state money to support certain movements and the artists within them. Instead of having artists exhibiting photos of the protests and uprisings, we invited them to the exhibition space. Some of the Occupy members who accepted this form of collaboration, such as Occupy Museums, were using the Biennale as a way to mediate and get their message through, but others didn't care about the audience, so the audience didn't respect them. The hospitality contract and the political potential were broken. I believed in the idea, but I disagreed with Artur on its implementation. He refused to curate the situation; I believed that only through curating and mediating the situation would it function performatively.

CC: In my understanding, being an artist is perhaps not a right but a privilege, and it's a privilege given by society to those who are able to show us the world in a different way. One has to respect that privilege, and that's why the question of audience is so important. With privilege comes responsibility. Artists must always respect the fact that an audience, a society out there, allowed them the time and space to do the work they do. Now, whether the artwork deals with questions of public good is another story, but artists are always responsible to society. I think the role of the artist is to figure out what to do with this responsibility.

This conversation took place in Autumn 2013.

CURATORIAL DICTIONARY: UNPACKING THE OXYMORON

tranzit.hu

Curatorial Dictionary is a long-term collaborative research project that was initiated by tranzit.hu in 2012. The project currently takes the form of an open-access, online, Hungarian and English language dictionary,[1] which aims to interpret the most frequently used but less clear-cut concepts of international curatorial-contemporary art discourse. In the dictionary, there are also suggestions for - the often missing - Hungarian equivalents of English terms. Of the terms we have worked with so far, six are included here: *collaboration*, *exhibition display*, *curatorial*, *discursivity*, *interpretation* and *performativity*.

The idea of a curatorial dictionary emerged during a reading seminar organised in preparation for one of the workshops of tranzit.hu's Free School for Art Theory and Practice in Budapest.[2] While discussing concepts used within international curatorial discourse and notions related to curatorial practice, we identified a gnoseological uncertainty. We could clearly point to relevant projects and authors/texts reflecting on specific concepts; yet - despite the vast amount of writing related to curating - we proved unable to determine more general textual surveys about the meanings and roots of these concepts.

Those involved in early discussions about the dictionary came together to form a working group. This included individuals who are active in Hungary within the field of contemporary art, curating, ethnography, visual culture and education: Balázs Beöthy, Nikolett Erőss, Zsófia Frazon, Eszter Lázár and Eszter Szakács. Paul O'Neill also contributed to the project as a respondent/advisor. After taking a more meticulous look at how concepts had come about within curatorial discourse, we found notions such as *performative curating, new institutionalism* or *collaboration* to be deliberately vague, as they attempt to delineate a particular practice rather than a theoretical line of enquiry. We also recognised that - as opposed to other theoretical-academic discourses - curatorial discourse is extrapolated from practice; concepts which are created are often 'propositions [for a certain curatorial] practice', and are 'employed to mark out a specific current discourse'.[3] Nevertheless, we decided to develop a general, meta-level project through which these concepts, their signification and discursive

1. See the project website of the *Curatorial Dictionary* at http://tranzit.org/curatorialdictionary/
2. *Curating and the Educational Turn* - seminar with Paul O'Neill and Mick Wilson within the framework of the tranzit.hu Free School For Art Theory and Practice, Budapest, 17-18 June, 2011.
3. Simon Sheikh, 'Burning from the Inside. New Institutionalism revisited' in Beatrice von Bismarck, Jörn Schafaff and Thomas Weski (eds.), *Cultures of the Curatorial.* Sternberg Press. 2012. p. 363.

formation could be more thoroughly understood, through which we could account for their relevance within curatorial praxis.

At the same time as we realised the inability of curatorial discourse to fully capture curatorial practice, we also identified a cultural and linguistic-epistemological gap. As native Hungarian speakers, we had to acknowledge that some of the basic concepts in English, such as *education*, are simply unavailable in the Hungarian language – there is no 'perfect' equivalent to its English meaning, not only linguistically but also conceptually. Moreover, we also wanted to question the hybrid language we use in Hungarian (common to many other non-English languages) when talking about curatorial work in Hungarian, the technical terms are given in English, making this discourse more opaque to non-English speakers. It also has to be noted that the prevalence of English terms in Hungarian is connected to fact that, so far, only a handful of the seminal texts around curating have been translated into Hungarian.(4)

Many of the objectives of this first phase were formed as we worked on the project, rather than following a predefined set of aims. During our initial discussions, it became clear that compiling an academic-encyclopaedic dictionary was not our goal. The working group wanted to go beyond linguistics, semantics and etymology, to focus not so much on defining the exact or 'proper' meanings of the concepts discussed but on understanding their contexts and relations. The *Curatorial Dictionary* therefore attempts to delineate the historical, socio-cultural contexts and artistic processes in which the examined terms are used and given signification. Hence, the project is also a meta-analysis; it looks at how different lines of discourse create meanings; it is a critical account of texts on contemporary art and curatorial practices.

In its first phase, the *Curatorial Dictionary* is, in some respects, comparable to Raymond Williams' *Keywords: A Vocabulary of Culture and Society* and its revised edition.(5) The *Keywords* project goes beyond a philological-etymological enquiry, and, unlike the undertakings of Oxford-style dictionaries, is concerned with the 'connection and interaction' between

4. See Zoltán Kékesi, Eszter Lázár and Tünde Varga (eds.), *A gyakorlattól a diskurzusig – Kortárs művészetelméleti szöveggyűjtemény* [From Practice to Discourse – Contemporary Art Theory Reader]. Magyar Képzőművészeti Egyetem / Hungarian University of Fine Arts. 2012. http://www.mke.hu/sites/default/files/szoveggyujtemenyTT_0406_0518.pdf

5. Raymond Williams, *Keywords: A Vocabulary of Culture and Society.* Oxford University Press. 1983 (Orig. 1976). As well as Tony Bennett, Lawrence Grossberg and Meaghan Morris (eds.), *A Revised Vocabulary of Culture and Society.* Blackwell Publishing. 2005.

words, rather than with the 'range and variation' of their meanings.[6] In this way, Williams attempts to map out a larger framework of words – a conceptual vocabulary of culture and society. In attempting to outline the framework for curatorial discourse, the dictionary in no way aimed to be comprehensive. The selection of concepts was based on the individual interests, and often divergent opinions, of the working group members; in this way, the dictionary is again grounded in discourse. Rather than offering a series of statements, it is based on our debates with one another as well as with publications on the examined concepts. When writing the definitions of terms, a common interest within the group was to understand the processes which yielded texts permeated with expressions such as 'change', 'shift', 'transition', 'transformation', 'turn' or 'old. vs. new'. Furthermore, in order to make the dictionary as flexible and as accessible as possible, the primary medium of the project is an open-access website.[7]

Understanding curatorial practice and discourse through the dictionary format, however, also raised concerns within the group. This approach was critiqued for the presumed disparity between the normative and restrictive framework of a dictionary and the disposition of curatorial practice towards always being in flux and moving between different disciplines. Nevertheless, it can be argued that the volume of textual production around curating since the early 1990s calls for analysis,[8] and a structuring survey of its elements and modus operandi is pertinent.

In practical terms, the interpretation of concepts takes the form of short essays – for want of a better category. For this current stage of the project, entries on some terms – such as *interpretation* and *exhibition display* – include more general remarks on practices in Hungary and in the Eastern-European region. When writing the texts, it was a consideration that, rather than just relying on reference materials, we should also reflect upon our artistic-curatorial-museological practices in Hungary. In this, we sought to deviate from the practice of citing a series of examples without explanations – although, in some entries, we felt the need to discuss relevant projects. This shift of focus from 'project-dropping' to meta-discourse analysis may also be related to the fact that we have not seen many of the best-known exemplary projects. Nevertheless, we now

6. Raymond Williams, Ibid. p. 19.
7. See the project website of the *Curatorial Dictionary* at http://tranzit.org/curatorialdictionary/
8. See Paul O'Neill, *The Culture of Curating and the Curating of Culture(s)*. The MIT Press. 2012.

have easier access to books and articles, which, for us, are often the primary site of encounter for such projects.

Within the texts, the contradictory pull between the presumed 'objectivity' of a dictionary and our socio-cultural specificities came to the fore when we attempted to provide examples (projects, exhibitions, institutions, spaces, etc.) of the concepts under discussion. We wanted to go beyond merely reiterating the globally renowned and often-cited projects. Instead, we aimed to reference examples that had taken place in Hungary or in Eastern Europe. However, we came to realise that the concepts we discuss in the dictionary have predominantly been developed in Western Europe and North America and that they might not always be relevant frameworks for interpreting practices which take place, for instance, in Hungary or the Eastern European region. In the upcoming phase of the *Curatorial Dictionary*, we plan - through international collaborations - to identify the dominant, 'international' curatorial discourse, by offering reflections and considering practices from various positions. At the same time, we also plan to map the local(ised) manifestations and relevance of the concepts in various geographical and geopolitical regions.

In many ways, *Curatorial Dictionary* also presents 'the curatorial turn' - the emergence of curatorial praxis as a composite of various discourses. One can trace the processes of this turn by examining adjacent discourses on *collaboration, exhibition display, the curatorial, discursivity, interpretation* or *performativity* - each of which offers a relevant perspective on processes that have primarily taken place in the contemporary art world since the 1960s. In turn, this implies that the curatorial field continues to be a field of contestation - defined and upheld by attempts to legitimise certain types of (curatorial) practice. An important means through which legitimisation takes place is writing and publishing.

Eszter Szakács

Collaboration [9]

Collaboration is the generic name for dialogical activities which bring about artworks, exhibitions or projects. Pre-eminently, these are situations in which a group of people - rather than an individual artist,

9. Collaboration and collaborator acquired negative meanings after World War II. They were used to refer to those who, during the French Vichy regime, cooperated with the German occupiers. Today, however, the word collaboration is applied as a synonym for 'working together'.

curator or participant – work and develop a concept together. Instead of following the long tradition of object-centred artistic production, these practices favour process – dialogue among diverse communities (→*discursivity*, →*performativity*). Collaborative practices often expand the terrain of contemporary art, in order to involve social, economic or political issues (→*curatorial*, →*interpretation*).

Depending on the combination of participants and the relationship between them, different but synonymous terms have evolved to name these processes, including cooperation, interaction, collective action or participatory practices.[10] Collaboration can take place between artists (artists' groups) and curators (collective curating); various partners active outside the art scene can also be involved. Collaboration is an open-ended concept, comprising several strategies.[11] In the case of cooperation (based on the notion of collaboration), this is of mutual benefit to the partners; however, with participation, members can only shape the unfolding of a situation, the framework of which has been predefined by someone else.[12] The realm of collaboration can also be extended with new terms – such as dialogical art, conversational art, littoral art or new genre public art – in which, in addition to the dialogical relationship between artists and their partners, the dialogue becomes a part of the 'work' itself.

The participants (artists, curators, actors from the social field) in contemporary collaborative art practices have an important position in mediating new social meanings through their shared responsibility as not only 'content' but also 'context providers'[13] (→*curatorial*). One of the most important aspects of all collaborations in art is that social criticism and social impact are mediated through art. Self-organisation[14], as a form of collaboration, is itself a productive and empowering strategy which could lead to broader cultural and social impact, linking new forms of inter-subjective experiences with political activism.

Collaboration carries with it important implications for the role of the viewer. Once a passive figure confined to visual perception, Minimalism, Installation Art and other spatial practices, especially Performance Art, have

10. See also Christian Kravagna, 'Working on the Community Models of Participatory Practice'. 1998. http://republicart.net/disc/aap/
11. Maria Lind, 'The Collaborative Turn' in Johanna Billing, Maria Lind and Lars Nilsson (eds.), Taking the Matter Into Common Hands: On Contemporary Art and Collaborative Practices. Black Dog Publishing. 2007. p. 17.
12. Ibid. p.15-31.
13. Grant Kester, *Conversation Pieces: Community and Communication in Modern Art*. University of California Press. 2004.
14. See also Stine Herbert and Anne Szefer Karlsen (eds.), *Self-Organised*. Open Editions-Hordaland Art Centre, 2013

reinvested the viewer with her/his bodily sensation, and physical activity has become vital to experiencing the artwork. This entails the emancipation of the viewer and the revision of traditional power relations defining artist-institution-viewer dynamics. Furthermore, while art was shifting from the practice of producing objects, Conceptualism, Happenings and Fluxus - informed by a wide range of performative practices - decoupled participation from physicality. These art practices therefore started to involve the audience in performing collective art-making, bringing art closer to everyday life and experience. Rather than accentuating the authorial position of the individual, those genres most appropriate to collective authorship were foregrounded by artists' groups in the 1960s. This can be examined as an antecedent to contemporary collaborative practices, in which joint initiatives - combining political engagement and activist endeavours - can be linked, first and foremost, to alternative forms of knowledge production.[15] Moreover, collaboration can also be considered within the trajectory of site-specific art practices since the 1960s, in which the remit of the site was expanded to include the public, and, later, the community.[16] (→ *interpretation.*)

Collaboration is also an important aspect of work between curators. In the case of collective curating - a growing tendency in the curatorial practice of recent decades - the curatorial vision is formed by multiple voices, rather than an individual (authorial) voice, and shared decision-making is accentuated during the realisation of the project. Collective curatorial methods are not only deployed by pilot initiations but also have a significant impact on the globalised biennial network, which is often manifested in the appropriation of (once) alternative methods.

The critical literature on collaboration takes up issues related to structure, working methods and motivation, the question of authorship (the responsibility of authors), the aesthetic and ethical parameters of collaborative processes and the outcome of projects. Among the writers and critics developing the theoretical foundation of such practices, Grant Kester and Claire Bishop represent a definitive, if fruitful, opposition. While valorising events and projects with the potential for social disruption, Bishop argues in favour of the autonomy of artists and the aesthetic criteria of their works,

15. Ibid. p. 16.
16. See also Hal Foster, 'The Artist as Ethnographer' in *The Return of the Real.* The MIT Press. 1996. p. 302-309; and Miwon Kwon, *One Place after Another - Site-Specific Art and Locational Identity.* The MIT Press. 2002; as well as Paul O'Neill, Claire Doherty (eds.), *Locating the Producers - Durational Approaches to Public Art.* Valiz. 2011.

which, in certain cases, might predominate over equality. By contrast, Kester argues for consensual collaboration, offering solutions to particular socio-political problems instead of cultivating the artist's privileged position. Such critical approaches towards relational art (→*performativity*) have also contributed to debates around dialogical, community-based art forms. Relational art requires participation, but its formalism is much criticised as the choreography of the work is principally predesigned by the artist, delimiting the subjective encounters that the works intend to establish within a hermetic, institutionally framed environment.

In the past few years, collaborative groups - comprised by flexible memberships and short-term projects - carved out new possibilities which could contribute to their effectiveness, thanks to global communication networks and the mobility of privileged actors. The increased mobility of otherwise institutionally empowered artists may, however, run the risk of producing superficial encounters with members of certain communities, which restrict shared interest and mutual understanding. Although collaborative practices characterise most of the socially-engaged and activist art projects that involve various communities and individuals, (→*discursivity*), they are increasingly criticised for instrumentalising collaboration to gain political legitimisation, justifying the artist's intention or the public funding invested in the project.

Nikolett Erőss and Eszter Lázár

Curatorial

The emergence of the curatorial as a concept since the 1990s may be considered part of an attempt to define the field of curatorial-cultural praxis in its broadest sense. In turn, this development may be situated in relation to the concomitant, and still debated, expansion of curating within the cultural field. Curatorial work no longer solely concerns the display of artworks and the task of exhibition-making; it is now also understood as a practice centred on longer-term, less object-orientated, discursive-educational projects that involve various people as instigators and actors (→*discursivity*, →*collaboration*). Subsequently, curatorial work has become more conceptual, increasingly concerned with process, knowledge and research-based endeavours. Likewise, expanded curatorial work enters into social and political discourses, inasmuch as many projects - with their thematics, research or statement - wish to contribute to socio-political realities, to understand or even change parts of the world around us (→*collaboration*).

Conceptualisations of the curatorial are manifold, and proponents of this notion possess varied interpretations as to its meaning, significance and modus operandi. Among other things, it has been understood as: something more than curating, as a form of critical thought that may be deferred in its manifestation[17] an expanded function of mediation that aims to question the status quo;[18] a dynamic constellation of activities with ways of dialogically working with others, which is also able to disrupt consolidated forms of practice.[19] However, as a common denominator, the curatorial may best be broadly understood as a way of working within the cultural field. At the same time, this notion can be viewed as an attempt to posit curatorial work as both a discipline and a socio-cultural practice for generating, contextualising and making art and ideas public. One is reminded here of Annie Fletcher's remark, in relation to the *Paraeducation Department*, which can be regarded as delineating the notion of the curatorial:

> *The mechanism of an exhibition is simply not enough to describe what goes on in art, or what goes on at the practice level. What we used to articulate in terms of particular artists' oeuvres, or curatorial oeuvres I suppose, should be democratised. That is what Paraeducation was about. I hope that everybody grasps the method - it's not an artwork, but just a method of working.*[20]

The curatorial as a methodology cannot, however, be ascribed to a specific set of practices or projects; its outcome can be a discussion, an exhibition, a space, a book, an action, a combination of all these or other, often intermediary, forms. Yet, one of the salient features of the curatorial may be its collaborative and collective character (→*collaboration* →*discursivity*). Working together curatorially could mean several individuals coming together, sharing responsibility for a project, having

17. Irit Rogoff, 'Smuggling - An Embodied Crticality'. 2006. http://eipcp.net/dlfiles/rogoff-smuggling. Also Irit Rogoff and Beatrice von Bismarck, 'Curating/Curatorial' in Beatrice von Bismarck, Jörn Schafaff and Thomas Weski (eds.), *Cultures of the Curatorial.* Sternberg Press. 2012. p. 21-38.
18. Maria Lind, 'The Curatorial'. *Artforum* October 2009. p. 103. Also Maria Lind (ed.), *Performing the Curatorial - Within and Beyond Art.* Sternberg Press. 2012.
19. Paul O'Neill, 'The Curatorial Constellation and the Paracuratorial Paradox'. *The Exhibitionist* No. 6. 2012. p. 55-60.
20. Annie Fletcher, 'On Curatorial Hypothesis'. Interviewed by Andrea Wiarda. *A Priori* No. 12. 2005. http://users.coditel.net/aprior.org/wiarda.html

trust in one another's work within that, as well as potentially realising a (plat)form that involves (many) others in a formative way. As usually many people are involved in such projects, they tend to be polymorphous; they are longer-term, complex and often research-based, with many levels of realisation, in a stage of perpetual becoming. This ever-becoming position reminds us of Irit Rogoff's identification of the curatorial within the gap (or *différance*) between a project's proposition and its inability to carry out that very proposition.(21) Although locating the workings of the curatorial in the negative hypothetical might be a bridge too far, the 'impossibility' of curatorial work is a familiar situation to many, as it is often the case that there is a gap between the intention of an exhibition or project and its (physical/concrete) realisation.(22)

It is also important to note that the concept of the curatorial is not embraced by the whole curatorial-contemporary art field. The dividing line between opponents and proponents seems to imply an oppositional understanding between exhibition-making practices and discursive practices as well as between artists and curators (→*discursivity*). One of the most outspoken critics of curatorial practices that do not concern exhibition-making is Jens Hoffmann, who has coined the term *paracuratorial.*(23) The para is derived from Gérard Genette's concept of *paratext*, which includes all the elements beyond the body text (blurb, back matter, typography etc.). Hence, the paracuratorial, in Hoffmann's sense, refers to all the activities which are either outside of exhibition-making, yet posited as the outcome of curatorial work (such as lectures, screenings) (→*discursivity,* →*performativity*), or which are 'exhibitions without art, working with artists on projects without ever producing anything that could be exhibited'.(24)

Beyond the debate about the centrality of the exhibition form, another criticism levelled against the curatorial is that it prioritises the figure of the curator. For instance, in an essay referencing the concept of the curatorial, Anton Vidokle understands the figure of the curator to be dominant over that of the artist in terms of the originator of art; hence he finds the concept of the curatorial useful only in re-inscribing the power

21. Irit Rogoff and Beatrice von Bismarck, op cit.
22. Ibid. p. 24.
23. Vanessa Joan Müller, 'Relays'. *The Exhibitionist* No. 4. 2011. p. 66-70.
24. Jens Hoffmann and Maria Lind, 'To Show or Not To Show'. *Mousse* No. 31. 2011. http://www.moussemagazine.it/articolo.mm?id=759

position of the curator.[25] The name itself is quite unfortunate, as it does seem to focus on the curator. Yet, the concept endeavours rather to denote a particular way of working, involving many participants and different levels of collaboration. In this way, the curatorial has the potential to become an encompassing idea within the contemporary art and cultural field.

Eszter Szakács

Discursivity

Discursive practices and their trajectory in contemporary art, since the second half of the 1990s, can be considered as an expansion of various discussions around contemporary art and its social function. Discursivity in art and curatorial practices also gained momentum when dematerialised mediums (i.e. lectures, symposia, discussions, talks, workshops) were initiated as projects in themselves. That is, discursive events that were previously regarded as supplements to the exhibition have taken centre stage within the exhibition space (→*exhibition display*, →*curatorial*). Discursive practices have not only changed the form, content and presentation mode of artworks (→*exhibition display*) but also the function of institutions, their exhibition policies and even the role of the actors within them (→*performativity*, →*collaboration*). At the same time, this discursive shift also indicates a perpetual critical assessment of these very changes.

Discursive practices are partly built on the traditions of Conceptual Art, which focused on re-assessing the meaning(s) of art, the function and social responsibility of museums or the social position and status of the artist (→*interpretation*, →*performativity*). In Post-Fordist society, art is regarded as a field of knowledge production, a(n intellectual) commodity. Artists reacted to the commodification of their work by either creating dematerialised artworks, which were difficult to sell, or by 'displaying' themselves in the exhibition space.

Increased discursivity met with the proliferation of new institutionalism, institutional criticism and new methods of curating (→*performativity*). The art institution has become an active space and a multifunctional platform; besides being a showroom, it is also a site for education and research,

25. Anton Vidokle, 'Art Without Artists?' e-flux Journal 16. 2010. http://www.e-flux.com/journal/art-without-artists/

and it even works as a community centre (→*performativity).*[26] Educational projects (workshops, discussion, schools etc.) within the art institution – which are distinct from museum pedagogy – can also be considered in the framework of 'the educational turn'.[27] This change indicates not only the renewed status and role of institutions but also, and in correlation with this, the repositioning of relations between the actors of the art world as well as their relation to the public. At the same time, the (authorial) position of the curator in shaping critical discourse became more pronounced, and the curatorial voice became equally crucial to that of the artist. Contemporary turns towards discursivity have become an integral part of artistic and curatorial practice, in which different discursive forms may be considered an act of artistic production. Consequently, the curator and the artist use similar working methods; rather than engaging in object-based practices, they prioritise performative and immaterial mediums (including verbal and written forms) (→*curatorial*).

Discursivity can be examined through different approaches:

The most elemental manifestation of discursivity in contemporary art is the flourishing of talk as an art form, which, in most cases, is intended as a one-way communication, fulfilled in the form of a lecture, delivered in a performative way.

The dialogue can be understood as an art form that requires at least a two-way communication, which is the prerequisite of communicative action. Discursivity within contemporary art is connected to various other tendencies in art (→collaboration, community art, dialogical art or socially-engaged art). Dialogue requires active, 'talking' participants with multiple voices and opinions around a chosen or given theme, in which dialogue becomes an integral part of the artwork through communication and exchange (new genre public art, littoral art, relational aesthetics, conversational art, dialogue-based public art).

Discursivity can be considered an open platform. Participants (curators, artists, critics, theoreticians, the public) in discursive practices can articulate their own views as members of a temporary community. The

26. Charles Esche, 'What's the Point of Art Centres Anyway? Possibility, Art and Democratic Deviance'. 2004. http://www.republicart.net/disc/institution/esche01_en.htm
27. Paul O'Neill and Mick Wilson (eds.), *Curating and the Educational Turn*. Open Editions/De Appel. 2010.

objective of dialogues between participants is that of effectively discussing differences of opinion, leading to a possible consensus or multiple outcomes.

As all of the aforementioned methods have witnessed an upsurge since the 1990s, one can characterise this phenomenon as a 'discursive turn' in contemporary art.(28)

Discursive practices in contemporary art, which are based on the premises of democratic methods, however, often seem to exclude, rather than include the audience. Discursive events within the contemporary art world frequently operate with an expert level of discourse that is not accessible to everyone, and often alienating forms are used (for example, empty tables, chairs and time schedules about the talks as display settings in an exhibition space). Discursivity can easily reach the end of its effectiveness when it is institutionalised and involved within mainstream practices, such as biennials ('discursive biennials'), when all the structures they should be critical about are accepted and applied as a framework to expand the possibility of the discursive.

It now seems that the expanded field of the discursive lies in its political potential (→*curatorial*). This is where the dominant, authorial voice turns into multi-layered voices, where curatorial and artistic practices can support each other, meet their extended possibilities and share their social responsibilities (→*collaboration*, →*curatorial)*. An actor of the contemporary art field, a cultural practitioner as a public intellectual, can become an agent in reformulating the basics of contemporary art, perhaps even as advocates in the cultural sector or as cultural policy-maker, dealing not only with different issues in contemporary art but also with the broader field of contemporary culture.

Eszter Lázár

Exhibition Display

Modes of display, formed through curatorial and institutional decisions, represent the primary communicative tool of exhibitions,

28. Mick Wilson, 'Curatorial Moments and Discursive Turns' in Paul O'Neill (ed.), *Curating Subjects*. Open Editions/De Appel. 2007. pp 201-216.

profoundly shaping visitors' perceptions. The history of exhibition and installation design, the analysis of the physical and interpretative environment, in and through which artworks and artefacts are presented, formed a neglected chapter in the history of art until the past two decades. With the recent proliferation of different exhibition formats and the increased self-reflectivity of curatorial strategies, exhibition display has become a significant field of both historical-theoretical, and artistic research.[(29)] New aspects of these enquiries include the relationship between exhibition display and the articulation of power or its role in activating and involving the audience. However, as exhibitions have been highly influenced by the display techniques of commercial and propaganda exhibitions since the early 20th century, the analysis of their display cannot be confined to the field of visual art. Application of the scientific understanding of human perception (take, for example, the myriad optical devices, the reorganisation of knowledge and the genealogy of the observer) have also had a definitive impact on the formation of exhibition design. Display orientates the visitor, builds, unfolds and masks relations, articulates political statements alongside aesthetic ones (→*interpretation*). For example, from the 1960s onwards, politically-engaged progressive art applied techniques of display which had previously been typical of propaganda exhibitions; prosaic, didactic modes of information visualisation, photographs, statements and diagrams became integral parts of art installations.

Along with the political upheaval of the late 1960s, the 'demystification of the hidden structures of the artworld'[(30)] challenged the well-established value system (→*interpretation*, →*performativity*). Revealing the preconditions for producing and displaying art within the institutional frame, display became a focal point for the critical engagement of artists and curators alike. Consequently, exhibition display – like the once-dominant model of the white cube – has become denaturalised. Informed by the conceptual tendencies and institutional critique of the late 1960s, artists (and increasingly curators) began to use exhibitions as their primary medium, bringing exhibition installation, interpretation and mediation into focus as part of their (often critical) analysis, to the point at which artworks and exhibition displays became equivalent (→*interpretation*).

29. See for example Reesa Greenberg, Bruce Ferguson and Sandy Nairne (eds.), *Thinking About Exhibitions*. Routledge. 1996.
30. Paul O'Neill, 'Action Man: Interview with Seth Siegelaub'. *The Internationaler* No. 1. 2006. p. 5-7.

The artist - abandoning her/his position as an uncompromised outsider, questioning the system and revealing hidden power relations (as in institutional critique) - positions herself/himself within the existing institutional structure, using and reshaping the given framework.

Learning from artistic practices (as well as interiorising criticism and, at the same time, extinguishing it), art institutions initiated self-reflective projects - often in collaboration with invited artists - which aimed to critically explore their context and position (→*interpretation*). Decades later, in the 1990s and early 2000s, 'new institutionalism' provided fertile ground for a self-reflexive understanding of exhibition display (→*performativity*). Nevertheless, in certain cases, the balance seemed to have shifted towards formal achievements, leaving the much-praised discursivity (which would be generated and served by the redesigned public spaces of the institutions, for example) to those who had already been involved in the discourse (→*discursivity*).

Right before the Millennium, growing interest in exhibition histories was substantiated by research into exhibition display and design. Taking the Museum of Modern Art (MoMA) New York as a case study, Mary Anne Staniszewski published an extensive volume on the complex political, ecological and cultural context of exhibition displays from the 1920s onwards. Staniszewski wrote about what she calls the collective 'amnesia' that pervades the history of exhibitions - the erasure of the exhibition as an aesthetic and historical category from the collective subconscious of art professionals. To counter this selective memory, her book, *The Power of Display,*[31] analyses progressive exhibition displays that were conceived by leading avant-garde artists of the early 20th century. In doing so, Staniszewski presents trend-setting examples of European exhibition design from the time MoMA was founded, and investigates the presentation strategies of design and propaganda exhibitions, as well as the various appearances of photography in the frame of exhibitions. In the meantime, she criticises MoMA for being much less innovative, as far as display techniques are concerned, than in its early years, for not intending to challenge the model of the white cube, and thus pushing all responsibility for the exhibitions' appearance onto exhibiting artists. This non-reflexive attitude on the part of the museum leaves the comments and critique of the commissioned artists working in collaboration with the

31. Mary Anne Staniszewski, *The Power of Display. A History of Exhibition Installations at the Museum of Modern Art.* The MIT Press. 1998.

institution unattended. At the same time, presentation of these critical works serves to prove the institution's flexibility and openness.

It is important to note that the new discipline of exhibition history - embedded in a broader tendency towards critically conditioned understandings of the past - has been worked out in the context of post-war Western Europe and the United States and is thus framed by the operational system of late capitalism. However, many of its historical and critical observations also hold true when applied to the former Soviet Bloc. In order to establish context-specific research in Eastern Europe, a constant re-evaluation of Western theories is needed. After the early years of the 20th century - when progressive design was a revolutionary tool in Eastern Europe and the Soviet Union - the subsequent decades brought about a dramatic decline in the public display of progressive art. In the countries of the former Soviet Bloc, the presentation of contemporary art suffered the same restrictive power of the state-maintained institutional system as art as a whole. There were no exhibition spaces dedicated to modern art, and the neo-avant-garde was banned from public spaces. On the rare occasions on which contemporary art was shown publicly, its modes of display did not differ significantly from those of classical art. Private apartments, studios, alternative spaces (for a certain period of time) beyond the control of the ruling power meant relative safety, if limited publicity, for illegal or non-supported artworks and events, whose display techniques were rather accidental; their importance and mediating power laid mostly in their ad hoc character. As far as exhibition history in the former Soviet Bloc is concerned, the basic research of the past, with its complex references to control mechanisms and propaganda, remains a rather untapped field for interdisciplinary research.(32)

Nikolett Erőss

Interpretation

Interpretation, interpretation-based presentation and display have always been part of museological and curatorial work in various forms. The 'interpretative turn' within social sciences has established new, complex, critical, self-reflective and inter-subjective methodologies. The concept of interpretation, the different approaches within

32. As an exception, see Zsuzsa László (ed.), *Parallel Chronologies - An Archive of East European Exhibitions.* tranzit.org. http://tranzit.org/exhibitionarchive

social sciences and artistic-curatorial practices, as well as the critical and research methodology based on theoretical concepts, emerged in the 1960s and '70s. This approach primarily appeared in Anglo-Saxon cultural anthropology and ethnography, as well as in European ethnology, shaping the whole spectrum of cultural-artistic representation and methodology.[33] The path along which the meaning of interpretation has expanded was, on one hand, related to the methodological crisis that occurred within the positivist human and social sciences of the 1960s. On the other hand, the change in the concept of interpretation was also related to the textual understanding of culture, cultural phenomena and artworks, which cannot be considered in isolation from the 'linguistic turn' of cultural studies; 'Culture as text' is a metaphor for the 'interpretive turn'.[34] At the same time, this approach also foregrounds the role of the reader who constructs works through interpretation (→*discursivity*).

The 'interpretative turn' within the social sciences did not mean the 'end' of one theory and the 'beginning' of another - in this sense, it cannot be considered a new scientific paradigm, as it only criticised the working methodologies (i.e. fieldwork) of anthropology and not the science as such. Through this critical method, a scientific praxis (empirical social sciences), previously considered only practical, 'turned into' an intellectual activity. The three best-known protagonists of symbolic anthropology (Clifford Geertz, Paul Rabinow and David Murray Schneider) arrived at correlations - through the self-reflexive articulation of the author's relation to interpretation and the affirmation of culture's symbolic meaning - which now form the methodological components of 'cultural turns'.[35] The key notions of this turn included editing, rhetoric, dialogue and translation as well as the author and the reader. In this sense, this new anthropological praxis connected with other fields - such as literature, film, theatre and the museum - which had always been closely related to representation, interpretation, textuality and semiotics. Underlined by interpretation (through exhibitions and the works of social scientists and artists), cultural representations and contexts were, from then on, undoubtedly infiltrated with the pursuit of various viewpoints, multiple

33. Paul Rabinow and William M. Sullivan, 'The Interpretive Turn' in Paul Rabinow and William M. Sullivan (eds.), *Interpretive Social Science - A Reader*. University of California Press. 1979.

34. Doris Bachmann-Medick (ed.), *Übersetzung als Repräsentation fremder Kulturen*. Schmidt Verlag. 1997. As well as Doris Bachmann-Medick (ed.), *Kultur als Text. Die anthropologische Wende in der Literaturwissenschaft*. Fischer. 1998.

35. See Doris Bachmann-Medick, *Cultural Turns. Neuorientierungen in den Kulturwissenschaften*. Rowohlts. 2009.

voices, transparency, intuition and the critical practice of (Bourdieusian) distinctions.

Museums of socio-anthropology and art began to integrate the concerns of these methodological changes into their exhibition praxes, with the discursive presentation of creators, authors and concepts (→*exhibition display* →*discursivity*). As a result, 'exhibiting cultures' became the object and subject of analysis within critical and curatorial work.[36] This practice can also be connected with institutional critique, which emerged within the art field in the 1960s. These changes are most evident in the chosen thematics, in the complexity and reflexivity of display as well as in the (trans)formation of discourses based on the normativity of canons and meta-narratives. While these methodological concerns came into view differently in art and socio-anthropological museums, what they had in common was their critical accounts of questions related to the socially constructed character of representation and the role of the object, the field/context and the museum/exhibition within the representational economy. This facilitated curatorial and artistic work in demonstrating the objects' change of contexts, generating debate and expanding the exhibition framework (→*discursivity,* →*performativity*). The display of social phenomena, the subjective elements of interpretation as a method for the production of meaning were all gaining ground within exhibition-making. The related concepts of 'writing culture' and 'exhibiting culture' were popularised by the titles of two seminal anthologies of anthropology.[37] Cross-referencing these two concepts opened up a new space within exhibition-making and the discourses around it, as well as in the positioning of representation and the narrative within the museum/exhibition.

Interpretation and (self-)reflectiveness can also be considered central elements in the emergence of conceptual-critical art practices and the curatorial role in the 1960s. On the one hand, artists began to deploy more conceptual, reflective and critical strategies, underscoring the socially constructed character of representation and that of the autonomy of the artwork and the gallery space. On the other hand, the curator began operating at a more visible level, acting as a defining figure

36. Ivan Karp and Steven D. Lavine (eds.), *Exhibiting Cultures – The Poetics and Politics of Museum Display.* Smithsonian Institution Press. 1991; and Allison James, Jenny Hockey and Andrew Dawson (eds.), *After Writing Culture – Epistemology and Praxis in Contemporary Anthropology.* Routledge. 1997.

37. James Clifford and George E. Marcus (eds.), *Writing Culture – The Poetics and Politics of Ethnography.* University of California Press. 1986., and Ivan Karp & Steven D. Lavine. Ibid.

within the exhibition, especially that of the group exhibition. The elevated importance of the curator can be seen as corollary to the 'demystification' of art and its institutions: that is, the endeavour to denaturalise the supposed autonomy of artistic production and exhibition-making, by accentuating all the elements - the curator being one of them - which affect art and exhibition processes.[38] Consequently, the curatorial-interpretive function started to become conceptual, rather than solely practical, coming to the fore predominantly in relation to the contextualisation and mediation of artworks.

An oft-cited, yet frequently criticised, point at which these methodological changes were made visible at an (art) institutional level was MoMA, New York. From the 1980s, the critical understanding of cultural anthropology and aesthetics jointly emerged in exhibitions staged there. An early and pivotal example was *'Primitivism' in 20th Century Art: Affinity of the Tribal and the Modern*, which drew heavy criticism for, among others things, making the distinction between ('Western/modern') 'art' and ('tribal') 'artefacts' from a Westernised and de-contextualising aesthetic-formalistic point of view.[39] In addition to the convergence of anthropology and art, it is worth noting the shift in importance of the site within artistic and curatorial practices. Since the 1960s, art's increased engagement with site-specificity - and hence with different communities - also necessitated an engagement with anthropological methodologies (→*collaboration*). The 'quasi-anthropological' paradigm within art practices - when 'art thus passed into the expanded field of culture that anthropology is thought to survey'[40] - also raised the ever-present issues of locality, globalisation, cultural translation and (re)presentation. These questions all pertain to another type of artistic-curatorial practice that surged during the formative years of globalisation post-1989: the biennial exhibition.

Emerging in the 1960s and cohering as a comprehensive methodology from the 1970s, critical interpretation has scarcely influenced the practices of museums, researchers and initiators in Hungary. State

38. Paul O'Neill, op cit. 2012.

39. For the critical legacy of *Primitivism* in terms of the art-artefact debate, see also, among others: the *Art/Artifact: African Art in Anthropology Collections* exhibition and catalogue (Susan Vogel (ed.), *Art/Artifact: African Art in Anthropology Collections*. The Center for African Art/Prestel Verlag. 1988) and its criticism by Alfred Gell in *The Art of Anthropology* (Alfred Gell (author) and Eric Hirsch (ed.), *The Art of Anthropology - Essays and Diagrams*. Athlone Press. 2006 [Orig. 1999]), as well as their cross-references in Hungarian by Péter György, A *Kalinyingrád Paradigma*. Magvető, 2009.

40. Hal Foster, op cit. See also Miwon Kwon, op cit., and Paul O'Neill and Claire Doherty, op cit.

socialism did not facilitate an undermining of the authoritarian attitude of state institutions, neither the showcasing of critical or relative standpoints. This seclusion only loosened up after the political changes of 1989; however, this was less evident in the mainstream than in the alternative and independent scenes.[41] This can clearly be attributed to the previously controlled political structures and to the lack of social, as well as institutional, mobility that was prevalent in Hungary in the 1980s. After 1989, the contemporary art scene (artists, curators, institutions) responded to the changes more promptly than the socio-anthropological museums. Just like the major collections built on the 19th-century concept of 'nation', socio-anthropological museums remain indebted to a critical and self-reflexive re-reading of the past (including their own). Nonetheless, there have been sporadic examples of this kind of re-assessment within temporary exhibitions. Contemporary artworks that relate critically to the society surrounding them are important indicators of, or even catalysts for, changes in exhibition display. In the case of socio-anthropological museums, this critical voice can be formed by the interpretative approach of a researcher or curator, which may also become visible to the public. If the autonomous voice of the author (both that of the artist and the curator) becomes part of, and defines, the exhibition, this may not only expand the scope of the work (the exhibition), but also that of reception and mediation.

Zsófia Frazon and Eszter Szakács

Performativity

Performativity is an interdisciplinary concept that emerged in linguistics[42], ethnology[43] and, later, in cultural and gender studies.[44] The performative is understood as the constitution of meaning through acts or practices. However, not all acts are necessarily performative; imitation may lack a constitutive effect on reality. Gaining authenticity (successful social performance) in segmented societies is a complex process. Recently,

41. Rita Kálmán, Katarina Šević et al. (eds.), *We Are Not Ducks On a Pond But Ships at Sea – Independent Art Initiatives, Budapest 1989–2009.* Impex/Kortárs Művészeti Szolgáltató Alapítvány. 2010.
42. J.L. Austin, *How To Do Things With Words.* Harvard University Press. 1962 (Orig. 1955).
43. Milton Singer, *When a Great Tradition Modernizes – An Anthropological Approach to Modern Civilization.* Praeger Publishers. 1972.
44. Judith Butler, *Gender Trouble – Feminism and the Subversion of Identity.* Routledge. 1990.

certain researchers have described our whole culture as performative.[45] The performative research method observes the conditions of meaning production through detailed analysis of the social, spatial, structural and physical conditions of the act, whether it is intentional or unintentional.

The aim of the performative approach to curating is to actively structure and mediate the relationship between art and its audience, as well as reconfiguring the relation between the curator and the artist. Relational works, in the Bourriaudian sense[46] not only ask the viewer to actively participate; they cannot be realised without this participation (→*collaboration*). Performative curatorial practices adapted the working models of relational aesthetics, inasmuch as the outcome and processes of performative curating are realised through the active participation of artist and viewer (→*collaboration*). Furthermore, the relational in contemporary art is also a form that calls the normal modes of exhibition production and display into question (→*exhibition display*).

To some extent, these practices rely on the institutional critique of the 1960s, but from a different perspective; instead of standing outside, they investigate the methods of the institution from within. Projects can take the form of events or situational interventions. Artists and curators collaborate to realise the work, and the institution is often transferred to a production site.[47] Performatively conceived exhibitions are self-reflective and employ experimental methods. Talks and discussions can be incorporated into the project as artworks (→*discursivity,* →*curatorial*), while artworks may take the form of exhibition decor, lighting or labelling design and gallery furniture. Other works move around, are added, taken away or placed outside of the institution. Performative curating is interested in *dialogue* ('a curatorial praxis that develops together with artistic practices and reacts to former curatorial strategies'), *transparency* ('curatorial and artistic production strategies [...] made transparent to the public') and *process* ('processual artistic and curatorial strategies can draft exhibition

45. J.C. Alexander, 'The Cultural Pragmatics of Social Performance: Between Ritual and Rationality. Blurred Boundaries: Rethinking Culture in the Context of Interdisciplinary Practices'. Academia Sinica, Taipei, Taiwan, 13-14 December, 2003. *Sociological Theory* No. 22.4. 2004. p. 527-573. As well as Erika Fischer-Lichte, *The Transformative Power of Performance – A New Aesthetics*. trans. Saskya Iris Jain. Routledge/Chapman & Hall. 2008 (Orig. 2004).

46. Nicolaus Bourriaud, Relational Aesthetics. trans. Simon Pleasance et al. les Presses du Reel, 2002. (Orig. 1998).

47. Maria Lind, 'Learning from Art and Artists' in Gavin Wade (ed.), *Curating in the 21st Century*. The New Art Gallery. 2000. p. 87-102.

practices which simultaneously promote, authorise and reflect')[48] (→*discursivity*, →*interpretation*).

Performative curatorial strategies were emboldened by the biennial boom of the 1990s, offering more opportunities to experiment with new formats beyond the bureaucratic bounds of the museum. However, many practitioners of this type of nomadic curatorial attitude became affiliated with different European institutions, providing the opportunity to elaborate on the experience within the frame of 'new institutionalism'. It is at this point that certain aporias pop up. As Simon Sheikh has noted, institutionalised critique cannot be the same as institutional critique.[49] It is also difficult to renew a public or even public attitude.[50] It is hard to defend experimental practices against populist political arguments – as it was demonstrated by the curtailment of certain institutions practising this paradigm, such as the Rooseum in Malmö (under Charles Esche) or Witte de With in Rotterdam (under Catherine David). Another critique of the relational approach (and new institutionalism) is that it 'risks setting up an unnecessary polarisation between self-reflexive open-ended practices and those which do not subscribe to a "post-medium" condition'.[51]

The era of new institutionalism may be in decline, along with the idea of the welfare state, but the performative could still prove to be a vital curatorial method. It may be best practised as an independent agent, frequently collaborating with artists and occasionally with institutions, with the curator taking the same amount of existential risk as artists typically do and inventing new methods of mediation. The role of art in society and the methodologies of art institutions can be challenged from unexpected angles, as we see now in Hungary after ideological measures, centralisation and cuts in state subsidies. A higher level of role-consciousness, solidarity and, consequently, new configurations of cooperation is desirable in such a situation. Reflection and self-reflection on the framework within which one is working has an important role in shaping the future.

Balázs Beöthy

48. Katharina Schleiben, 'Curating Per-Form'. 2002. http://www.kunstverein-muenchen.de/03_ueberlegungen_considerations/en_performative_curating.pdf
49. Simon Sheikh, op cit.
50. Alex Farquharson, 'Bureaux de change'. *Frieze* No. 101. September 2006. p. 157 and p. 159.
51. Claire Doherty, 'The Institution is Dead! Long Live the Institution! Contemporary Art and New Institutionalism'. 2004. http://engage.org/publications/..%5Cdownloads%5C152E25D29_15.%20Claire%20Doherty.pdf

Biographies

Balázs Beöthy

Balázs Beöthy is an artist, curator and editor of exindex (http://exindex.hu/), based in Budapest. He studied art, theology and media science. He participated in numerous exhibitions, including the 4th International Istanbul Biennial, *Beyond Art* at the Ludwig Museum, Budapest, *man fügt eins zu, man zieht eins ab* at Künstlerhaus Bethanien, Berlin and *On Difference2* at Kunstverein Stuttgart. His works are present in several private and public collections. His curatorial projects are in most cases developed in partnership with others. He publishes regularly online and offline. Since 2012, he has been a working group member of the *Curatorial Dictionary* project of tranzit.hu.

Hyunjoo Byeon

Hyunjoo Byeon is a curator based in Seoul. Her curated projects include *Artsonje Lounge Project: nowhere* (Artsonje Center, Seoul, 2012), *Tourist's Dream* (Project Space 2 at Iniva, London, 2010) and Jason Underhill's *Sing Your Heart Out*, part of *Event Horizon*, *GSK Contemporary* (Royal Academy of Arts, London, 2008-09). She co-curated several exhibitions with Christine Takengny including *Flexible Aura* (Brain Factory, Seoul, 2009) and *Visual Vocabulary* (The Gallery at Willesden Green, London, 2008). From 2011 to 2013, Byeon was curator at Artsonje Center, Seoul, where she worked for the exhibitions such as *Simon Fujiwara* (2013), *Shinro Ohtake* (2012-2013), *Lee Bul* (2012), *Hein-kuhn Oh: Middlemen* (2012), and *Abstract Walking - Sora Kim project* (2012). She has achieved her MFA in Curating from Goldsmiths, University of London; lectured at colleges including Kaywon University of Art and Design; contributed to art magazines and publications including Contemporary Art Journal and *Dual Mirage*; and translated *Curating Subjects* (Open Editions, 2007) into Korean that was co-published by The Hyunsil Publishing and Samuso: Space for Contemporary Art in 2013.

Carson Chan

Carson Chan (1980) is an architecture writer and curator, pursuing a PhD in Architecture at Princeton University. After working for Barkow Leibinger Architects and the Neue Nationalgalerie's architecture exhibitions department in Berlin, with Fotini Lazaridou-Hatzigoga, he founded PROGRAM in 2006, a non-commercial initiative for art and architecture collaborations. He has variously curated and overseen more than 30 international exhibitions of contemporary art and architecture. His writing on art, architecture and contemporary culture appears in books and periodicals worldwide, including Kaleidoscope, where he is a Contributing Editor, and 032c (Berlin), where he is Editor-at-Large. Chan has interviewed a broad range of contemporary practitioners, including Thomas Demand,

Udo Kittelmann, William T. Vollmann, MVRDV, Ute Meta Bauer, Greg Lynn, Rick Owens, Hans Kollhoff and David Simon. With Nadim Samman, Chan curated the 4th Marrakech Biennale 2012, presenting newly commissioned works by more than 40 artists, architects, writers, musicians and composers at 5 locations throughout the city. Chan was Executive Curator of the Biennial of the Americas 2013, in Denver, Colorado. Also in 2013, Chan co-organized a conference at Yale School of Architecture with David Andrew Tasman and Prof. Eeva-Liisa Pelkonen, bringing together leading and emerging scholars researching both historical and contemporary practices of architecture exhibition making.

Nikolett Erőss

Nikolett Erőss is a curator based in Budapest, Hungary; currently working at the Ludwig Museum - Museum of Contemporary Art, Budapest. After receiving her diploma in art history, she started working at C3: Center for Culture & Communication Foundation as a new-media art curatorial assistant, then later as an editor of the on-line magazine, exindex (http://exindex.hu/). She was a board member of the Studio of Young Artists Association, Budapest, Hungary as well as co-curator of the Studio Gallery. She ran Trafó Gallery, Budapest between 2006 and 2011. Over the course of almost five years, she curated at Trafó Gallery numerous exhibitions, talks and programs, and took part in various international collaborations. She lectures at the Hungarian University of Fine Arts, Budapest where she teaches contemporary art and theory with a special focus on exhibition history, new museology, public art, site-specificity and participatory practices. Since 2012, she has been a working group member of the *Curatorial Dictionary* project of tranzit.hu.

Chris Fite-Wassilak

Chris Fite-Wassilak is a write and a curator based in London. He is a regular contributor to Art Monthly, Art Papers, Art Review, and Frieze. Publications include Gavin Murphy: On Seeing Only Totally New Things, (Dublin: Royal Hibernian Academy and the Irish Architecture Foundation, 2013), and the Memory Marathon Catalogue, (London: Serpentine Gallery and Koenig Books, 2014).

Olga Fernández López

Olga Fernández López is an academic researcher and teacher. Since 2009 she lectures at the History and Theory of Art Department, Universidad Autónoma de Madrid. She has been a visiting lecturer at the Curating Contemporary Department (Royal College of Art). She was Chief Curator and Research and Education Responsible at the Museo Patio Herreriano (Valladolid, Spain) between 2001 and 2006. She researches about the specificities of the exhibition medium and its critical possibilities for curatorial practice and has published various articles on these topics.

Kate Fowle

Kate Fowle is chief curator at Garage Museum of Contemporary Art in Moscow and director-at-large at Independent Curators International (ICI) in New York. From 2009-13 she was the executive director of ICI. Previously she was the inaugural international curator at the Ullens Center for Contemporary Art in Beijing (2007-08) and chair of the Master's Program in Curatorial Practice, which she co-founded in 2002 for California College of the Arts in San Francisco. Before moving to the United States Fowle was co-director of Smith + Fowle in London. From 1994-96 she was curator at the Towner Art Gallery and Museum in Eastbourne, East Sussex. Fowle's recent writing includes catalogue texts on Doug Aitken, John Baldessari, Harrell Fletcher, Ilya Kabakov, Robert Longo, Ari Marcopoulos, Sterling Ruby, Qiu Zhijie, and Althea Thauberger. She has written on curating and exhibition practices for numerous publications and magazines, including Parkett, Modern Painters, Mousse, Art in America, Manifesta Journal, the Exhibitionist, and Frieze.

Maja & Reuben Fowkes

Drs. Maja and Reuben Fowkes are art historians and curators whose interests in the field of art and ecology are manifest in their curated exhibitions, symposia and writings, exploring key ideas and practices around green curating, environmental art history and the sustainability of contemporary art. Their work also focuses on the theory and aesthetics of East European art from the art production of the socialist era to contemporary artistic responses to the transformations brought by globalisation. Maja has a PhD from University College London with a thesis on Central European Neo-Avantgarde Art and Ecology under Socialism, while's Reuben's thesis at Essex University was on socialist realist public monuments in post-war Eastern Europe. Maja is the author of *The Green Bloc: Art and Ecology under Socialism* (CEU Press, forthcoming). Their current engagements include curating an exhibition of Hungarian artist Csaba Nemes at Museum of Modern and Contemporary Art Rijeka (summer 2014), an article on Green Critique in a Red Environment in Art Margins Journal (June 2014), as well as a year-long River School on the Danube on art and wilderness. They work out of Budapest and London through the Translocal Institute (www.translocal.org).

Zsófia Frazon

Zsófia Frazon is an ethnographer, currently working at the Museum of Ethnography Budapest. Since 2005, she has been organising at the Museum of Ethnography Budapest the MADOK Research Program, which aims to set up and run cooperation between museums in Hungary for studying contemporary society and culture. She has curated various exhibitions and projects at the Museum of Ethnography Budapest, including *Plastic* (2006/2007); the *EtnoMobil* project (2009-2011), which is an archive, an exhibition and a web2 site based on collaboration and participation; and the study-exhibition *Objective-Case* (2011-2012), aimed primarily for students in higher education. Her research fields include contemporary consumerism, the role of objects in personal lifestyle, urban culture and subcultures, as well as modern and post-modern everyday life and their representation in contemporary art. Her book *Museum and Exhibition - The Space of Reshaping* (Budapest-Pécs, 2011) discusses the diverse strategies museums apply to display objects and to represent social and cultural worlds. Since 2012, she has been a working group member of the *Curatorial Dictionary* project of tranzit.hu.

Liam Gillick

Liam Gillick was born in Aylesbury, England in 1964. Following his studies in Fine Art at Goldsmiths' College 1987 he held his first solo exhibition at Karsten Schubert Gallery in London in 1989. Gillick's work has subsequently been included in numerous important exhibitions including Documenta and the Venice and Berlin Biennales. Solo museum exhibitions have taken place at the Museum of Contemporary Art in Chicago, The Museum of Modern Art in New York and Tate in London. Gillick's work is held in many important public collections including the Centre Pompidou in Paris, The Guggenheim Museum in New York and Bilbao and the Museum of Modern Art in New York. Over the last twenty five years Gillick has also been a prolific writer and critic of contemporary art - contributing to Artforum, October, Frieze and *e-flux Journal*. He is the author of a number of books including a volume of his selected critical writing. High profile public works include the British Government Home Office (Interior Ministry) building in London and the Lufthansa Headquarters in Frankfurt. Throughout this time Gillick has extended his practice into experimental venues and collaborative projects with artists including Philippe Parreno, Lawrence Weiner and Louise Lawler.

Georgina Jackson

Georgina Jackson is a curator and writer. She was Exhibitions Curator at Dublin City Gallery The Hugh Lane between 2005 and 2008 where she co-curated *TACITA DEAN* (2007), *Ellen Gallagher Coral Cities* (2007) and was assistant curator on *Beyond the White Cube: a retrospective of Brian O'Doherty/Patrick Ireland* (2006) and *The Studio* (2006). Between 2009 and 2011 she was a curator-in-residence at The Mattress Factory Art Museum, Pittsburgh, where she curated *Neighbo(u)rhood* (2011) and *Nothing is impossible* (2010). From 2008 until 2012 she was a research scholar at the Graduate School of Creative Arts and Media, Dublin, where she completed a curatorial practice-based PhD mapping and exploring the altering terms of large-scale international group exhibitions and the political since 1989 and initiated an exhibition histories research group under the umbrella term 'the enquiry'. She has lectured at Dublin Institute of Technology and the National College of Art & Design, Dublin, and contributed to journals such as Printed Project and Art & the Public Sphere. She is currently Director of Exhibitions & Publication at Mercer Union, a centre for contemporary art, in Toronto.

Eszter Lázár

Eszter Lázár is a curator, lecturer, and currently a PhD candidate in the Cultural Studies Program at the University of Pécs, Hungary. She studied art history and cultural anthropology. She works as a curator at the Hungarian University of Fine Arts, Budapest where she is a board member of the Exhibition Committee. Since 2009, she is also an assistant lecturer at the Art Theory and Curatorial Studies Department at the Hungarian University of Fine Arts, Budapest. Between 2002 and 2010, she was the chief curator at the Karton Gallery & Museum in Budapest. She curated various exhibitions and projects, including *Intimations of the Past* (2006), *Models for a Fictional Academy* (2006), *Visibility Works* (2007) at the Barcsay Hall at the Hungarian University of Fine Arts, Budapest; *Over the Counter - The Phenomena of Post-socialist Economy in Contemporary Art* (2010), with co-curator Zsolt Petrányi at Műcsarnok / Kunsthalle, Budapest; and *Middle East Europe / Strategies of Re-enactment* (2012) at Labor, Budapest. She was an editorial board member of the on-line reader of contemporary art theory *From Practice to Discourse* (Budapest, 2012). Since 2012, she has been a working group member of the *Curatorial Dictionary* project of tranzit.hu.

Sidsel Nelund

Sidsel Nelund is an art writer and PhD fellow working on the concept of knowledge production in contemporary art. She lives and works in Copenhagen and collaborates with artists on art projects mainly in Beirut,

Copenhagen and Santiago de Chile. She holds an MA in Aural and Visual Cultures from Goldsmiths University of London and an MA in Modern Cultures from the University of Copenhagen, where she is now a recipient of the Mads Øvlisen PhD Scholarship within art history and arts-based research.

Paul O'Neill

Dr. Paul O'Neill is a curator, artist, writer and educator based in New York and Bristol. He is Director of the Graduate Program at the Centre for Curatorial Studies, Bard College in New York. Paul has co-curated more than fifty exhibition projects across the world including: *The Curatorial Timeshare, Enclave, London* (2013); *Our Day Will Come*, Part of *Iteration: Again, Hobart, Tasmania* (2011); *We are Grammar*, Pratt Institute, Manhattan Gallery, New York (2011); *Coalesce: happenstance, SMART*, Amsterdam (2009); *Making Do, The Lab*, Dublin (2007); *General Idea: Selected Retrospective*, Project Art Center, Dublin (2006); *Tonight*, Studio Voltaire, London, (2004); and *Are We There Yet?* Glassbox, Paris (2000). He is international tutor on the de Appel Curatorial Program since 2005, Amsterdam and he has held numerous research and lecturing positions at Goldsmiths, University of London; Middlesex University; The Graduate School of Creative Arts and Media, Dublin and the University of the West of England, Bristol. Between 2001-03, he was the Gallery Curator-Director of London Print Studio Gallery. Paul's writing has been published in many books, catalogues, journals and magazines and he is a regular contributor to *Art Monthly.* He is reviews editor for *Art and the Public Sphere Journal* and is an editor of Afterall's *Exhibition Histories* Series. He is on the editorial board of *The Exhibitionist and The Journal of Curatorial Studies.* He is editor of the curatorial anthology, *Curating Subjects* (2007), and co-editor of *Curating and the Educational Turn* with Mick Wilson (2010), both published by de Appel and Open Editions (Amsterdam and London), and author of *Locating the Producers: Durational Approaches to Public Art* (Amsterdam, Valiz, 2011), edited with Claire Doherty. He is author of the critically acclaimed book *The Culture of Curating and the Curating of Culture(s)*, (Cambridge, MASS., The MIT Press, 2012).

Simon Sheikh

Dr. Simon Sheikh is a curator and theorist. He is Reader in Art and Programme Director of MFA Curating at Goldsmiths, University of London. He is a correspondent for *Springerin*, Vienna, and a columnist for e-flux Journal, New York. He is currently a researcher for the on-going *Former West* project, initiated by BAK in Utrecht. He was Coordinator of the Critical Studies Program, Malmö Art Academy in Sweden, 2002-2009 and Curator at NIFCA, Helsinki, 2003-2004. Curatorial work includes exhibitions such as *Circa Berlin*, Nikolaj - Copenhagen Contemporary Art Center, 2005, *Capital (It Fails Us Now)*, UKS, Oslo, 2005 and Kunstihoone, Tallinn, 2006, *Vectors of the Possible*, BAK, Utrecht, 2010, *All That Fits: The Aesthetics of Journalism,* QUAD, Derby, 2011, *Do You Remember the Future?*, Etagi, St. Petersburg, 2011, and *Unauthorized,* Inter Arts Center, Malmö, 2012. Recent publications include the anthologies *We are all Normal* (with Katya Sander), Black Dog Publishing, London 2001, *Knut Åsdam* (monograph), Fine Arts Unternehmen, Zug, 2004, *In the Place of the Public Sphere?*, b_books, Berlin, 2005, *Capital (It Fails Us Now)*, b_books, Berlin, 2006, and *On Horizons* (with Maria Hlavajova and Jill Winder, BAK, 2011. A collection of his essays is forthcoming from b_books.

Henk Slager

Henk Slager is Dean of MaHKU (Utrecht Graduate School of Visual Art and Design), Visiting Professor of Artistic Research (Finnish Academy of Fine Arts, Helsinki), Tutor at de Appel Curatorial Programme (Amsterdam), and curator of a.o. *Flash Cube* (Leeum, Seoul, 2007), *Shelter 07* (The Freedom of Public Art in the Cover of Urban Space, Harderwijk, 2007), *Translocalmotion* (7th Shanghai Biennale 2008), Nameless Science (Apex Art, New York, 2009), *Critique of Archival Reason* (RHA Dublin 2010), *As the Academy Turns* (Collaborative project Manifesta, 2010), *Any-medium-whatever* (Georgian Pavilion, Venice Biennale, 2011), *Temporary Autonomous Research* (Amsterdam Pavilion, 9th Shanghai Biennale), *Offside Effect* (1st Tbilisi Triennial, 2012) and T*he Judgment is the Mirror* (Living Art Museum, Reykjavik, 2013). He recently published *The Pleasure of Research* (Helsinki, 2012).

Eszter Szakács

Eszter Szakács is a curator and researcher based in Budapest. She studied art history and American studies. She currently works at the contemporary art organisation tranzit.hu in Budapest. At tranzit.hu, since 2011, she curated the project of The Pseudo Race Group *Liberagility* (2012), and is the editor and working group member of the long-term collaborative research project *Curatorial Dictionary*. She is a guest lecturer at the Art Theory and Curatorial Studies Department at the Hungarian University of Fine Arts, Budapest on the practices and discourses of curating in Hungary and Eastern Europe post-1989. Previously she worked at Műcsarnok / Kunsthalle, Budapest as an assistant curator (2008-2010).

tranzit.hu

tranzit.hu is a contemporary art organisation that was launched in Budapest in 2005. It is part of the East-Central European network called tranzit, which consists of local units working independently in Austria, the Czech Republic, Hungary, Romania and Slovakia. tranzit.hu initiates discursive, educational, research, exhibition and publishing projects in Hungary and internationally. tranzit.hu encourages self-organisation as well as the encounter of different contexts and groups of people, and does so in constant mediation. Also through pilot projects, tranzit.hu aims to create a space where culture is produced, rather than perceived, where ideas are tested and can be debated - especially in awareness of a conservative backlash. tranzit.hu projects include the educational platform Free School for Art Theory and Practice (ongoing since 2006), the visual culture blog *tranzitblog* (ongoing since 2007), the curatorial research project *Parallel Chronologies - An Archive of East European Exhibitions* (ongoing since 2009) the anthology *Art Always Has Its Consequences - Artists' Texts from Croatia, Hungary, Poland, Serbia, 1947-2009* (Sternberg Press, 2011), the Catalyst Award (annually since 2010) or the Action Day series (2013-2014), a civil debate and action forum on the current possibilities of contemporary art in Hungary.

Jelena Vesić

Jelena Vesić is independent curator, writer, editor and lecturer. She was co-editor of *Prelom* - Journal of Images and Politics (Belgrade) 2001-2009 and co-founder of independent organization Prelom Collective (Belgrade) 2005-2010, active in the field of publishing, research and exhibition practice. She is also co-editor of *Red Thread* - Journal for social theory, contemporary art and activism, (Istanbul) and member of editorial board of *Art Margins* (MIT Press). Her recent curatorial projects are: *Oktobar XXX: Exposition - Symposim - Performance*, Cultural Centre Theatre, Pančevo 2012/Bone Festival, Bern, 2013; *Against Art: Goran Đorđević - Copies* (1979-1985), Museum of Contemporary Art and City Gallery, Ljubljana-Belgrade, 2012/13; *Lecture Performance*, Museum of Contemporary Art and Koelnisher Kunstverein, Cologne-Belgrade, 2009/2010; *Political Practices of (post-) Yugoslav Art: RETROSPECTIVE 01*, Museum 25th of May, Belgrade, 2009.

Marion von Osten

Marion von Osten is an artist, writer, researcher and exhibition maker.
She is a founding member of the Center for post-colonial knowledge and culture (CPKC) and kleines postfordistisches Drama (kpD) in Berlin as well as of the media collective Labor k3000 Zürich. Beyond her artistic practice, she initiates long term research and collaborative project exhibitions, like: *Aesthetics of Decolonization*, ith Zurich, 2014-2016 (with Serhat Karakayali); *Tricontinental*, Tensta Konstall, Stockholm, 2014-2015; *Model House—Mapping Transcultural Modernisms*, Academy of Fine Arts Vienna, 2010-2013; *Action! painting/publishing*, Les Laboratoires d'Aubervilliers, Paris, 2011-2012; *In the Desert of Modernity—Colonial Planning and After*, Casablanca, 2009, Berlin, 2008 (with Tom Avermaete & Serhat Karakayali); *Projekt Migration*, Cologne, 2002-2006 (with Aytac Erylmaz, Martin Rapp, Regina Röhmhild, Kathrin Rhomberg) and *TRANSIT MIGRATION*, Zürich, Frankfurt 2003-2005. *Atelier Europa*, München 2004 (with Sören Grammel), *Be Creative! The Creative Imperative*, Zurich, 2003 (with Peter Spillmann). Publications include: *Transcultural Modernisms*. Ed. Model House Collective, Vienna/Berlin, 2013, *Das Erziehungsbild. Zur visuellen Kultur des Pädagogischen*. Ed. with Tom Holert, Vienna, 2010; *The Colonial Modern. Aesthetics of the Past. Rebellions for the Future.* Ed. with Tom Avermaete and Serhat Karakayali, London/Berlin 2010; *Projekt Migration*. Ed. Kölnischer Kunstverein et al, Cologne 2005; Norm der Abweichung. T:G 04, Zürich/Vienna, 2003; *MoneyNations*. Ed. with Peter Spillmann, Vienna 2003; *Das Phantom sucht seinen Mörder. Ein Reader zur Kulturalisierung der Ökonomie*. Ed. with Justin Hoffmann,Berlin 1999.

Joanna Warsza

Joanna Warsza is a curator, researcher and writer in the fields of visual and performing arts and architecture. Currently she is Head of the Public Programs for Manifesta 10 in St. Petersburg, Russia. She was the curator of the Georgian Pavilion at the 55th Venice Biennale and associate curator of the 7th Berlin Biennale. Joanna works mostly in the public realm, examining social and political agendas, such as the invisibility of the Vietnamese community in Warsaw, the phenomenon of the Israeli Youth Delegations to Poland (with *Public Movement)*, or the legacy of post-Soviet architecture in Caucasus. In 2006 she founded a Laura Palmer Foundation for curatorial projects that she run till 2011. She edited of *Stadium X-A Place That Never Was* (2009), *Forget Fear* (2012) and *Ministry of Highways: A Guide to the Performative Architecture of Tbilisi* (2013). She has been appointed the Head of the CuratorLab at Konstack in Stockholm. Joanna lives and works in Berlin and Warsaw.

Mick Wilson

Mick Wilson (BA, MA, MSc, PhD) artist, educator and researcher, is Head of the Valand Academy of Arts, Gothenburg University, Sweden; Editor-in-chief of *PARSE* Journal for Art and Research; member of EARN, European Artistic Research Network; and chair of the SHARE Network. He was formerly founder Dean of the Graduate School of Creative Arts and Media, Ireland; and first Head of Research, NCAD, Ireland. Edited volumes include (with Schelte van Ruiten) *SHARE Handbook of Artistic Research Education* (2013); and (with Paul O'Neill) *Curating and the Educational Turn* (2010). His recent writing has focused on pedagogical rhetoric and epistemic politics. He lives and works in Sweden.

Vivian Ziherl

Vivian Ziherl is Curator at If I Can't Dance, I Don't Want to Be Part Of Your Revolution, Amsterdam. Recent projects include Landings (with Natasha Ginwala) at Witte de With Center for Contemporary Art and partner organisations including Rietveld Academie Studium Generale, Tropenmuseum Amsterdam, Stedelik Museum Amsterdam, BARBERSHOP, Campo Adentro and David Roberts Art Foundation, among others and *StageIt! Part 1 & 2* (with Hendrik Folkerts) at the Stedelijk Museum, 2012/2013. Vivian was the founding contributing editor of *Discipline Magazine*, and her writing has appeared in periodicals including *Frieze, e-flux Journal, Witte de With Review, Pages Magazine, LEAP Magazine, Metropolis M, Eyeline* and the *Journal of Art (Art Association of Australia and New Zealand)*. Vivian is the recipient of a curatorial fellowship with Institute of Modern Art, Brisbane.

Editors' Acknowledgments

We, the editors are grateful to all the authors for their considered contributions, and for persevering with us throughout the editorial process. We wish to thank the de Appel Arts Center, Open Editions, the Center for Curatorial Studies at Bard College (CCS Bard), and Valand Academy of Arts for their generosity in supporting this co-publication and for making it possible. We would especially like to acknowledge Tom Eccles, Lorenzo Benedetti, Ann Demeester, Guus van Engelshoven and David Blamey for their on-going support.

We would also like to thank all the following for their generosity, exchange of ideas and critical dialogue at vital moments during the development of the project: 100% Proof, The Exhibitionist, Art & the Public Sphere Journal, BROWN&BRÍ (Rachel Brown / Brighdin Farren), Charles Esche, Ingrid Elam, Annie Fletcher, Liam Gillick, Sarah Higgins, Daniel Jewesbury, Suzanne Mooney, Johan Oberg, Mats Olsson, Lívia Páldi, Sarah Pierce, Sabina Sabolović, What How and for Whom (WHW), Nuno Sacramento, Lucy Steeds and Vivian Ziherl.

We would like to acknowledge the contribution made by different student groups with whom some of the ideas informing the construction of this anthology were first tested out in classroom discussions, seminars and workshops. These include the de Appel Curatorial Programme participants 2012-2013, the students, graduates and faculty of CCS Bard College Graduate Program, Bard College 2013-2014, tranzit.hu's Free School for Art Theory and Practice and the doctoral researchers at GradCAM 2011-2012.

We wish to thank the de Appel Curatorial Programme, Amsterdam; A*Desk, Barcelona; Latitude 53, Edmonton, Alberta; tranzit.hu, Budapest; World of Art, SCCA-Ljubljana, Centre for Contemporary Arts and GradCAM Ireland for enabling us to develop some of our ideas in public and for those essential moments of discursivity that drove the project forward, and finally to all the artists, curators, educators, writers, galleries and arts organisations who have helped this project to take form.

Series Editor
David Blamey

Editors
Paul O'Neill
Mick Wilson

Proofing
100% Proof

Design
Jonathan Hares

Design Layout
Joseph Pochodzaj

Font
Stephan Müller
Unica Neue Regular & Light

Cover Paper
Neenah Lahnstein
Neobond 200gsm

Publisher
Open Editions / de Appel

E-orders:
Open Editions
orders@openeditions.com
+44 (0)20 7830 9779

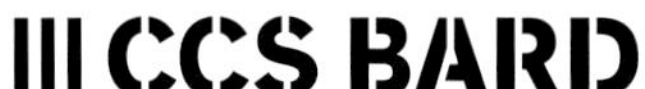

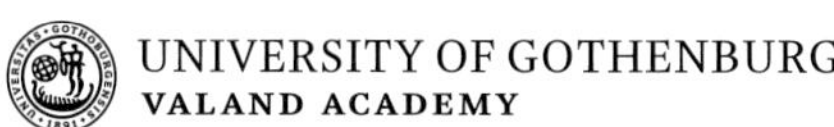